A Garland Series

RENAISSANCE DRAMA

A COLLECTION OF
CRITICAL EDITIONS

edited by
STEPHEN ORGEL
The Johns Hopkins University

A Critical Edition
of James Shirley's
ST. PATRICK FOR IRELAND

JOHN P. TURNER, JR.

GARLAND PUBLISHING, INC.
NEW YORK & LONDON • 1979

All volumes in this series are printed on
acid-free, 250-year-life paper.

Library of Congress Cataloging in Publication Data

Shirley, James, 1596–1666.
  A critical edition of James Shirley's St. Patrick for
Ireland.

  (Renaissance drama)
  Includes index.
  1. Patrick, Saint, 373?–463?—Drama. I. Turner,
John P., 1943–   II. Title. III. Title: St. Patrick for
Ireland. IV. Series.
PR3144.S26 1979   822'.4   78-66857
ISBN 0-8240-9729-7

F O R E W O R D

The following text was submitted to the faculty of
the Graduate School, Indiana University, Bloomington,
Indiana, in partial fulfillment of the requirements for
the degree of Doctor of Philosophy in the Department of
English in 1972. Since that time, although several other
of Shirley's plays have received editorial attention,
no new critical or editorial work on St. Patrick for
Ireland has come to my attention. I wish to thank the
many libraries (mentioned on pp. 8 and 9) who kindly
allowed me to examine their copies of the play. Special
mention should be made of the Provost and Fellows of Eton
College. In addition, I would like to thank the members
of my thesis committee, particularly the chairman, Charles
R. Forker, for his constant help and counsel, and Hugh
MacMullan, for his kindness and encouragement.

1

T A B L E   O F   C O N T E N T S

L I S T   O F   A B B R E V I A T I O N S

Q   St. Patrick for Ireland. The first Part. Written by
     James Shirley. London, 1640, reissued 1657.

BB.   Frater B. B., tr. Jocelinus, Monk of Furness, "The Life
     of the Glorious Bishop S. Patricke . . ." in Thomas
     Messingham's Florilegium Insulorum Sanctorum. The
     translation is appended to Alphonso de Villegas' Lives
     of the Saints in two of its editions: St. Omers, 1625
     and Rouen, 1636.

Chetwood.   William Rufus Chetwood, ed. A Select Collection of
     Old Plays. Dublin, 1750, rpt. London, 1751. St. Patrick
     for Ireland is one of the plays in this collection.

Donovan.   Jeanne Adele Donovan. "A Critical Edition of James
     Shirley's St. Patrick for Ireland" (unpub. Master's thesis,
     Univ. of Ill., 1947).

Gifford.   William Gifford and Alexander Dyce, ed. The Dramatic
     Works and Poems of James Shirley . . . . 1833; rpt. New
     York: Russell and Russell, 1966.

MacMullan.   Hugh MacMullan, ed. St. Patrick for Ireland . . .
     (unpub. thesis, Oxford Univ., 1931).

Armstrong.   Ray Livingstone Armstrong, ed. The Poems of James
     Shirley. New York: Columbia Univ. Press, 1941.

Abbott.   Edwin A. Abbott. A Shakespearian Grammar. 3rd ed.,
     1870; rpt. New York: Dover, 1966.

Bullen Collection.   A. H. Bullen. A Collection of Old English
     Plays. 4 vols., 1883; rpt. New York: Benjamin Blom, 1964.

Dodsley.   Robert Dodsley. A Select Collection of Old Plays,
     ed. William Carew Hazlitt. 4th ed. London, 1874.

Forsythe.   Robert Stanley Forsythe. The Relations of Shirley's
     Plays to the Elizabethan Drama. 1914; rpt. New York:
     Benjamin Blom, 1965.

Forker.   Charles R. Forker, ed. James Shirley, The Cardinal.
     Bloomington, Ind., 1964.

Nason.   Arthur Huntington Nason. James Shirley, Dramatist.
     1911; rpt. New York: Benjamin Blom, 1967.

OED. The Oxford English Dictionary . . .

Partridge. Eric Partridge. Shakespeare's Bawdy. New York:
    Dutton, 1960.

Tilley. Morris Palmer Tilley. A Dictionary of the Proverbs
    in England in the Sixteenth and Seventeenth Centuries.
    Ann Arbor: Michigan Univ. Press, 1950.

The citations from Shakespeare are to G. B. Harrison, ed. The
    Complete Works of William Shakespeare, New York, 1948,
    rpt. 1968. Other major works cited by author are as
    follows:

Beaumont, Francis and John Fletcher. The Works of Beaumont
    and Fletcher, ed. A. H. Bullen (Variorum Edition).
    4 vols. London, 1904-12.

Chapman, George. The Plays of George Chapman: The Comedies,
    ed. Allan Holaday and Michael Kiernan. Urbana: Illinois
    Univ. Press, 1970.

------------. The Tragedies of George Chapman, ed. Thomas
    Marc Parrott. 2 vols., 1913; rpt. New York: Russell and
    Russell, 1961.

Chaucer, Geoffrey. The Works of Geoffrey Chaucer, ed. F. N.
    Robinson. 2nd ed. Boston: Houghton Mifflin, 1957.

Dekker, Thomas. The Dramatic Works of Thomas Dekker, ed.
    Fredson T. Bowers. 4 vols. Cambridge, Eng.: Cambridge
    Univ. Press, 1953-61.

Donne, John. The Poetical Works, ed. Herbert J. C. Grierson.
    1929; rpt. Oxford: Oxford Univ. Press, 1971.

Ford, John. 'Tis Pity She's a Whore, ed. N. W. Bawcutt.
    Lincoln: Univ. of Nebraska Press, 1966.

Greene, Robert. The Plays and Poems of Robert Greene, ed.
    J. Churton Collins. 2 vols. Oxford, 1905.

Heywood, Thomas. The Dramatic Works. 10 vols., 1874; rpt.
    New York: Russell and Russell, 1964.

Kyd, Thomas. The Spanish Tragedy, ed. Andrew S. Cairncross.
    Lincoln: Univ. of Nebraska Press, 1967.

Lyly, John. The Complete Works of John Lyly, ed. R. Warwick
    Bond. 3 vols. Oxford, 1902.

Marlowe, Christopher. The Works and Life of Christopher
    Marlowe, ed. R. H. Case. 6 vols. London and New York,
    1930-33.

Middleton, Thomas. The Works of Thomas Middleton, ed. A. H.
    Bullen. 8 vols., 1885-86; rpt. New York: Russell and
    Russell, 1964.

Milton, John. Complete Poems and Major Prose, ed. Merritt Y.
    Hughes. New York: Odyssey, 1957.

Sidney, Sir Philip. The Prose Works of Sir Philip Sidney,
    ed. Albert Feuillerat. 4 vols. Cambridge, Eng.: Cambridge
    Univ. Press, 1962.

Spenser, Edmund. The Faerie Queene, ed. J. C. Smith and E. de
    Selincourt. London: Oxford Univ. Press, 1912, rpt. 1965.

Tourneur, Cyril (?). The Revenger's Tragedy, ed. R. A. Foakes.
    Cambridge, Mass.: Harvard Univ. Press, 1966.

INTRODUCTION

I. THE TEXT

A. The 1640 Edition

St. Patrick for Ireland: The First Part was first published in quarto in 1640. All indications point to its being
published independently of any other works, although in several surviving copies the text has been bound together with
other plays of the period, and rows of ornaments at the head
of the text on A 3 and possibly also on the imprint appear to
be from the same setting as in the edition of The Constant
Maid of the same date.[1] The text, by the standards of the
day, is a good one, and it is not unlikely that Shirley took
pains to see his work through the press. St. Patrick was
entered in the Stationers' Register on 28 April 1640 along with
The Constant Maid for the bookseller Richard Whitaker. The
form of the entry is as follows:

Master   Entred for his Copies under the hands of
Whitaker.   doctor WYKES and Master ffetherston Warden

           two Playes. viz. . . xij[d]

              Saint PATRICK for Ireland. and

              The Constant Maide. by JAMES SHIRLEY.[2]

[1] Walter Wilson Greg, A Bibliography of the English
Printed Drama to the Restoration (London, 1939-60), II, 594.

[2] Edward Arber, ed. A Transcript of the Registers of
the Company of Stationers of London 1554-1640 A. D. (London,
1877, IV, 482.

No subsequent edition was printed in the seventeenth century, and no second part is known to have been written. In 1657, however, the unused sheets of the 1640 printing were bound together with those of The Constant Maid (also originally printed for Whitaker in 1640) and both were issued together under the general title Two Playes by the bookseller Joshua Kirton, who had come into possession of the Whitaker copyrights on 7 March 1653 upon the death of Whitaker.[3] Collation of both extant copies of the 1657 re-issue had shown it to be identical in all respects to that of 1640 except for the replacement of the title page.

For the present edition I have fully collated thirty copies of St. Patrick for Ireland with the aid of the Hinman collator at Indiana University. The copies at the University of Illinois and at the Huntington Library (my copy-text) I have examined firsthand, and others I have procured in photo-duplicates. No substantive variants were noted in the thirty copies collated, a fact that makes it highly probable that no variants occur in the other extant copies.[4] A list of the copies collated follows:

[3]A Transcript of the Register of the Worshipful Company of Stationers from 1640-1708 A. D. (London, 1913), I, 412.

[4]The only other extant copy I was able to locate is in the possession of the Bishop of Ely in England. I was unable to secure a photoduplicate. It is probable that other copies exist, but I was unable to locate them. I am indebted to William H. Bond of Harvard University for his assistance in filling out my census of copies.

C	University Library, Cambridge, England
CH	Huntington Library, San Marino, Calif.
CN	Newberry Library, Chicago, Ill.
DML	Dublin Municipal Library, Ireland
EC	Eton College Library, England
EN	National Library of Scotland, Edinburgh
IU	University of Illinois Library, Urbana, Illinois
L I and II	British Museum, London
LC	Library of Congress, Washington, D. C.
LVD	Dyce Collection, Victoria and Albert Museum, London
MB	Boston Public Library, Boston, Mass.
MH	Harvard University Library, Cambridge, Mass.
MMc	McMaster University Library, Hamilton, Ontario, Canada
MWe	Wesleyan University Library, Middletown, Conn.
MWiW-C I and II (1657)	Chapin Collection, Williams College, Williamstown, Mass.
NE	University of Newcastle Library, Newcastle-upon-Tyne, England
O I, II, and III	Bodleian Library, Oxford
OW	Worcester College Library, Oxford
PU	University of Pennsylvania Library, Philadelphia, Pa.
T	Texas Christian University Library, Fort Worth, Tex.

TU I, II, and III   University of Texas Library,
Austin, Tex.

WF I and II (1657)   Folger Shakespeare Library,
Washington, D. C.

Y   Yale University Library, New
Haven, Conn.

The collation of St. Patrick for Ireland: The First Part
is as follows: Quarto, A to I (seven full sheets).

[A 1] Title page beginning "S^T· PATRICK / FOR / IRELAND."
(see illustration on page 1)

[A 1^V] Blank

[A 2] Row of ornaments and "The Prologue." (28 lines,
"We know not what will take, . . .")

[A 2^V] "The names of the Actors."

A 3 (the only signature in the quire) Row of ornaments
and beginning of text ("Act. I.")

[A 3^V] through [I 3^V] Text of play (five acts in verse
and prose)

[I 4] Text concluded, rule, "The Epilogue." (12 lines,
"How e're the Dyce run Gentlemen, . . ."), and
"FINIS."

[I 4^V] Blank

St. Patrick for Ireland contains thirty-six unnumbered
leaves. The gatherings are regularly signed like B (B, B 2,
B 3) except that A is unsigned on A 1 and A 2. A running
title, "St. Patrick for Ireland." appears throughout the text
([A 3^V] through [I 4]). There are catchwords at the foot
of each page of text; irregularities occur between [B 4]

and [B 4^V] ("Enter" / "End."); B 2 and [B 2^V] ("Patr." / "Pat."); [D 4^V] and E ("King." / "Kin."); E and [E 1^V] ("Ba." / "Bar."); [F 3^V] and [F 4] ("Eme." / "Em."); H and [H 1^V] ("Now" / "2 Now"); and H 2 and [H 2^V] ("1 Sould. The" / "1 The").

The first leaf is missing in both MWiW-C and WF II, the general title page "Two Playes" (reprinted on page 2 of this edition) having taken its place. And in TU III, the first leaf is missing with no replacement. The last leaf is missing in L I and IU.

It seems that John Raworth, the printer, departed from the usual use of one or two skeletons in the printing of the play. Charlton Hinman has shown for instance that the running titles, headlines, and rules were consistently used for the same page in each forme of the Shakespeare First Folio.[5] However, we do not find a similar case in St. Patrick. For example, on signature [A 3^V] the running title contains several distinctive letters. The "a" in "Patrick" is broken in a way that cuts across two of the lines of the letter, and the top of the "f" in "for" makes it distinguishable from the "f's" in the other running titles. If St. Patrick for Ireland had been set up the same way as the First Folio, with the running titles remaining part of the skeleton forme, we would expect these distinctive pieces of type to reappear on [B 3^V], [C 3^V], and so on. However, the running title appears at the

[5]Charlton Hinman, The Printing and Proofreading of the Shakespeare First Folio (Oxford, 1963), I, 172.

head of the following leaves: [A 3^V], [B 3^V], [C 4^V], [D 3^V], E 2, F 2, G 2, H 2, and I. Moreover, the first setting of running titles omits the final period in [A 3^V]. It apparently was first added on [B 3^V] and appears thereafter. This arrangement indicates that the printer did not consistently retain the running titles as a part of the skeleton, although some attempt was made to do so.

It is difficult to account for these irregularities. Most likely the lack of rules or headlines in the book made it easier for the compositor to treat the running titles as part of the text. It seems that he did not break down the title, however, since the same pieces of type always occur together. Moreover, the fact that the distinctive title occurs only once in each quire suggests that one forme was being set up while the other one was in the press, since if the formes were set up one at a time, it would seem likely that it would appear twice in each quire.

Despite the fact that the above evidence makes it possible that two compositors set the type for St. Patrick, each working from a different type case, the evidence does not bear out this assumption. The play contains some variant spellings, but these are not distinctive or consistent enough to warrant the conclusion that they represent the habits of different men. Moreover, many times these spellings occur on the same page (e.g., bloud and blood on [B 4^V]). Distinctive types do not occur regularly or often enough to provide any evidence either way.

For the most part, the text is fairly well printed. Aside from a high incidence of ambiguous punctuation, the text is easy to read and contains few troublesome errors; most of these are obvious misprints. There are several badly inked letters in some of the copies, but none gives any doubt as to its intended form. Blurring or faintness because of imperfect inking occurs occasionally, but it does not obscure the meaning of the play. Misspacing occurs only a few times. Throughout, the text is set up in ordinary Roman type face, but italics are consistently used for speech headings, proper names, and stage directions, as well as for gnomic emphasis in the prophecy (I.i.59-61) and for the songs throughout the play.

The punctuation is very light throughout. As in most printed plays of the period, it is rhetorical rather than grammatical or logical. Usually a comma is used for intermediate stops within a speech. Occasionally we see a semicolon, but usually only in passages where there are already a number of commas and a heavier stop is needed to distinguish this pause from the others. Percy Simpson's rules,[6] despite their elasticity, are of very little use with the erratic punctuation of this text. Several times question marks and exclamation points occur, but in other circumstances they are omitted. In one case (II.i.13) the colon seems to have been used as an exclamation point.[7] One explanation for such irregularities

[6] Shakespearian Punctuation (Oxford, 1911), passim.

[7] Simpson, p. 73, has listed this as common usage in the Renaissance.

is that St. Patrick partakes of both old and new systems of punctuation.

The compositor observed the usual seventeenth-century practice of distinguishing syllabic -ed in an adjective or past participle from the unsyllabic ending by using -ed for the former and 'd for the latter (for example, starved for starv'd [I.i.6] but pleas'd for pleased [Prologue, 10]). Some exceptions occur, but they are usually cases where -ed is used for the unsyllabic ending as in modern usage.

As my collation shows, St. Patrick for Ireland was not corrected in press. Minor variations do occur, but without exception only in cases involving punctuation. Poor inking or damaged type seems to account for each instance. In any case it is improbable that a seventeenth-century proofreader would loosen the chase of an entire forme merely to make a few minor corrections in punctuation, at the same time letting more obvious errors in the same forme stand uncorrected.

The lining of the verse in the 1640 edition most always reflects the rhythm of Shirley's poetry. Gifford's edition of 1833 (as we shall see later) often forces Shirley's lines to fit strict iambic pentameter to the detriment of the author's loose, conversational style. Often, however, Gifford seems to be correct and Q wrong. As W. W. Greg points out,

> . . . an author's scribal practice was often lax:
> he would run short lines on to others merely for
> convenience of writing or to economize space . . . .
> Moreover, an author sometimes crowded additions into
> the margin of his manuscript in such a way that the
> metrical structure was obscured, in which cases the
> printer was reduced either to setting them as prose

or to cutting them up as best he could in accord-
ance with his own ideas of verse. Also the absence
of capitalization in the manuscript tended to obscure the distinction between verse and prose, and
it is not uncommon to find the printer mistaking
one for the other. It follows that as a rule no
great importance attaches to the line division in
early printed texts, and an editor may be mainly
guided by his own sense of the fitness of the verse.[8]

Despite the general faithfulness of the printed text to
the rhythm of Shirley's verse, some problems of the type Greg
discusses do occur in Q. Most of these can be traced to problems of space, either in the printed text or in the manuscript.
For example, Q prints the following statement by Dichu and
Archimagus' response in four lines:

Dichu. Call this good man your father, Boyes.

Archimagus. He's mad, and I am frantick at this base
    Apostasie. My Lord, think how you may
    Provoke our gods, and the King anger. (I.i.263-266)

Gifford correctly rearranges this consistently iambic verse
(three and a half metrical lines) on five lines of type:

Dichu. Call this good man your father, Boyes.

Archimagus.   He's mad,
    And I am frantick at this base Apostasie.
    My Lord, think how you may provoke our gods,
    And the King anger.

Evidence of a similar economy appears in the occasional running
together of two lines of type. For example,

Conallus. Father. Archimagus. The King. (IV.ii.27-28)

seems to be two partial verse lines rather than a part of one
single verse line. Stage directions are also occasionally
crowded in this way (e.g., I.i.77).

We learn from the imprint on the title page that St.

---

[8] Walter Wilson Greg, The Editorial Problem in Shakespeare
(Oxford, 1967), p. liii.

Patrick for Ireland was "Printed by J[ohn] Raworth for
R[ichard] Whitaker." For some years previous to 1640, Shirley's
plays had been published by William Cooke, most often in
partnership with Andrew Crooke. Usually their printer was
Thomas Cotes, although Crooke and Cooke had hired John Norton
to print The Example (1634), The Gamester (1633), and The Duke's
Mistris (1635/6). The relationship of Shirley with Andrew
Crooke and William Cooke was a long and apparently profitable
one. However, upon Shirley's return from Ireland in 1640,
this relationship came to an end. Allan H. Stevenson suggests
that the break might have been a result of the carelessness of
Thomas Cotes' press corrector, possible mishandling of his
plays by Andrew Crooke, or a dwindling demand for plays.[9] In
any case, Shirley apparently delivered the manuscripts of St.
Patrick for Ireland and The Constant Maid soon after his return
from Ireland in April of 1640.[10] These, however, were the only
plays which Whitaker published or Raworth printed. It is possible, then, that Raworth might have neglected to proofread
St. Patrick for Ireland, a circumstance that could account for
Shirley's ceasing to do business with Whitaker, as well as
for the fact that no press corrections show up in a collation
of thirty copies.

Richard Whitaker's bookshop was at the King's Arms in

[9] Allan H. Stevenson, "Shirley's Publishers: The Partnership of Crooke and Cooke," The Library, 4th ser., 25 (1945),
158-159.

[10] Allan H. Stevenson, "Shirley's Years in Ireland," RES,
20 (1944), 27.

St. Paul's Churchyard from 1619 to 1648. Richard was in partnership with his brother Thomas, and, according to Henry R.
Plomer, the two "had an extensive business, and published much
of the best literature of the period."[11] John Raworth was a
London printer in the parish of St. Bennet, Paul's Wharf, from
1638 to 1645.[12] He must have had a good reputation because
he was among the twenty printers who were licensed by Star
Chamber Decree in 1637.[13] Whitaker also achieved distinction
in his lifetime, having been made a warden of the Company of
Stationers in 1643.[14]

It is possible to reach some tentative conclusions about
the kind of manuscript that Raworth received for printing in
1640. W. W. Greg defines two broad categories of manuscripts
from which plays were printed in the seventeenth century. In
the first category belongs the author's rough draft, or "foul
papers," (or a scribal transcript of same) which is a copy
"representing the play more or less as the author intended it
to stand, but not itself clear or tidy enough to serve as a
prompt book."[15] The other kind which has relevance to our
inquiry is the prompt-book itself, which was prepared by the

[11] A Dictionary of the Printers Who Were at Work in England, Scotland and Ireland from 1640 to 1667 (London, 1907),
s.v. "Richard Whitaker."

[12] Plomer, s.v. "John Raworth."

[13] Arber, IV, 532.

[14] Plomer, s.v. "Richard Whitaker."

[15] Walter Wilson Greg, The Shakespeare First Folio (Oxford,
1955), p. 106.

theatrical company from the author's "foul papers" or fair
copy for use in producing the play in the theater. Manuscripts
of the first type produce printed texts of a higher authority
than the second, since they have been tampered with much less
by persons other than the author, and therefore more clearly
reflect his intention.

According to Greg, there are several kinds of evidence
that help to reveal what sort of manuscript lies behind a
given text. "If an author gets embrangled in a speech, he
may impatiently pass on in the heat of composition, intending
perhaps to go back to it, or perhaps content to leave it for
the copyist to untangle."[16] Such "embranglement" may lie
behind Corybreus' speech at III.ii.104-108:

> Not but with those
> They mean especiall grace to; such as they
> Know must hereafter shine above with them,
> Though meerly mortals, are ador'd. And seldom
> Visit the world . . . .

Gifford finds the passage incomprehensible, and suggests that
"a careless printer" has dropped out words between ador'd and
And seldom.[17] He may be right. But it is also possible that
the difficulty of this passage was a characteristic of Shirley's own foul papers.

"Ghost characters," or characters introduced by a stage
direction but not used on stage (either for a speech or to
perform a necessary function), are also an indication of a
play's having been set from the author's manuscript. Such a

[16] The Shakespeare First Folio, p. 111.

[17] Gifford, IV, 405.

character (or perhaps characters) is the "Guard" which accompanies the King and Archimagus on stage at IV.ii.112.1.

The language of stage directions can also provide similar evidence. Throughout the play there are many stage directions which show the author's conception of a scene, rather than the information necessary for a theatrical prompter to do his job. Often props are included in the description. For example, "Enter Angell Victor, bearing a banner with a crosse."[18] Or the setting is described, as with

> Recorders. The Altar prepar'd, with Ferochus and Endarius, as before. Leogarius, Conallus, Archimagus, Magitians, Ethne, Fedella; a sacrifice of Christian bloud.
> (IV.ii.0.1-3)

Or descriptions of the costumes may be given ("Enter . . . Corybreus . . . habited gloriously, and representing Cean-crochi"[19] and "Enter Corybreus as before habited"[20]). Also there are several vague entrances and exits ("Exeunt Leogarius, Queen, Conallus, &c. [and Magitians]"[21] and "Enter St. Patrick, and his traine"[22]). In one place (IV.ii.112.2) the author has told the actors how to play the scene ("Ferochus, Endarius confidently meet the King"), and in another (III.ii.144.1-2) he gives information about the progress of the play ("The Devils rejoycing in a dance conclude the Act.").

[18] I.i.142.1.

[19] III.ii.23.1-2.

[20] IV.i.187.

[21] II.ii.67.1.

[22] III.i.84.1.

Confusion in the designation of characters in the text constitutes further evidence that the play was printed from authorial papers.[23] There are several minor cases of erratic character designation in the 1640 edition of St. Patrick for Ireland. Leogarius, the King, is called by his name in the first act, but simply "King" later in the play. In Act II Ferochus and Endarius are representing Jupiter and Mars at the altar. The stage direction indicates that "the Idol that presented Jupiter moveth." Later (II.ii.35.3-4) one of the speeches is assigned to "Jupiter." Nowhere is there any indication of which character, Ferochus or Endarius, impersonated Jupiter. We can assume that a theatrical company would have made a firm decision on this matter by the time the play was produced. Another irregularity of a similar nature is the large number of characters called "Priests." In "The names of the Actors," the Druid priests are called "Priests" and St. Patrick's followers "Religious men." However, often in the play itself the Druids become "Magitians." The Christian monks, then, are several times referred to as "Priests." This confusion is quite natural in an author's manuscript, but unacceptable in a prompt-book.

In short, while none of the bits of evidence is conclusive in itself, the sum total of such details makes it likely that St. Patrick for Ireland was printed from the author's holograph (or a scribal transcript of that holograph) rather

[23] The Shakespeare First Folio, p. 113.

than the prompt-copy owned by the Dublin theater. And this
conclusion is borne out by what we can learn about Shirley's
activities and his relations with his publishers (see pp. 15-16
above). Shirley's manuscript must have become the property
of Whitaker by the time he entered it in the Stationers'
Register in 1640. Shirley probably delivered it to Whitaker
upon his return to London. It is unlikely that he had any
intention of producing it in London. The play's special Irish
theme and story would have less appeal in England. Further,
since we know that Shirley took great pains in the printing of
his plays before he went to Ireland, often participating
personally in all stages of the printing and publishing,[24] we
can assume the case was similar with St. Patrick. Certainly
we can assume that Shirley took great interest in the printing
of his own plays from the available evidence.[25]

---

[24] Stevenson, "Shirley's Publishers," p. 143.

[25] Stevenson, "Shirley's Publishers," p. 158 suggests
that the blunder of Crooke and Cooke in assigning The Ball
to Chapman might have been responsible for the end in Shirley's
long business arrangement with them. Shirley also very system-
atically arranged his own poems in the 1646 volume (Armstrong,
p. xxix). A similar case is indicated further in the dedica-
tions to The Wedding, The Grateful Servant, Love's Tricks,
The Maid's Revenge, The Opportunity, and The Imposture.

B.   Subsequent Editions

After its first appearance in 1640 and re-issue in 1657,
St. Patrick for Ireland was not published again in the author's
lifetime.   In 1750 William Rufus Chetwood, a Dublin thespian
and historian of the Irish theater, edited a number of plays,
including St. Patrick, which had relevance to his country's
theatrical history.[26]   This volume was re-issued in London the
next year.   Chetwood attempted to update the play for an
eighteenth-century reading public, introducing much editorial
emendation silently.   For the most part he modernized the
spelling and punctuation (often obscuring the intended meaning
of the author).   He also failed to include either the Prologue
or the Epilogue in his text of the play.   Except for the fact
that I have adopted his punctuation in a majority of cases,
Chetwood's edition is far removed from the original text, and
therefore is of little scholarly authority or importance.

The next edition was equally unauthoritative.   In 1833
the Reverend Alexander Dyce published Shirley's complete works
in six volumes.[27]   William Gifford had done most of the editing
of the plays at the time of his death, and Dyce took over, putting together the last volume, writing a life, and seeing the
whole through the press.[28]   Gifford was the sole editor of

[26] William Rufus Chetwood, A History of the Irish Stage
(Dublin, 1750).

[27] William Gifford and Alexander Dyce, eds., The Complete
Poems and Plays of James Shirley (London, 1833).

[28] The Quarterly Review, XLIX (April and July, 1833), 2.
According to the Wellesley Index to Victorian Periodicals, the
author of this piece was Henry Hart Milman, an amateur poet who
was also dean of St. Paul's.

<u>St</u>. <u>Patrick</u> <u>for</u> <u>Ireland</u>, which appears in volume IV. The Gif-
ford-Dyce edition, while it prevented complete nineteenth- and
twentieth-century ignorance of Shirley's works, is unacceptable
by modern bibliographical standards. Gifford modernized the
spelling and punctuation, listed only a few variant readings,
bowdlerized and emended the text unjustifiably, and provided
little guide to Shirley's work beyond simple biographical
details, many of which have now been proved inaccurate or
incomplete.[29] This edition, reprinted in 1966 by Russell and
Russell of New York, is still the only available collection of
Shirley's complete works.[30]

[29] The work of A. H. Nason has been the most significant
contribution to biographical scholarship on Shirley since Gifford and Dyce. The other important contributions are the
articles by Allan H. Stevenson, cited above, the introduction
to Armstrong's collection of the poems, and an article by Albert
C. Baugh, "Further Facts About James Shirley," RES, VII (Jan.,
1931), 62-66, which deals with questions of Shirley's marriage,
his years of teaching, and the question of his having taken holy
orders.

[30] Since the publication of the Samuel A. Tannenbaum <u>Eliza-
bethan</u> <u>Bibliographies</u> in 1946, a number of plays have been edited
as doctoral dissertations. Under the directorship of G. E.
Bentley, several graduate students edited some of Shirley's plays
at the University of Chicago: A. H. Carter, ed. <u>The</u> <u>Maid's</u>
<u>Revenge</u> (1940); Henrietta L. Herod, ed. <u>Changes</u>, <u>or</u> <u>Love</u> <u>in</u> a
<u>Maze</u> (1942); Edward Huberman, ed. <u>The</u> <u>Politician</u> (1946); Theodore
K. Niles, ed. <u>Hyde</u> <u>Park</u> (1940); John F. Nims, ed. <u>Love's</u> <u>Cruelty</u>
(1945); Esther M. Power, ed. <u>The</u> <u>Wittie</u> <u>Faire</u> <u>One</u> (1942); Stephen
H. Ronay, ed. <u>The</u> <u>Gamester</u> (1948); and Frances F. Senescu, ed.
<u>The</u> <u>Bird</u> <u>in</u> a <u>Cage</u> (1948). In addition, several other plays have
received serious editorial attention: Marvin G. Morillo, <u>The</u>
<u>Humorous</u> <u>Courtier</u> (unpub. diss., U. of Mich., 1958); Mumper Nixon,
<u>Love's</u> <u>Tricks</u> (unpub. diss., U. of Penna., 1959); Kenneth J.
Ericksen, <u>The</u> <u>Young</u> <u>Admiral</u> (unpub. diss., Rice U., 1967); and
Robert J. Fehrenbach, <u>The</u> <u>Politician</u> (unpub. diss., U. of Mo.,
1968). <u>The</u> <u>Lady</u> <u>of</u> <u>Pleasure</u> appears in Vol. II of Richard C.
Harrier's <u>Jacobean</u> <u>Drama</u> (New York, Anchor Books, 1963) and in
A. S. Knowland's <u>Six</u> <u>Caroline</u> <u>Plays</u> (London, Oxford Press, 1963),
which also includes <u>The</u> <u>Wedding</u>. John Stewart Carter's University
of Chicago dissertation was the basis of his edition of <u>The</u> <u>Trai-
tor</u> (Lincoln, Nebr., U. of Nebr. Press, 1965). C. R. Forker has
edited <u>The</u> <u>Cardinal</u> (Bloomington, Ind., Indiana Univ. Press, 1964).

Gifford's nineteenth-century audience was a cultivated but unscholarly one. This accounts for the fact that his textual apparatus consists of little more than an occasional brief explanation of an archaic word or a footnote explaining a change he has made in the text. He also occasionally makes shrewd observations which lack any documentation whatsoever. The lines of the play are not numbered, and the printer seems to have made quite a few mistakes in setting the type from Gifford's manuscript.

Aside from his unjustifiable emendations, the most annoying characteristic of Gifford's edition is his insistence on strict metrical regularity throughout St. Patrick for Ireland. Often he inserts words in brackets, omits words, expands Shirley's characteristic contractions silently, and changes the flexible, relaxed verse of the play into a strict and unbending iambic beat. Much of the flavor of Shirley's verse, as well as the variety of his prosodic effects, is lost when wo' not becomes will not, ha' have, 'em them, ye you, and so forth.

But despite the lack of modern bibliographical procedure in Gifford's edition, many things about it remain valuable. His obvious care in the reading of the text and his intelligent interpretations of the stage directions still command respect, as do several well-founded emendations. He tends to see the play in terms of the nineteenth-century stage instead of the seventeenth, and finds it necessary to localize each scene specifically. But these localizations are usually borne out by the text or by the source. Although he subdivided Shirley's

five acts into scenes, these divisions are always ones which
the text itself implies by a cleared stage.

St. Patrick for Ireland was edited in a B. Litt. thesis
at Oxford by Hugh MacMullan in 1931.[31] Since it has never been
published and does not appear in any of the standard bibliog-
raphies or lists of theses, it is virtually unknown, even to
specialists. Moreover, this edition presents a "diplomatic"
text which attempts to reconstruct exactly (even down to the
ornamental letters, rules, and press errors) the 1640 quarto.
In recent years this extremely conservative kind of edition has
lost much favor. Nonetheless, MacMullan's textual apparatus
within this old-fashioned system is consistent and rigorous.
Moreover, his introduction contains much valuable information
on the sources and analogues of the play, as well as a lengthy
review of the critical scholarship and some aesthetic observations of his own. MacMullan, however, has little respect for
the play as a work of art. He tends to dismiss the curious
blend of genres in the play, the theatrical effectiveness, and
the poetry as hack work. Although I would not maintain that
this play demands the highest place in the dramatist's canon,
Shirley's art in St. Patrick deserves more consideration than
it has received from MacMullan and others. The play is a unique
work in the dramatist's canon and also an important historical
document. It provides evidence for insights into the nature of
Irish and other non-London stages in the early seventeenth century.

[31] "A Critical Edition of James Shirley's St. Patrick for
Ireland" (B. Litt. thesis, Oxford, 1931).

Despite his failure to appreciate <u>St</u>. <u>Patrick's</u> importance and significance, MacMullan, along with Gifford, remains
the most influential editor of <u>St</u>. <u>Patrick</u> upon my own work.
He has kindly offered assistance to me in the preparation of
my text, has sent me a copy of his thesis (which otherwise would
have been unavailable to me), and generally offered encouragement. I am also deeply indebted to him in my commentary on the
text.

Since MacMullan's edition only one other has appeared, so
far as I know. This is an M. A. thesis submitted to the University of Illinois (1947) by Jeanne Adele Donovan.[32] It is a
modern-spelling edition including few emendations. The few
emendations attempted, however, are often unacceptable by modern
bibliographical standards. Her criteria for emendation are
more often subjective or aesthetic than bibliographical and,
therefore, she replaces some perfectly good seventeenth-century
words with ones which she feels Shirley would probably have
preferred.

[32] Jeanne Adele Donovan, "A Critical Edition of James
Shirley's <u>St</u>. <u>Patrick</u> <u>for</u> <u>Ireland</u>" (M. A. thesis, U. of Ill.,
1947).

C. The Present Edition

My edition of St. Patrick for Ireland: The First Part
provides Shirley's play with its first critical old-spelling
text. It also attempts to set up an apparatus that will serve
the needs of both the scholar and the university student. As
Fredson T. Bowers points out, "A critical old-spelling edition
attempts to establish the text of the literary work concerned
and thereby to become a definitive edition."[33] Consistent with
modern editorial practice as defined by Professor Bowers (as
well as Charles R. Forker and R. J. Fehrenbach, whose editions
of Shirley's The Cardinal and The Politician, respectively, are
models for my own edition of St. Patrick), I have tried so far
as possible to recover the intentions of the author as these
would be represented by his own completed manuscript.

Accordingly my text rests upon a full collation of thirty
copies of Q (see pp. 7 and 8 above), including both surviving
copies of the re-issue of 1657, this being the only edition
published during the author's lifetime. In general, I have
retained the accidentals (spelling, punctuation, and capitalization) of my copy-text (CH), and have emended only when I
thought Shirley would have authorized a change himself (for
example, when a stage direction is obviously omitted or when
a speech is misattributed), or when the quarto reading creates
insurmountable problems for the modern reader. Naturally
punctuation, since it is the least reliable factor in seventeenth-century printed texts, has undergone the most change.

[33] Textual and Literary Criticism (Cambridge, Eng., 1959,
rpt. 1966), p. 119.

I have also collated the four later editions of the play using Q as the control. Although none of the variants introduced by later editors has genuine authority, some of them have historical interest, and I have recorded the substantive ones to show where I have accepted or rejected previous emendations. In all cases where I have adopted the emendations of previous editors or emended myself, I have done so only when such alterations could be justified by modern bibliographical principle. With a few exceptions to be explained in a moment, no emendations have been made silently. Substantive changes will be found in my textual footnotes and justified by commentary; non-substantive changes are listed in the appendix entitled "Emendations of Accidentals." In my text I have changed the punctuation of Q as little as possible, although it has often been necessary to emend in order to convey the sense of the play to the modern reader. In most cases I have substituted semicolons for ambiguous commas, except where a colon is necessary, on the assumption that this practice involves the least departure from the 1640 text. As noted above all such emendations are recorded. The only silent changes or exceptions fall within the following categories: I have modernized the old long s, as well as updated the practice of interchanging i and j and u and v. All speech prefixes and abbreviations in stage directions have been expanded. I have normalized the spacing of contractions and silently corrected turned letters. Ornamental letters, the capitals following them, running titles, catchwords, and signatures are all omitted or modernized.

In rearranged verse lines (which are listed in the emendations) I have silently changed capital and lower case letters to fit the new structure. I have italicized all speech prefixes and stage directions except for proper names within the stage directions, which have been consistently cast into Roman type.

I have centered without comment the more important stage directions, as well as all the entrances, and lines have been silently indented to indicate that they are part of a verse line. In emending stage directions, or adding new ones, I have always tried to be faithful to Shirley's intentions and the conventions of the seventeenth-century theater, while attempting to make the actions on stage as clear as possible. All additions are indicated by square brackets.

Although I have tried not to over-regularize Shirley's meters in the play, there are often sound bibliographical reasons for relining speeches. Such relineation is carried out under the principles set forth on pp. 13 and 14. I have listed all of these changes in relineation in the "Emendations of Accidentals," and my debt, if any, to previous editors has been acknowledged. In the spacing of the text on the page, I have tried to show the metrical structure of the lines by indenting when a new speech begins in mid-line. The numbers in the right margins therefore refer to metrical lines rather than lines of type except, of course, in the prose passages. This procedure was made customary by Capell and is

used by Professor Forker in his edition of The Cardinal,[34]
as well as in most modern dramatic editions.

Another practice which I have consistently adopted is that
of numbering the lines of stage directions that take up more
than a single line of type.[35] Stage directions take the number
of the preceding spoken line, followed by a full stop and the
number of the line of the stage direction. Thus, III.ii.144.2
refers to a part of a stage direction in Act III, scene ii,
which occurs on the second line after line 144. When a stage
direction begins a scene, it is numbered 0.1, 0.2, and so forth.

Although Q is divided only into acts, I have numbered by
scenes in order to be consistent with the system of reference
conventionally used in printed editions of Renaissance drama.
However, I have printed the text without suggesting locations,
and I have bracketed the missing act and scene divisions in
order to emphasize the continuous movement of the play so characteristic of the drama of the day.

Apart from this introduction, my textual apparatus consists
of the following:

1) Textual footnotes (restricted to substantive or semi-
substantive variants)

2) A running commentary on the text

3) A list of emended accidentals

4) A glossarial index to the commentary.

[34] (Bloomington, Ind., 1964).

[35] Forker, p. xxxii.

The textual footnotes appear at the foot of each page, divided
from the rest of the page by a horizontal rule. In order to
conserve space, these have been limited to substantive or semi-
substantive departures (either my own or those of previous
editors) from the 1640 edition. Departures from Q that concern
only the accidentals of the text (punctuation, lineation, spelling, and so forth) are listed in an appendix. In cases where
I have accepted the emendation of a previous editor, I have
indicated the earliest editor to introduce it. If I have
accepted an emendation in spirit, but have not used the exact
wording of the previous editor (as, for instance, in an added
stage direction), I have recorded the fact in the footnote but
have not given the previous editor's exact wording. If I have
rejected a significant emendation of a previous editor, that
is also recorded, but my historical collation (included in the
textual footnotes) does not include minor matters such as
relineation, modernized spelling, or other changes which do
not affect meaning. In the form of my footnotes, I follow the
practice of Professor Forker.[36] The reading to the left of
the bracket is that of my edition. If no siglum follows the
bracket, the emendation is my own. Variant readings within a
single footnote are separated by semicolons.

The following examples should help clarify my form:

zeales] Q; zeal Gifford. (I.i.39)

The above note indicates that I have retained Q's reading "zeales"

---

[36] Professor Forker adopts this practice from that of The
Revels Plays under the general editorship of Clifford Leech.
See Forker, p. xxxiii.

and rejected Gifford's emendation "zeal."

    *binds∧] Gifford; binds: Q.   (II.i.13)

This note indicates that I have adopted Gifford's omission of punctuation, removing the colon of Q. The caret indicates the absence of punctuation. The asterick indicates that the emendation is justified in the running commentary below. My practice in recording non-substantive emendations is explained at the beginning of "Emendations of Accidentals."

My own commentary on the text appears at the foot of the text. For the most part, this consists of glosses of difficult terms or explications of difficult or obscure passages. As noted above I also discuss textual matters here, including any reasons I have had for accepting or rejecting the emendations of previous editors. Because Shirley borrowed much from his fellow dramatists, I have tried to include citations of parallels between St. Patrick for Ireland and other works by Shirley himself and other writers of the period. While I have attempted to make my annotations as complete as possible, I have taken pains not to let them become unwieldy or to take the emphasis off Shirley's distinctive use of language for dramatic effect. In order that this edition may be more useful to students of seventeenth-century English, the glosses have been indexed at the end of the thesis.

In the commentary, my debt to MacMullan will be immediately obvious. I have appropriated many of his excellent footnotes, always with acknowledgement. I have also made extensive use of the OED, which is not often cited in the notes except in

unusual or problematic cases. Also I have relied heavily on
Abbott's <u>Shakespearian</u> <u>Grammar</u> and Simpson's <u>Shakespearian</u>
<u>Punctuation</u> for matters of elucidation which do not always
find their way into the footnotes. If the reader finds references incomplete, I direct his attention to the list of
abbreviations and major works cited, which precedes this
introduction.

II. THE DATE AND FIRST PRODUCTION OF THE PLAY

When on May 12, 1636, the London theaters were closed because of an outbreak of plague[37] Shirley, as well as other dramatists of the time, were left without the means to perform their plays. Shirley, however, had been invited to go to Dublin to participate in a new theatrical enterprise. Thomas Wentworth (later Earl of Stafford) had become Lord Deputy of Ireland in 1633. His administration was fraught with perils, since he had to defend a shaky compromise between three groups of "Irish" citizens, the Irish (Catholic and uncivilized, who were completely opposed to English rule), the "new English" (English landowners and settlers of the last fifty years), and the "old English" (those who accepted the rule of the English as long as their rights to religion and property were not threatened).[38] As William Smith Clark points out, Wentworth assumed his responsibilities with two goals in mind:

> first, to make Ireland a profitable tributary to the crown; second, to make her chief city beautiful and fashionable as befitted the capital of the English viceroy.[39]

One of the things he did to achieve the second of these goals was to lure a shrewd Scottish dancing master, John Ogilby,

[37] Nason, p. 93.

[38] These categories are defined by C. V. Wedgewood in Thomas Wentworth: A Reevaluation (London, Jonathan Cape, 1961), p. 129.

[39] The Early Irish Stage (Exford, 1955), p. 26.

to Dublin. Ogilby observed that the cultural climate was
right in Dublin for a professional playhouse similar to those
found across the channel in London. He established the first
professional playhouse on Irish soil in Werburgh Street soon
after his arrival. It is probable that Wentworth himself,
assisted by Ogilby, undertook to persuade the most prominent
playwright of the day, James Shirley, to join the company of
the first Irish theater while Wentworth was visiting England
between June and November of 1636.[40]

Allan H. Stevenson gives several reasons for fixing the
date of Shirley's departure for Ireland in late autumn or
early winter of 1636. First of all, Shirley probably did not
take Wentworth's offer seriously until the London theaters
had been closed by plague. He might even then have had reason
to wait hopefully for their reopening in the near future.
Furthermore, during the summer and fall of 1636, there were
rumors of pirates as well as several confirmed incidents in
St. George's Channel and the Irish Sea. It was very dangerous
to cross from England to Ireland in times like these, but one's
chances of safety were significantly improved by travelling in
one of the King's own ships. Wentworth had come to England on
the guard ship Ninth Lion's Whelp in June.[41] Since the Whelp

---

[40] Allan H. Stevenson, "Shirley's Years in Ireland,"
RES, XX (1944), 20. Shirley probably had had some previous
personal contact with Ogilby at the Phoenix Theater (Bentley,
II, 517-518) and this probably encouraged him to go to Ireland.
Schipper (p. 189) also points out that Shirley may have known
George Fitzgerald, the Earl of Kildare, at St. Albans.

[41] Stevenson, p. 21.

appears to have been busy fighting pirates during most of the summer and fall, it is probable that Shirley went to Ireland with Wentworth on November 23, 1636.[42] Finally there is the statement of a Dublin historian, D. A. Chart, who set down what Stevenson believes to be authentic tradition when he wrote that "James Shirley, the last of the giant brood of playwrights who succeeded Shakespeare, came to Dublin in the train of the great Lord Deputy."[43]

Shirley probably left Ireland and returned to London permanently by 1640. Ordinarily we might infer this from the date on the London edition of St. Patrick for Ireland, since Shirley was normally in London in order to see his plays through the press. However, there is some evidence that Shirley's publishers, Andrew Crooke and William Cooke, had set up a Dublin bookshop to deal with the publication of Shirley's plays while he was in Ireland.[44] Nonetheless, Shirley's dedication to Captain Richard Owen in The Opportunity (1640) indicates that the play was "emergent from the press"[45] upon his return. From careful consideration of the incidents described in that dedication, Stevenson has concluded that Shirley left Dublin on

[42] Stevenson, p. 22

[43] Stevenson, p. 22, quotes D. A. Chart, The Story of Dublin (London, 1907), p. 218.

[44] Allan H. Stevenson, "Shirley's Publishers," pp. 152-158.

[45] Gifford, III, 369.

Owen's ship, along with Wentworth, on April 4, 1640, probably
arriving in London\about the middle of that month.[46]

If it is safe to assume that Shirley arrived in Dublin
in November of 1636 and left in April of 1640, it follows with
fair probability that St. Patrick for Ireland was written
between these dates. There is good evidence that the play
was written specifically for the new theatrical enterprise in
Dublin. The subject matter is taken from Irish Catholic legend,
and the Epilogue speaks of it as "your story, native knowne"
(line 7). La Tourette Stockwell has provided documentary
evidence to show that the Dublin theater in Werburgh Street
opened its doors for the first time at the beginning of the
theatrical season (i.e., in mid-autumn) of 1637.[47] It is
reasonable to assume, as Stevenson does, that The Royal Master
was the first play to be presented in the Dublin theater.
"The trailing cloud of commendatory verses in the quarto of
1638 clearly celebrates a memorable occasion."[48] Moreover, the
dedication of The Royal Master to the Earl of Kildare has Shirley calling that play "the first fruits of my observance to
your lordship."[49] On the basis of Miss Stockwell's evidence
and the New Year's Eve Epilogue to the play, we may assume that
The Royal Master was presented before Wentworth and his court

[46] Stevenson, "Shirley's Years in Ireland," pp. 26, 28.

[47] Dublin Theaters and Theatre Customs (Kingsport, Tenn.,
1938), p. 2.

[48] Stevenson, "Shirley's Publishers," p. 155.

[49] Gifford, IV, 103.

on 1 January 1637/38, probably not long after its premier at
the Werburgh Street theater.

Since much of Shirley's time during his Dublin employment
was taken up with the revision of other plays (e.g., Jonson's
The Alchemist and Fletcher's The Night Walker), it is reasonable to assume that his comedy, Rosania (later printed in 1652
under the title, The Doubtful Heir), was written for production
the next season (1638/39). Albert Wertheim[50] points out that
Shirley's prologues became increasingly bitter, however, as
time went on and the enterprise in Dublin began to look more
and more like failure. Wertheim quotes from two of Shirley's
prologues to illustrate the point. First, The Irish Gentleman:

> It is our wonder, that this faire Island, where
> The aire is held so temperate (if there
> Be faith in old Geographers, who dare
> With the most happy, boldly this compare)
> That to the noble seeds of Art and Wit,
> Honour'd else-where, it is not naturall yet.
> . . . .
> While others are repair'd, and grow refin'd
> By Arts, shall this onely to weeds be kinde?
> Let it not prove a storie of your time,
> And told abroad to staine this promising Clime,
> That with, and soule-enriching Poesie,
> Transported hither must like Serpents dye,
> Unkinde to both alike, shall the faire Traine
> Of Virgin Muses onely here be slaine?[51]

Second, Shirley's Dublin prologue to Middleton's No Wit, No Help
Like a Woman's (called in Dublin No Wit to a Woman's:

> We are sorrie Gentlemen, that with all our paines
> To invite you hither, the wide house containes

[50] "The Presentation of James Shirley's St. Patrick for
Ireland at the First Irish Theater," N & Q, n. s., XIV (June,
1967), 212-213.

[51] Armstrong, p. 29.

No more. Call you this terme? if the courts were
So thin, I thinke 'twould make you Lawyers sweare
. . . .
Ile tell you what a Poet sayes, two yeare
He has liv'd in Dublin, yet he knowes not where
To finde the City: he observ'd each gate,
It could not run through them, they are too strait:
When he did live in England, he heard say,
That here were men lov'd wit and a good play;
. . . .
But they doe not appeare, and missing these,
He sayes he'll not beleeve your Chronicles
Hereafter, nor the Maps, since all this while,
Dublin's invisible, and not Brasile.[52]

Shirley's increasing bitterness leads Wertheim to conclude that

St. Patrick for Ireland was probably the playwright's last-

ditch attempt to draw audiences to the Werburgh Street theater.[53]

The spectacular nature of the play suggests this, as well as the

conscious attempt to select this important Irish event, St. Pat-

rick's arrival on the Irish shores, for the subject matter. So

it seems logical to assign the composition of St. Patrick for

Ireland a date late in 1639, and to posit its presentation dur-

ing the season of 1639-40. This hypothesis is further borne

out (if we accept Stevenson's theory of a Dublin representative

of Cooke and Crooke's bookshop) by the fact that Shirley waited

till he returned from Ireland to publish the play.[54] If the

[52] Armstrong, p. 29.

[53] Wertheim, p. 213.

[54] Previous to Stevenson's article, most commentators
assumed that Shirley made a brief return to London in March
or April of 1637 (see Schipper, p. 189). Very recently, Anna
Maria Crinò (p. 19) has accepted (with Nason, pp. 109-115)
that he made two brief return trips. These suppositions, however, are based solely on the evidence of the London publication
of several of Shirley's plays in the years we assume he was in
Ireland. The Dublin bookshop theory seems much more probable
given the vicissitudes of ship travel in those days.

play had been written and presented earlier, he probably would
have delivered it to John Crooke in Dublin, and it would have
been published in London by Crooke and Cooke. However, if it
was written and presented immediately before Shirley's return
to England, Shirley most likely would simply have taken it
with him. Upon arriving in London and finding fault with the
printing of other plays (see pp. 15 and 16 above), he may have
decided to secure new publishers for St. Patrick for Ireland
and The Constant Maid.

As for the first production of St. Patrick for Ireland,
we can assume that it was, like The Royal Master, "Acted in
the new theater in Dublin: and before the Right Honorable the
Lord Deputy of Ireland, in the Castle."[55] The theater in Werburgh Street was located not far from Dublin castle, where
Wentworth had taken up residence. This "pretty little theater"[56]
was probably conceived along the lines of the private theaters
of London. The plays seem to have been written for a coterie
rather than a public theater audience, though not for royalty.[57]
Shirley was used to writing for coterie audiences which were
upper-class and sophisticated when he was working in London.
Though the Dublin audience was of more or less the same social

[55] From the title page of The Royal Master, quoted in
Nason, p. 97.

[56] John Aubrey, Brief Lives, ed. Andrew Clark (Oxford,
1898), II, 102.

[57] The sophisticated nature of the repertoire is obvious
from the lists of plays which were performed there, e.g.,
St. Patrick, The Royal Master, The Doubtful Heir, The Alchemist, The Irish Gentleman, No Wit, No Help Like a Woman's, etc.

class, being composed chiefly of Anglican upper classes trans--
ported from London,[58] Shirley's problem in Dublin was that he
assumed the Dubliners would have the same tastes as his London
audiences, so he offered the usual Fletcherian fare. These
plays, it turned out, were too esoteric for the Dublin boondocks.

Although built with the tenants of Dublin Castle in mind,
the theater in Werburgh Street was, after all, a commercial
venture. Therefore, as Clark suggests, Ogilby probably used
the theaters of London as a model. The Werburgh Street theater
therefore most likely had

> like structural arrangements and small capacity--accom-
> modating, say, three to four hundred people. It may be
> imagined as a modest rectangular building of timber and
> brick, lighted by wall candelabra. At the back of the
> pit (and possibly at the sides) there was perhaps a
> narrow gallery with one or two of the castle notables
> or other "persons of honour."[59]

Such a description parallels closely the speculation concerning
the "private" theaters in London during the period. Although
there is no direct evidence, several facts lead G. E. Bentley
to suggest that the Werburgh theater may have had connections
with the Phoenix in Drury Lane. Aubrey makes a statement about
John Lacy (the well-known Restoration actor) indicating that
he was apprenticed to John Ogilby, and that he was a member of
the Phoenix company in 1631. In the second place, Ogilby's

---

[58] Stephen J. Radtke in _James Shirley, his Catholic
Philosophy of Life_ (Washington, D. C.: Catholic U Press, 1929)
has made much of St. Patrick as a "play based on Catholic
traditions" (p. 41). The content of St. Patrick, however, is
exploited for entertainment rather than religious purposes.
The Protestant composition of his audience reinforces this idea.

[59] Clark, pp. 29-30.

dancing was particularly spectacular--the kind which was popular in the theaters. Moreover, since Shirley had been chief
poet for the Phoenix, it is possible it was there that Ogilby
made his acquaintance.[60]

If the connection between the Phoenix and Werburgh actually
existed, it would follow that the Dublin house resembled the
one in Drury Lane. Bentley's research indicates the usual
stage, with the interesting possibility that it may have been
equipped for the use of scenery. "The evidence is not conclusive to demonstrate such a radical innovation, but the inconclusive evidence of something different in Drury Lane should
be noticed."[61] A stage sketch among the Inigo Jones materials
at Chatsworth shows an arched proscenium, a stage set with sky
borders, a backdrop showing an encamped army, and so forth.
The sketch is marked "for ye cokpitt for my lo Chamberlain
1639." The question, of course, is which stage is being
referred to. It could have been the Phoenix (formerly called
the Cockpit) or perhaps a court theater. In short, though the
evidence is inconclusive, there is a possibility that the model
for the Werburgh Street theater was among the most modern of
the London theaters.

At the time of the opening of the Dublin theater, there
were itinerant actors in the country. Wentworth's household
put on several plays while he was Lord Deputy, the parts being

[60] Bentley, II, 517-518.
[61] Bentley, VI, 51.

taken by "his lordship's gentle [folk]."[62] There were also
actors of the commoner sort who were something of a public
nuisance. An act of the Irish parliament in 1636 denounced
"'common players of enterludes' as rogues and vagabonds and
classed them with jugglers and other low entertainers."[63]
Clearly, however, Ogilby would not have wished to staff his
theater with talented servants or performing riffraff.

Where, then, did the actors come from? Stevenson points
out that "the Londoners of Dublin would prefer to import not
only a dramatist and plays but some good professional actors
from London."[64] He goes on to theorize that, since certain
leading actors of Queen Henrietta's men are not heard of after
the breakup of the group in 1636/37, they may have gone to
Dublin. One of them, William Robbins, was a famous comedian
who, if he did go to Dublin, probably presented an excellent
Rodamant in St. Patrick for Ireland. Stevenson's speculation,
in short, suggests that St. Patrick might have been presented
with considerable polish.

One other matter about the first presentation of Shirley's
play remains to be considered. Although the earlier plays
presented in Werburgh Street were either revisions of standard London dramas or new plays written for an audience with
similar tasts, St. Patrick for Ireland seems to be a play
which reflects Shirley's revised attitude about the level of

[62] Aubrey, II, 101.

[63] Allan H. Stevenson, "James Shirley and the Actors at
the First Irish Theater," MP, XL (1942), 148.

[64] Stevenson, "Shirley and the Actors," p. 149.

his audience's sophistication. As Wertheim states, Shirley makes use of many tricks and theatrical effects to woo his Irish audience.[65] The play contains several impressive miracles, moving statues, flames behind the altar, and even a burning house, into which Milcho throws himself near the climax of Act IV. Shirley seems to have desired his Dublin audience to learn as many of the effects of the English stage as possible in one play. Moreover, there are many songs throughout the play, and the play offers quite a bit of slapstick comedy, as well as fantastic costumes for the spirits and for Corybreus when he is impersonating Ceanerachius. At the climax of the play, Shirley makes a theatrically effective use of the trap doors on stage when St. Patrick performs his startling feat, in full view of the audience, of driving away Ireland's snakes and serpents, which have crept out of the earth to destroy him.

> The presentation of the serpents on stage would have been no mean feat for Caroline stagecraft even in England, and Shirley was clearly aware that these serpents plus the sudden sinking of the magician would provide a breathtaking finale for the Dublin theatergoers.[66]

We can only guess at how this scene was realized on stage. Perhaps snakes from beneath the stage were operated by rods as in some Western European puppet drama. Or, more likely, actors, fantastically dressed to suggest serpents, crept across the stage and then retreated through the trap at St. Patrick's command. Such staging could have been derived from the masques

[65] Wertheim, p. 213. Anna Maria Crinò (p. 136) also believes that the spectacle was designed to attract and sophisticate the relatively unsophisticated Dubliners.

[66] Wertheim, p. 213.

which were then in vogue in London. From the complex collection of theatrical effects we find in this play, we can see
how much the Caroline stage was capable of. We can also
surmise that with this play Shirley was striving to save
the theater, perhaps trying to lure the merchants and middle
classes of Dublin with his flashy play about one of their
national heroes.

Despite Shirley's efforts to create a spectacular show,
however, St. Patrick for Ireland was probably not very suc-
cessful. In the prologue Shirley promises, "First welcome
this, you'll grace our Poet's art, / And give him Courage for
a second part."[67] Apparently the audience did not "welcome"
the play, because there is no indication that Shirley ever
wrote a sequel, and he departed for England, never to return,
shortly after the play was presented. Several commentators
have speculated about the possible content of a second part
of St. Patrick for Ireland, since the play seems to be a
complete whole without one. George P. Krapp suggests that
the second part might deal with the popular legend of St. Patrick's purgatory,[68] but, as MacMullan points out, there was a
wealth of material in Shirley's source (see appendix) "for a
continuation of the struggle between Leogarius and Patrick
which the first part leaves in abeyance."[69]

[67] Prologue, 11. 27-28.

[68] The Legend of St. Patrick's Purgatory (Baltimore,
1900), p. 6, n. 2.

[69] MacMullan, p. vi, n. 3.

Although St. Patrick for Ireland was entered in the Stationers' Register on 28 April 1640, it seems never to have been licensed for production in London. Its subject matter is taken from Irish Catholic legend, and the play was intended for an Irish audience, but London theaters produced plays throughout the Renaissance dealing with stories set in many foreign and exotic countries, among them Spain and Italy. The fact that Shirley was an English Catholic, and therefore familiar with the prejudices of his predominantly Protestant countrymen at this particualr time, as well as the play's having been unsuccessful in Dublin, may have persuaded him not to attempt to have St. Patrick produced in London. Furthermore, since Shirley is writing down to his Dublin audience, he knew his traditional London audience would find the pyrotechnics insulting and worthy of more crudely popular theaters.

After Shirley's death, the stage history of the play is a complete blank. The London Stage[70] lists no subsequent performance, and there is no record of St. Patrick's having been produced professionally in Ireland in later years. It is possible, of course, that the play has been produced by amateurs, but inquiries (to the dramatic club of Trinity College, Dublin, for example) have produced no response.

---

[70] The London Stage 1660-1800: A Calendar of Plays Entertainments & Afterpieces Together with Casts, Box-Receipts and Contemporary Comment (Carbondale, Ill., 1960-   ).

III. SOURCES AND INFLUENCES

Most commentators upon the works of James Shirley have
noted that the dramatist's works are highly derivative.
Henry Hart Milman, in "The Works of James Shirley," pointed
out that the possibilities for dramatic invention in the
Renaissance had pretty well been exhausted by the height of
Shirley's career.[71] The drama had, in Forsythe's words,
"become conventionalized" and dramatists had begun to derive
their inspiration mainly from works of the earlier writers, rather than from "life and genuine realism."[72] As a
result, the plots of Shirley's plays represent a combination
of materials from various sources.

> Shirley had no scruples about revising the plots
> which he borrowed. He not only changed their
> catastrophes to suit himself, but introduced new
> episodes, new incidents, new devices, new char-
> acters, and new characterizations. These are
> new only in the sense that they are the play-
> wright's addition, for in fact they often have
> many parallels in earlier plays.[73]

This is not to suggest that Shirley was an arrant plagiarist,
however. His originality lies not so much in new and fresh
invention, but in the way he combined secondhand materials
for dramatic effect and cleverly unified various elements
into his plots and situations.

[71] Quarterly Review, XLIX (1833), 14.

[72] Forsythe, p. 49.

[73] Forsythe, pp. 50-51.

St. Patrick for Ireland, like the rest of the works in
Shirley's canon, is analogous to a large number of plays by
earlier dramatists. Forsythe points out that many of the
incidents and characters in St. Patrick are similar to those
employed by other dramatists of the period.[74] A careful
examination of these plays, however, has not indicated that
Shirley consciously imitated these plays (except, perhaps,
in the few cases I shall consider later in this introduction).
Rather he probably synthesized a number of familiar, conventional elements and refined upon them in order to produce
St. Patrick for Ireland. Moreover, this synthesis was probably
not a fully conscious process but rather the natural result of
a skilled playwright's being closely in tune with the traditions
of his art.

Nevertheless, several commentators have suggested specific
sources for the plot of the play. Gerard Langbaine, in An
Account of the English Dramatic Poets,[75] listed "Bede's Life
of Patrick, Siegebert, Baronius, Bale, and John Kirke's Seven
Champions of Christendom" as possible sources for the St. Patrick material, as well as "his life in English in Twelves."
Adolphus William Ward suggested that Calderon's El Purgatorio
de San Patricio might be added to the list,[76] and Gifford

[74] Forsythe, pp. 223-231.

[75] (Oxford, 1691), p. 483.

[76] A. W. Ward, A History of English Dramatic Literature
(London, 1899), III, 100.

vaguely alludes to "Bede, and other early historians, and
. . . The Life of St. Patrick."[77]

Hugh MacMullan points out in his own discussion of the
sources that by 1640 there were only four lives of St. Patrick in general circulation: the one supposedly written by
Bede (published in Opera Bedae . . . , Basel, 1563, actually
written by the monk, Probus); Capgrave's Nova Legende Anglie
(published by Wynkyn de Worde in 1516); Philip O'Sullivan's
Patriana Decas (Madrid, 1629); and that of Jocelyn, Monk of
Furness. The last named work appears in Latin in Thomas Messingham's Florilegium Insulorum Sanctorum (Paris, 1624) and
in an English translation by a Frater B. B., "The Life of the
Glorious Bishop S. Patricke . . ." appended to Alphonso de
Villegas' Lives of the Saints in only two of its many editions:
St. Omers (?), 1625 and Rouen, 1636.[78]

Of these four, MacMullan states, the life by Jocelyn is
the only one which contains all the incidents of Patrick's
life that Shirley uses in St. Patrick for Ireland. Capgrave's
life is quite similar to Shirley's play, but this writer uses
different spellings for the names Milcho (Miluch) and Conallus
(Conaldus), does not use the names Ethne and Fedella for those
characters, and does not mention Emeria at all. Since the life
in Bede and O'Sullivan's work are both even further removed
from St. Patrick for Ireland, it is probable that Jocelyn's
work is the source for Shirley's play.

[77] Gifford, IV, 364.

[78] Hugh MacMullan, "The Sources for Shirley's St. Patrick
for Ireland," PMLA, XLVIII (1933), 806-807.

Of the two forms in which Jocelyn's life appears, it is probable, as MacMullan points out,[79] that Shirley used the English translation by Frater B. B. It contains all the incidents used in St. Patrick for Ireland, and in two cases agrees more closely with Shirley's play than does the Latin life. The episode in which St. Patrick drinks the poisoned wine is more circumstantial in the Latin than in the English version:

> Vir vero Domini calice accipiens, & nomen Domini
> invocans: illum inclinavit & quidquid in potu
> pertiferum positum fuit, in volam propriam absque
> reliqui liquoris admixtione refudit: . . . ex eo
> bibens nullam lesionaut molestiam penitus sensit.

On the other hand, B. B. says Leogarius "offered the saint a poysoned cuppe, which to the great astonishment of all the company, he drunk off without receaving any dommage thereby . . .";[80] the chief deity of the Druids is called Ceancroithi in the Latin work,[81] Ceancrochie in B. B.,[82] and Ceancrochi, Ceanerachius, and Ceanerochi in St. Patrick for Ireland. These details seem to suggest that Shirley used the translation by B. B. as the source for his play.

From his source Shirley took the following incidents: the prophecy of St. Patrick's conversion of Ireland (appendix, pp. 16-17); the conversion of Dichu (p. 17); Milcho's suicide (p. 19); the conversion of the Queen (pp. 25-26); the poisoned

[79] MacMullan, "The Sources," p. 807.

[80] See BB, p. 27.

[81] Messingham, p. 27.

[82] See BB, p. 33.

cup (p. 27); Conallus' conversion and the prophecy of his
future (p. 32); the banishing of the snakes (pp. 88-89); and
Emeria's baptism (p. 19). In addition the story of St. Patrick's slavery in Milcho's house (pp. 7-9) is reported, and
the vision exhorting him to convert Ireland is described
(pp. 11-12). The King's attempt to avenge himself upon Dichu's
sons is also described, but in Jocelyn they are to be starved
rather than thrown from a rock.

Shirley derived the names of Leogarius, Corybreus (Coibre),
Conallus (Conall), Dichu, Ferochus (misprinted as Fiechus by
B. B but corrected at the end of the work), Endarius, Milcho,
St. Patrick, Victor, Ethne, Fedella, and Emeria (Jocelyn has
two characters named Emeria) from his source. However, he
changed a few of the relationships, and expanded the stories
to make them more interesting. For example, Jocelyn dwells
only briefly on the story of the two sons (in Jocelyn, brothers)
of the king (see appendix, pp. 31-32), but Shirley expands this
into a central conflict of his tragicomic subplot. Jocelyn's
account of Emeria is even briefer (p. 19), and from this Shirley gets the idea for the story of his heroine's suffering.
Shirley has taken Jocelyn's brief narratives, integrated them
carefully with the main plot and, as MacMullan points out,

> The dramatist has shown much dexterity in using his
> slight materials; for there is considerable complica-
> tion in his narrative of the Princes and Milcho's
> daughter, complications that are in no way suggested
> by B. B.'s simple narrative.[83]

[83] MacMullan, "The Sources," p. 809.

And Ethne and Fedella are changed from a brief account (p. 34) into a more complex role as the young and vivacious lovers of Ferochus and Endarius, an addition which provides a pleasant love-comedy plot, as well as an opportunity for the dramatist to elicit more sympathy for the two young men under the tyrannous edict of Leogarius.

Jocelyn's narrative obviously is intended for a much different audience than St. Patrick for Ireland. Dedicated to "the Catholickes of Ireland," the life attempts to exhort readers to Christianity. It is a typical Saint's life, a series of episodes held together mainly by the character of Patrick himself, which attempts to give a detailed picture of the saint and his work, with the goal of providing an example for the faithful. Jocelyn's work is a document of the Counter-Reformation, founded on the assumption that Catholicism is the only true Christianity. Shirley's play shows more interest in the conflict between paganism and Christianity in general than in Catholicism specifically. Despite the fact that Shirley was himself a Catholic, his vagueness about Catholic issues in this play is probably explained by the fact that the more wealthy and sophisticated members of his audience were Protestants. Shirley attempts to present an arresting theatrical experience and to unify his material effectively within the five-act dramatic structure. In order to do this he transformed his source and added material from other sources to endow his story with unity and coherence.

The story of Emeria and Corybreus, with Corybreus masquerading as a god, is perhaps taken from the story of Mundus and Paulina. This tale appears in various places and in various forms, among them Josephus, (Book XIII, chap. IV), Gower's Confessio Amantis (Book I, 11. 761-1059), Boccaccio's Decameron (Day IV, novel 2), and Bandello (Part III, novel 19). Of these, Bandello gives the narrative its fullest treatment. Paulina, a foolishly devout young wife of an older man, is visited in her chamber several times by Mundus, who disguises himself as the god Anubis (in Boccaccio, the lover disguises himself as the archangel Gabriel). Finally the visitor is surprised by a servant or the husband and jumps naked from the window into a nearby canal. When his ruse is discovered he is banished from the kingdom.

It is obviously not possible to say that Shirley borrowed specifically from this tale since, as MacMullan points out, there are other similar tales in which young men disguise themselves in order to gain access to the chambers of foolish women.[84] The purpose of the tale of Mundus and Paulina, moreover, is entertainment. The familiar story of the clever young cuckolder who gets caught has bawdry for its chief appeal. Shirley's situation is more complex. The major difference here is that Emeria is confronted with a choice between her ideal of chastity and the dictates of her religion, which religion Shirley considers as false as Corybreus' costume. Since it has this theme, the story fits well into the central conflict of the play, that between paganism and Christianity.

[84] MacMullan, "The Sources," p. 811.

The episode of the magic bracelet, which Corybreus uses to make himself invisible and which Rodamant later finds, is also quite similar to a familiar plot, although the parallel here is much closer than is the case with the story of Mundus and Paulina. MacMullan points out that the play by I. C., A Pleasant Comedy Called the Two Merry Milkmaids (London, 1661, but probably written about 1620,[85] probably provided the source for this incident. I. C.'s play has a ring in it which is used by various characters to make themselves invisible. A clown, Smirke, kisses Julia while he is invisible.[86] In St. Patrick for Ireland Rodamant kisses Fedella under similar circumstances. Fredericke in I. C.'s comedy then gains possession of the ring, kicks Callow and Ranoff, and mocks Ferdinando and Cornelius.[87] In St. Patrick for Ireland Rodamant kicks Ferochus and Endarius and makes fun of them. Finally a spirit retrieves the ring from Smirke, giving him cramps in the hand.[88] When a spirit takes the bracelet from Rodamant in V.i, the latter receives pains in the wrist. Such fun, however, was commonly exploited on the Renaissance stage.[89] A scene in Shirley's own The Lady of Pleasure (IV.i) takes place in the dark with the characters unable to see one

---

[85] Greg, A Bibliography, III, 486.

[86] I.C., A Pleasant Comedy of Two Merry Milkmaids (London, 1661), Sigs. L 4r-[M IV].

[87] I. C., K 3r-K 4v.

[88] I. C., O 3r

[89] Robert R. Reed, Jr., The Occult on the Tudor and Stuart Stages (Boston, 1965), p. 128.

another, despite the fact that they can be plainly seen by
the audience, and such devices continue to entertain spectators
even in our own day, as for example in Peter Schaffer's Black
Comedy.

There are two extant plays in which St. Patrick appears
as a character: Calderon's El Purgatorio de San Patricio and
John Kirke's Seven Champions of Christendom. Although earlier
commentators have considered these dramas possible sources for
St. Patrick for Ireland, it is unlikely that Shirley borrowed
from them for the character of his hero. Calderon's play
deals primarily with the legend of St. Patrick's purgatory,
and devotes much of its attention to Patrick's adventures with
Ennius, a character who does not even appear in Shirley's play.
Kirke's play contains more emphasis on the dealings of its many
sorcerers than on the story of St. Patrick and his conversion
of the Irish.

This latter play, however, may have influenced Shirley's
characterization of his villain, Archimagus. Sorcerers were,
by this time, popular types on the Renaissance stage, as well
as in non-dramatic literature. The characters Ormandine and
Argalio, like Archimagus, are able to summon spirits by their
commands, and attempt to keep the people in the kingdom slaves
to paganism. But here the similarities end. Kirke's two
magicians dominate the stage with their cheap wand-waving
antics, whereas Archimagus is characterized as the quintessence
of Druidism over whom Patrick must triumph in order to bring
Christianity to Ireland.

It is likely that Archimagus represents Shirley's use of
a theatrical tradition, rather than his being a character
borrowed from a specific source. Sorcerers, witches, and magic
of various kinds appealed to Tudor and Stuart audiences, as the
many plays containing episodes of magic and sorcery attest.
Forsythe (p. 223) lists seventeen plays which contain sorcerers
similar to Archimagus. Of these the character seems most like
Friar Bacon in Greene's Friar Bacon and Friar Bungay. One of
Bacon's speeches, as a matter of fact, is quite close to one of
Archimagus', but it seems likely that they both derived from
occult books popular at the time (see the commentary, I.i.21-30).
The name "Archimagus" might very well have been taken from Spenser's Faerie Queene, despite the fact that the two characters
are really not alike. Various magicians and devils meet fates
similar to that of Archimagus (for example, the fiends in Dekker's If This Be Not a Good Play, the Devil Is In It, [V.iii.
149] and Harpax in Dekker and Massinger's The Virgin Martyr,
[V.ii.238]), but it is likely that Shirley got the idea from
his source (see appendix, pp. 28-29.). Indeed Shirley's character seems a composite of all the magicians in Jocelyn's life,
the dramatist having kept the whole of the previous theatrical
tradition in mind as he wrote.

Sorcerers often had a clownish servant (for example,
Wagner in Marlowe's Doctor Faustus, Miles in Greene's Friar
Bacon and Friar Bungay, the clown in Rowley's Birth of Merlin,
and Suckabus in Kirke's The Seven Champions of Christendom),
and it is therefore not surprising that Shirley provided one

for Archimagus in this play. Rodamant is similar to Wagner
in his attempts to perform magic in II.i, and the numerous
non-magical comic scenes show him to be related to many of
the stock clowns in the drama of the period.

The same is true of the other "original" characters, the
soldiers in V.i and the Bard whom Shirley introduces into his
play. The crude, lustful soldiers who threaten Emeria represent typical figures (see the commentary, V.i.16). The Bard,
as Forsythe suggests (p. 224), is similar to the Harper of
Peele's Edward I, but Shirley adds to his conventional function
a typical carpe diem song and uses him to provide an unregen-
erate, worldly character from whose example Patrick is able to
make a moral point.

Two other plays have been suggested as minor sources for
St. Patrick for Ireland. Gifford mentions that Shirley "seems
to have had the Cave of Belarius [in Cymbeline] in view,"[90] in
devising his location for V.ii. Forsythe (p. 230) points out
that Shakespeare's Timon of Athens and Beaumont and Fletcher's
Cupid's Revenge and The Knight of Malta also have woodland
caves, which might be sources. MacMullan, however, remarking
that it is difficult to pin down the playwright's borrowings
specifically, suggests that Shirley might have been influenced
by Shakespear's play. MacMullan notes a kinship between the
two plays in terms of tone or mood, but does not insist upon a
clear or conscious relationship. Both plays have a bittersweet
tone or atmosphere of the kind that often informs tragicomedy.

[90] Gifford, IV, 437.

The other play often mentioned as a source, Dekker and
Massinger's The Virgin Martyr, has been pointed out by Forsythe
(pp. 221-231) and A. W. Ward[91] as being very close to St. Patrick for Ireland. Indeed the two plays have much in common.
Leogarius resembles Dioclesian, the tyrannous king of Rome,
and Theophilus, the cruel persecutor of Christians. Theophilus' later conversion, however, makes him also very much
like Shirley's Dichu. The saintly Dorothea resembles St. Patrick, her guardian angel resembles Victor, and Archimagus is
very much like the devilish Harpax. Dekker and Massinger's
play also contains low comic characters, Spungius and Hircius,
who perform functions similar to those of Rodamant and the
Bard, and the sisters Calista and Christeta are somewhat like
Ethne and Fedella, in that they are votaries in the Roman
temple, schooled by Theophilus, as Ethne and Fedella are
trained by Archimagus.

It must be admitted that all these comparisons are general
and circumstantial. There is no real evidence that characters
in The Virgin Martyr, however similar to those in St. Patrick,
were inspirations for Shirley's. MacMullan points out that
Forsythe and Ward were unaware of Shirley's source and therefore "ascribed to Dekker and Massinger's influence incidents
in Shirley's play which are drawn from [Jocelyn's] life of
Patrick."[92] Nevertheless, MacMullan continues, there are

[91] Ward, III, 100, n. 4.

[92] MacMullan, "The Sources," p. 812.

remarkable similarities between the two plays. He cites the following passages by way of example:

> Unto those gardens, whose immortall flowers
> Staine your imagin'd shades, and blest abodes.
> (St. Patrick for Ireland, I.i.212-213).

and

> The power I serue
> Laughs at your happie Arabie, or the
> Elizian shades, for he hath made his bowers
> Better indeed then you can fancy yours.
> (The Virgin Martyr, IV.iii.90-93).

This slight similarity between the two plays, as well as other even less obvious ones, is probably best explained by the derivative nature of the art which Shirley, Dekker and Massinger all practiced in the Caroline period. The age was a Christian one, and all three authors had access to the same body of religious literature. This, in addition to the fact that both plays are equally full of clichés, proverbs, and conventional expressions, would account for the similarities.

It is clear, however, that similarities in tone and theme exist between St. Patrick and The Virgin Martyr. They come from a tradition which Elida Maria Szarota calls "Martyrdramas."[93] In the Middle Ages in England, as well as in most of Europe, there existed a popular religious drama of saints, martyrs, and miracles. A saint's play, according to Mary del Villar, "is a play that has a saint as its protagonist or a miracle as its main action."[94] The Digby play, The Conversion of Saint Paul,

---

[93] Künstler, Grübler, und Rebellen: Studien zum europäischen Märtyrerdrama des 17. Jahrhunderts (Berne, Francke Verlag, 1967).

[94] "Some Notes on the Medieval Saint's Play" (unpub. M.S.), p. 2.

is an early example of the type.[95] The main interest, of
course, is in the conversion of Paul, but the play presents
comic scenes featuring devils and blundering servants which
are thematically related to the main plot in much the same
way as the activities of the comic characters in St. Patrick
relate to the story of the saint.

Examination of other early saints' plays suggests that
many of the scenes in Shirley's plays are stock features of
the genre. Miss del Villar points out that popular motifs
and stage conventions recur throughout the history of the
form.

> The toppling of heathen idols, for instance, that
> occurs in [the Digby] Mary Magdalene is a motif
> of pious legend adopted with enthusiasm in the
> drama, the earliest dramatic instance that I know
> of being the toppling of Tervagan in Jehan Bodel's
> Jue de S. Nicholas. The brutal irony of jailers
> and torturers, which presumably resulted from
> the imposition of medieval realism upon pious
> legend, can be found in the earliest vernacular
> plays, also.[96]

In short, Shirley shows a consistency with tradition in some
of the episodes which he selects for presentation in St. Patrick.

This hagiographic type of play died out in England during
the Reformation, as might be predicted. We find plays featuring saints during the sixteenth and seventeenth centuries, but
these saints are minor characters, introduced as historical

---

[95] F. J. Furnivall, ed., The Digby Mysteries (London, 1882),
pp. 25-52.

[96] del Villar, "Some Notes," p. 4.

figures or as Jeremiah-like prophets. St. Anselm in Rowley's
The Birth of Merlin is such a prophet, as is St. Eugenius in
Henry Shirley's The Martyred Soldier. The seventeenth century
saw the renewed popularity of the Martyrdrama, however. No
doubt encouraged by the Counter-Reformation and the ascendancy
of the Baroque temper, the drama of saints, martyrs, and miracles enjoyed a brief popular recrudescence. Szarota explains
this phenomenon further by pointing out that these dramas
celebrate a disappearing type--the embodiment of an absolute
human ideal.[97] Naturally these plays were most popular in
Catholic countries (Lope de Vega in Spain and Corneille in
France wrote several dramas of the type).

The Virgin Martyr and St. Patrick for Ireland, however,
are the major representatives of the type in England. Both
contain miracles, virgins threatened by heathen ravishers,
and saintly or angelic saviors. Each has as its basic conflict
the struggle between Christianity and paganism, with the result-
ing triumph of Christianity. In short, it is likely that The
Virgin Martyr, rather than being a source for Shirley's play,
is rather another example of a type. This type, though perhaps
rare in English drama, was popular and well developed on the
stages of Western Europe in the seventeenth century.

A more positive case for borrowing from earlier drama--
in this case from Webster's The White Devil--can however easily
be made. Webster uses the word "lost" as a motif in his play,
having various characters repeat it throughout the course of

[97] Szarota, p. 5.

the drama. This repetition plays on the various senses of the
word. The possibility of Websterian influence on Shirley is
perhaps strengthened slightly by the frequently reworked similarities between The Duchess of Malfi and The Cardinal (see
Forker, pp. xlviii-liii). For example, at the beginning
Bracciano uses the word in the sense of "confused, without
direction," or "totally smitten by love," since he desires to
possess Victoria Corombona, another man's wife. But by the
end of the play he and the other characters use the word in
the sense of "separated from the possibility of salvation,
condemned to hell for transgressions." This constant repetition is an ironic device, used by Webster to underline the
moral implications of his tragedy. Similarly, Shirley's
characters in St. Patrick for Ireland repeat the same word
throughout his play. The irony, moreover, is similar. The
magician's statement, "We are lost" (I.i.1) is ironically
echoed later:

> Dichu. Oh, I am lost.
>
> Patrick. Thou art found.

Dichu is using the word in its original sense (I.i.279-280),
as the magician used it earlier. But Patrick is reminding
Dichu of its religious meaning. The word, moreover, is used
a number of other times throughout the drama, each time sound-
ing the theme of religious conversion and making Shirley's
point about Christian salvation.

It is, of course, impossible to tell which source Shirley
borrowed from or even that it was necessary to borrow at all in

order to add interest and unity to Jocelyn's narrative. Forsythe lists many other anologous scenes and characters too
numerous to mention here.[98] It is likely that Shirley's
familiarity with much previous Renaissance drama helped him
to enrich and unify the story of the conversion of the Irish.

[98] Forsythe, pp. 223-231.

IV. THE PLAY

St. Patrick for Ireland has been no better received by
Shirley's commentators than it apparently was by the audience
at the first Irish theater. Nason considers it "beneath
remark,"[99] W. A. Neilson calls it "a hodge-podge,"[100] and
MacMullan states that it is "commonplace."[101] Although I
would not maintain that it deserves the highest place in
Shirley's canon, it does deserve more attention than it has
heretofore received. St. Patrick for Ireland, despite its
many conventional elements, is, in many ways, an atypical
play in the canon of English Renaissance drama as a whole and
of other works by its author. Other Renaissance plays exist
in which saints appear, notably Kirke's Seven Champions of
Christendom, Henry Shirley's The Martyred Soldier, and Rowley's A Shoemaker, A Gentleman and The Birth of Merlin. St.
Patrick for Ireland, however, unlike these earlier plays,
attempts to concentrate on important events in the life of
one particular saint.

Shirley adapts the medieval saint's life (a story containing more or less biographical material serving as an
example to the faithful) to the purposes of the chronicle play
(a dramatic recreation of history). But obviously neither of

[99] Nason, p. 318.

[100] The Cambridge History of English Literature, VI, 206.

[101] MacMullan, p. xxxix.

63

these generic classifications is sufficient to describe
St. Patrick for Ireland.

F. E. Schelling's idea that the main concern of the play
is religious[102] seems to me oversimple. Shirley's choice of
the St. Patrick legend as his subject matter suggests that the
playwright might have been interested in drawing local Irish
Catholics to the Werburgh Street theater. But the patrons of
the venture, Stafford and his staff, were Anglicans. For
such a mixed audience, we should expect Shirley to write a play
which avoided too much emphasis on Catholicism, directing their
attention instead to issues more closely connected with the
development of Ireland as a nation, rather than the specific
bringing of Catholicism to its shores. And this is more or
less what Shirley has done in this play. He seems to be more
interested in St. Patrick as a Christian character than as a
Catholic one. St. Patrick's activities as a bishop are only
lightly touched upon and, most significantly, Shirley omits
any reference at all to Patrick's visit to the Pope in Rome,
(see appendix, pp. 13-15). The playwright is clearly cele-
brating the triumph of Christianity over paganism, and the
subsequent change in Ireland from tyrannous, benighted barbar-
ism, with accompanying bad government, to the civilized and
supposedly learned and compassionate government predicted in
V.iii.11-20. The implication here, of course, is that the
greatness of Ireland continued to develop and reached a kind
of fruition in the viceregency of Stafford.

[102] The English Chronicle Play (New York, 1902), p. 207.

Indeed the relation of the two main plots (the conversion of the Irish and the story of Emeria, Conallus, and Corybreus) indicates, as MacMullan states, that Shirley was "intrigued with the problem of good and evil, especially as it was concerned with chastity and libertinism."[103] Such interest was not unique with Shirley, of course. Earlier dramatists of the day were exploiting the popular taste for tragicomedy. Whether, as Schelling would have it,[104] elements inherent in the genre itself caused its "decline," or, as Ribner suggests,[105] because of the inevitable admixture of historical romance, the chronicle play had become more and more "romantic." By Shirley's day such plays were set in the remote and legendary past and placed special emphasis on questions of morality, particularly as they extended to wronged women. Marvin T. Herrick points out that Renaissance idealism had led to the cult of the feminine. With tragicomic writers like Cinthio, for example, more and more emphasis is placed upon "women and domestic virtue."[106] This made his plays didactic, and it is this didacticism which begins to pervade English drama more and more as historical plays become tragicomic.

W. H. Hickerson has provided perhaps the most useful generic classification of plays like St. Patrick for Ireland

[103] MacMullan, p. xxvii.

[104] Schelling, p. 275.

[105] Irving Ribner, The English History Play in the Age of Shakespeare (Princeton, 1957), p. 271.

[106] Tragicomedy: Its Origin and Development in Italy, France, and England (Urbana, Ill., 1955), p. 66.

in his distinction between "compound" and "complex hybrid plays." The compound hybrid play is one which consists of "two or more parallel independent plots, one of which must be typically tragicomic."

> This type of play contains two or more entirely independent narratives of relatively equal importance, related to each other in only the most superficial fashion. Frequently the parallel plots contain subordinate actions which add to the intricacy of the play and which give even to a minor plot containing them the structure, scope and diversity of a complete Elizabethan play. The principal characters of the plot are kept apart . . . . The events of any given plot in a compound hybrid play do not consequently affect the course of action in any other plot.[107]

The complex hybrid play is a bit different, however. It

> attempts to create a semblance of unity of impression by subordinating its diverse plots to a general plan, the denouement of which involves all of the principal characters of the play and solves all of the complications of the subordinate actions. In contrast to the compound hybrid play, which contains a complete tragicomic action as one of its parallel independent plots, the complex hybrid play contains tragicomic elements diffused throughout the play, but no sustained or unified tragicomic plot . . . .[108]

St. Patrick for Ireland is thus to a certain extent a hybrid play. Conallus, Corybreus, and Emeria and their problems are unrelated to the tribulations of St. Patrick, except insofar as the saint solves Emeria's problems at the end of the play. It is thus not really reasonable to object to it,

[107] W. H. Hickerson, "The Significance of James Shirley's Realistic Plays in the History of English Comedy" (unpub. diss., U. of Mich., 1932), pp. 24-25.

[108] Hickerson, p. 25.

as does the reviewer in an American Quarterly Review article,[109]
that it is "an extraordinary jumble of the grave and the gay,
of scenes of the utmost seriousness and the most nonsensical
buffoonery . . . ." St. Patrick for Ireland is typical of an
age which enjoyed a fullness and complexity in its drama, and
to apply to it the critical standards of a later age is unfair
and unprofitable. But we must also recognize that in many ways
Hickerson's definition of the "complex hybrid play" applies to
St. Patrick as well. There is a "general plan" to the play,
but it is a thematic one, rather than being purely mechanical.

Despite the fact that some might think, with MacMullan,
that the story of Emeria and Conallus is by far the most
interesting plot,[110] it is related thematically to the St. Patrick material, and together they relate to a central issue.

The central issue of the play is the change in Ireland
from paganism to Christianity. Act I opens with a scene between
Archimagus and his magicians in which the moral and religious
condition of the Irish is carefully presented. Shirley has
drawn from black magic here in order to show Druids as anti-
thetical to Christians. This is no simple, sympathetic, bucolic
Druidism of the sort we find in Beaumont and Fletcher's Bonduca,
but a darkly malignant, evil religion whose chief priest is in
league with devils, the archenemies of Christianity. Archimagus
controls spirits and devils by the force of his art, but these

[109] XVIX (1833), 149.

[110] MacMullan, pp. xix-xx.

spirits are powerless in the face of St. Patrick's heavenly power. Patrick's subsequent triumph over Archimagus is a result of this superiority, and Patrick states near the end of the play (V.iii.11-20) that prosperity, good government, and learning will come to Ireland now that its Prince, Conallus, has accepted Christianity.

Emeria's plight, to a certain extent, is related to the moral situation in pagan Ireland. Corybreus disguises himself as one of the Druid gods, and she is powerless to resist his advances. However, the conversations between her and the disguised Corybreus (III.ii.42-144) underline the weaknesses of a depraved and benighted paganism. Emeria's devotion necessitates her subservience, but she several times points out that gods should not act this way.

> Doe our gods practise this? (III.ii.104)

> I thought the gods above had been all honest.
> (III.ii.113)

>   Can a Deitie
> Breath so much impious language, and reward
> Vertue with shame?   (III.ii.130-132)

> Oh help, some man; I dare not call upon
> The gods, for they are wicked growne . . . .
> (III.ii.139-140)

Corybreus argues from good pagan authority that he is, indeed, a god, and that gods do "practise this."

> 'Tis in them chastitie; nor is it sin
> In those we love to meet with active flames,
> And be glad mothers to immortall issues:
> How oft hath Jove, who justly is ador'd,
> Left heaven, to practise love with such a faire one?
> The Sun, for one embrace of Daphne, would
> Have pawn'd his beames: not one, but hath sometimes
> Descended, to make fruitfull weake Mortalitie.
> (III.ii.114-121)

That such rhetoric, coupled with Corybreus' disguise, is effective in this situation, indicates the moral vacuum of Ireland without Christianity.

A somewhat similar case is the plot between the young lovers Ferochus, Endarius, Ethne, and Fedella. When Leogarius condemns Ferochus and Endarius to death, he shows a complete lack of the kind of mercy expected in a Christian king. Then the two young men, in II.ii and IV.ii, disguise themselves as idols in the temple, an action that suggests that their masquerade is as false as the idols themselves. Furthermore, their dalliance with Ethne and Fedella in the temple, sanctioned by Archimagus, the chief priest, at the end of II.ii would have been blasphemous in a Christian church.

Rodamant's attempts to conjure at the beginning of II.i are, like Wagner's in Doctor Faustus, a parody of sorcery in general. By his actions, the servant ridicules and undercuts Archimagus' activities. His actions in attempting to hang himself also suggest a parody of Judas Iscariot, and his poetry to the Queen pokes fun at Corybreus' conventional courtly wooing of Emeria. The Bard, of course, provides Patrick with a convenient example that he uses to make a moral point about the nature of Christian conversion.

Moreover, many times throughout the play various elements relate symbolically or thematically to the larger issue. For example, the word "lost", with theological implications is a repeated motif in the play. Several times "blood streaming in the firmament" is mentioned (IV.i.227-228 and IV.ii.25-26) which

relates to a famous line in Marlowe's Doctor Faustus, "See
where Christ's blood streams in the firmament" (V.ii.148).
Milcho's death to a certain extent is a pagan anti-type of
Christian martyrdom, and Archimagus' attempt to poison Patrick
with a cup of wine is a grisly parody of the Eucharist. Moreover, there are constant puns on words like "grace" throughout
the play, and all of these elements echo and reinforce the
story of Patrick's Christian mission.

Despite the proliferation of plots, however, the play
moves swiftly to its climax. The inevitability of the conclusion is underlined by the prophecy (I.i.55-62) and also by the
audience's familiarity with the legend. The play deals succes-
sively with the various conversions and the deaths of the more
villainous antagonists, Milcho, Corybreus, and Archimagus;
includes some stock saint's play scenes moves fairly briskly
to the high point, the expulsion of the snakes. Despite the
promise in the epilogue of a second part (apparently never
fulfilled), however, the play ends on a rather incomplete
note. Patrick still faces major difficulties since Leogarius
has not been converted and is still plotting against the
saint, and since Emeria, despite the fact that she has been
avenged, still remains a wronged woman. This sort of
problematic ending, however, is typical of tragicomedy, and
Shirley's plays of this period, The Duke's Mistress, The Gentleman of Venice, The Politician, and A Bird in a Cage are all
characterized by a certain bitterness and a disillusionment
about the possibility of justice in the world.

But except in the case of Leogarius, evil is punished in this play. Milcho, Corybreus, and the villainous Archimagus all die violently for their transgressions. Their deaths, however, cannot really be called tragic in any sense. Their characters are fairly obvious throughout the play, and they remain static figures whose fall is not accompanied by any gradual increase of weakness. But as Edward Huberman has pointed out, Shirley is most often interested in situation rather than character. Shirley's characters ordinarily do not show much of a spiritual conflict and, except in a few cases, there is not usually an inner struggle in the minds of any of his persons. "The evil ones are simply wicked, and understand and accept the fact."[111] Shirley's main point in St. Patrick for Ireland is that the coming of the Christian message banishes evil as surely as St. Patrick banished the snakes.

The other characters, for the most part, also exist to serve their various plots. Ferochus, Endarius, Ethne, and Fedella are typical lovesick adolescents, who are in the main undifferentiated. Conallus' virtue is uncomplicated and direct, as is the goodness of Dichu and the Queen once they are con- verted, despite the fact that this conversion takes place too swiftly for modern taste. Emeria, on the other hand, is a bit more complex and more sympathetic because we see her conflict with herself and with Corybreus in III.ii. She does not, however, approach the complexity and fullness of character- ization of some of the women of earlier dramatists.

[111] Edward Huberman, "An Edition of James Shirley's The Politician" (unpub. diss., U. of Chicago, 1946).

It has been mentioned elsewhere that Shirley was an accomplished poet--"one of those post-Elizabethans--Fletcher being another--to whom the best impulse towards poetic imagery noticeable in our drama was communicated after Shakespeare."[112] But his verse is most often smooth and conversational, not often given to the kind of effect which results in a conceit, and not usually profoundly individualistic or consciously powerful. Jacob Schipper points out that Shirley's verse is often very close to prose, despite the fact that it is "sorg-faltig und fliesend."[113]

The verse in St. Patrick for Ireland, for the most part, is brisk and conversational. It does not usually get in the way of the action nor, to any extent, add much psychological depth to the characters. There is not great use of metaphor, except of the conventional kind, as can be seen in the commentary in the numerous similarities between Shirley's verse and that of his fellow dramatists. MacMullan criticizes Shirley for this conventionality and cites Corybreus' speech to Emeria in the garden as an example of Shirley's subservience to tradition.

[112] A. W. Ward, III, 555.

[113] James Shirley, Sein Leben und Seine Werke (Vienna, 1911), p. 357. Other authors have made disparaging comments about Shirley's artistic gifts, following the example of Dryden's "MacFlecknoe," where Shirley was compared to Shadwell, the "Last great prophet of tautology" (line 30). Among the more recent is C. S. Lewis in his essay, "Variation in Shakespeare and Others" in Rehabilitations (London, 1939), pp. 159-180. Lewis makes strongly disparaging comments about Shirley's talent. He accuses Shirley of mindless padding of poetic speeches, rather than true dramatic poetic characterization.

> Yes, and my rivalls too <u>Emeria</u>,
> And now they court thy beauty in my presence,
> Proud erring things of nature; dost not see
> As thou dost move, how every amorous plant
> Doth bow his leavy head, and becken thee?
> The winde doth practise dalliance with thy hairs
> And weave a thousand pretty netts within
> To catch it self. That violet droop'd but now,
> How tis exalted at thy smile, and spreads
> A virgin bosome to thee. There's a rose
> Would have slept still within his bud, but at
> Thy presence, it doth open his thin curtains
> And with warm apprehension looking forth
> Betrayes her love in blushes. And that Woodbine
> As it would be divorc'd from the Sweet-bryer,
> Courts thee to an embrace. It is not dew
> That like so many pearls embroider all
> The flowers, but teares of their complaint, with feare
> To loose thee, from whose eye they take in all
> That makes them beautifull, and with humble necks
> Pay duty unto thee their onely spring.
>
> (II.i.167-187)

MacMullan points out that "the metaphors are those of any cavalier poet. They have not even the merit of being distinctive
of the style of any one of that large group of versifiers.
They are indeed 'court praise.'"[114] On the whole I disagree.
The above passage is rather pretty and perhaps better than
MacMullan allows, though certainly not Shakespearean. Moreover, the passage is appropriate to the position it holds in
the play. We might consider the effect if Shirley had introduced brilliant, stunning, and highly original poetry into this
particular situation. Corybreus most likely would have appeared
a more sympathetic character than the dramatist means him to
be. Emeria's objections to the speech as "court praise"
(II.i.188), are no doubt Shirley's also. A similar case can
be made for Archimagus' "mere bombast."[115]

[114] MacMullan, p. xxxv.

[115] MacMullan, p. xxxvi.

> A whirlewind snatch 'em hence, and on the back
> Of his black wings transport these fugitives,
> And drop their cursed heads into the sea . . . .
> (I.i.182-184)

This is not only overdone (causing the audience to dislike
Archimagus), but it is also highly conventional (the figure
is used often by Webster). This is the way Shirley's audience
expected magicians to talk. Patrick, on the other hand, a
sympathetic character, often has the best lines, as we might
expect:

> I came not hither
> Without command, Legat from him, before
> Whose angry breath the rocks doe breake and thaw,
> To whose nod the mountaines humble their proud heads;
> The earth, the water, aire and heaven is his,
> And all the stars that shine with evening flames,
> Shew but their trembling when they wait on him . . . .
> (I.i.201-207)

And the passage which MacMullan quotes as a "fine speech" also
contains some good poetry:

> In vaine is all your malice, Art, and power
> Against their lives, whom the great hand of Heaven
> Daines to protect; like wolves you undertake
> A quarrell with the Moone, and waste your anger . . . . .
> (V.iii.91-94)

But, as MacMullan points out, these and other set lyrical
pieces more often impede the progress of the play by a beauty
which calls attention to itself, rather than fulfills a dramatic purpose.

The images in the play, it must be confessed, are more or
less conventional ones. The play contains many proverbs, as
well as several echoes of other dramatists of the day, along
with the addition of material which Shirley no doubt picked up
from everyday experience. Though there are three or four

classical allusions, Shirley does not demonstrate himself to
be any great scholar. Most of his poetic figures evoke a
short, brief, and fairly unarresting analogy which is easily
forgotten and does not stand in the way of the dramatic effect.
This simplicity is perhaps another evidence of Shirley's
bowing to popular taste in the hope of attracting the Irish
audience. Exceptions occur, however, most notably Milcho's

> And from my vexed heart exhale a vapour
> Of execreations, that should blast the day,
> And darken all the world. (IV.i.292-294)

I would agree with MacMullan[116] that this expression is clumsy,
ineffective, and bombastic. Perhaps this is another example
of Shirley's use of inflated verse to suggest the character
of one of his villains. But all in all, although Shirley's
verse seems appropriate to the drama of St. Patrick, it is not
memorable. Edward Huberman's evaluation of the dramatist's
verse in The Politician might serve as well as a description
of the poetry in St. Patrick for Ireland:

> Shirley's imagery is clear, adequate, and rarely,
> if ever, strained or forced; but it suffers from its
> very moderateness, and is often lacking in fervor and
> warmth. There seems to have been little place in the
> poet's consciousness for the richness of pictorial
> association which might have attended his use of
> imagery. The spring at which the earlier poets had
> drunk was beginning to run dry.117

However deficient Shirley's poetry is in this play, the
playwright shows himself an extremely capable manager of stage
spectacle in St. Patrick for Ireland. Swinburne was one of

[116] MacMullan, p. xxxvi.

[117] Huberman, p. 79.

the first to notice that the first scene of the play effectively catches the interest of an audience: "The style is a
little fresher, the movement more lively, and the actions
more amusing,"[118] than in most of his other dramas.

Albert Wertheim, in his article on Shirley's stagecraft
in this play,[119] has speculated on the staging of St. Patrick
for Ireland. The first act opens with the entrance of Archimagus and his fellow Druids "no doubt dressed in fantastic and
elaborate costume."[120] The dramatic opening lines

    1. Magitian. We are undone.

    2. Magitian.   We are lost.

are terse and to the point, carrying an effect not unlike the
short opening line to Webster's The White Devil:

    Lodovico. Banisht!

Soon after Archimagus' interchange with the magicians,
three spirits enter, no doubt dressed fantastically and speaking their lines "with exaggerated gesture."[121] The entrance of
St. Patrick and his train provides a dramatic contrast with

---

[118] Algernon Charles Swinburne, Contemporaries of Shake
speare (London, 1919), p. 301.

[119] Albert Wertheim, "The Presentation," pp. 212-215.

[120] Wertheim, p. 213.

[121] Wertheim, p. 214. Professor Wertheim informs me that
he was referring to the "antic gestures" frequently employed in
antimasques. Such "gestures" were probably grotesque and the
spirits made to look ugly or frightening in much the same way
as the witches at the beginning of Jonson's Masque of Queenes
(Jonson, VII, 277-317). Moreover, the entrance of the spirits
functions in true antimasque tradition, providing a contrast
for what is the climactic spectacle of the first act, the entrance of St. Patrick and his train.

the magician- and spirit-ridden environment of Druid Ireland.
Shirley is evoking a kind of pageantry and pomp with the Latin
song and the angel carrying a cross. Such spectacle should
have impressed his spectators.

A number of miracles and "surprizing scenes" take place
throughout the play. Dichu is paralyzed and then cured at
his conversion; Rodamant is killed by poison and then revived
by Patrick; the saint leads some of the characters safely from
Milcho's house, which the officer has set aflame; Milcho commits
suicide by jumping into the flames; Archimagus is swollowed up
by the earth and sent to hell; and finally, at the climax of
the play, St. Patrick banishes the snakes (perhaps actors cos-
tumed gaudily and spectacularly like snakes or some sort of
mechanical devices operated from the trap like rod puppets).[122]
They disappear into the same trap used a short time later for
Archimagus' disappearance.

> Since St. Patrick has said that he shall free Ireland
> from 'venonous natures,' it would be fitting that the
> evil magician fall into the same trap door through
> which his serpents have just made their exit.[123]

[122] Professor Wertheim doubts that actors were used for
snakes. In such a case Shirley would probably have provided
stage directions for the actors, he feels. We have seen above,
however, (pp. 16-20) that the 1640 text was probably set up
from Shirley's foul papers, rather than from a prompt book (or
none at all), since the author assumes that such details will
be worked out in production. Shirley might have left the problem to the stage manager, who might have solved it in either of
the suggested ways. Because of the other antimasque-like scene
(the entrance of the spirits at I.i.136), it seems likely that
Shirley also used actors here.

[123] Wertheim, p. 215.

Other arresting spectacles are provided by the two scenes set in the Druid temple, II.ii and IV.ii. In Act II the altar upon which Ferochus and Endarius represent idols is "discovered," perhaps on the inner stage, and, after a great deal of ritual and pageantry (including "a sacrifice of Christian bloud"), the idol representing Jupiter moves and speaks to the worshippers and a flame goes up behind the altar. These effects, along with the dance of the devils at the end of III.ii, the clever business involving the magic bracelet which makes its wearer invisible, and the many songs throughout the play, were obviously intended to impress and entertain Shirley's audience.

In short, despite the fact that St. Patrick for Ireland has been criticized for being "merely" theatrical, it is clear that theatricality is its raison d'etre. Shirley was trying desperately to revive the failing theatrical venture in Dublin with a flashy, spectacular play utilizing Irish history and legend. The interest the play holds for us today lies not so much in its artistic or poetic excellencies, for surely in this respect it is merely ordinary. But St. Patrick for Ireland comes down to us as an example of the theatrical experience which Caroline stagecraft could provide for an audience. Clearly such stagecraft evinced a high degree of sophistication, and Shirley demonstrates that he was a clever manipulator of theatrical devices who could use his theater to the fullest to provide his audience with entertainment.

S^{T.} PATRICK FOR IRELAND

The names of the Actors.

[Prologue and Epilogue.]

Leogarius, Monarch of Ireland.

Corybreus,
      his Sons.
Conallus,

Dichu, A Noble-man.

Ferochus,
      his Sons.
Endarius,

Milcho, A great Officer.

Archimagus, The chife Priest, a Magitian.

Two other Priests.

St. Patrick.

Victor, his Angell-Guardian.

St. Patrick for Ireland] MacMullan notes that the title is in the form of a slogan. "St. George for England" occurs in the title of William Smith's lost play, as well as in Marlowe's Edward II (III.iii.33-34), "Alarum! to the fight! Saint George for England, / And the Baron's right" (MacMullan, p. 97).

The names of the Actors.] follows Prologue in Q.

Leogarius] The names Leogarius, Corybreus (Coibre), Conallus (Conall), Ferochus (Fiechus), Endarius, Milcho, St. Patrick, Victor, Ethne, Fedella, and Emeria all appear in BB.

Archimagus] The word "Archimage" was often used in the period to denote a chief magician or enchanter. Forsythe points out (p. 221) that "The name of Archimagus suggests a recollection of [Archimago in] The Faerie Queene."

Victor, his Angell-Guardian] The idea of a guardian angel is common in Elizabethan drama. Cf. Angelo in Dekker and Massinger's The Virgin Martyr and the good angel in Marlowe's Doctor Faustus. See also BB, p. 8.

Bards.

Rodamant, Archimagus' Servant.

Souldiers.

Angels.

Religious men.

Servants.

[Snakes.]

Queene.

Ethne,
      her Daughters.
Fedella,

Emeria, Milcho's Daughter.

        [Scene: Ireland.]

    Rodamant] Shirley may have taken this name from the Saracen leader in Ariosto's Orlando Furioso. The name was also commonly used to describe a great braggart or boaster.

    Emeria] MacMullan points out that the Latin word, emerio, means "to deserve, to merit" (p. 99). See also BB, p. 19, where Milcho has two daughters, both of whom are named Emeria.

THE PROLOGUE.

We know not what will take; your pallats are

Various, and many of them sick I feare:

We can but serve up what our Poets dresse,

And not considering cost, or paines to please,

We should be very happy, if at last,   5

We could find out the humour of your taste,

That we might fit, and feast it, so that you

Were constant to our selves, and kept that true;

For some have their opinions so diseas'd,

The Prologue. (Chetwood omits)

*9. diseas'd] Gifford, MacMullan; displeas'd Q, Donovan.

1-10. The comparison of a play to a feast was a fairly
common one in the period. Shirley appeals to his audience's
palates also in the prologues to The Duke's Mistress, The
Doubtful Heir, and in several of his Irish prologues. Jonson
uses the figure in prologues to Epicoene and Volpone.

2. Various] varied.

3. dresse] prepare for use as food.

6. humour] disposition.

7. fit] furnish food for.

9. diseas'd] "Diseas'd" could become "displeas'd" by
a compositor's momentary eyeslip to "pleas'd" in line 10. The
fact that the expression "diseas'd opinion" was somewhat of a
cliché at the time reinforces this emendation. Cf. Shakespeare's The Tempest: "be cured / Of this diseased opinion,
and betimes" (I.ii.296-297) and the quotation from The Alchemist in the following note.

82

They come not with a purpose to be pleas'd: 10

Or like some birds that leave the flowry fields,

They only stoop at that corruption yeilds.

It were a custome would lesse staine the times,

To praise the vertues, when you chide the crimes.

This is but cold encouragement, but we   15

Hope here are few of those, or if there be,

We wish 'em not infectious, nor confine

We censures; woo'd each soule were masculine:

For your owne sakes we wish all here to day,

Knew but the art and labour of a Play;   20

Then you would value the true Muse's paine,

The throwes and travell of a teeming braine.

*21. Muse's] Donovan substantively; Muses Q; muses' Gifford.

9-10. For . . . pleas'd] Cf. Jonson, The Alchemist:
"He hopes to find no spirit so much diseased, / But will with
such fair correctives be pleased" (Prologue, 17-18).

12. that corruption] that which corruption; Shirley has
omitted the relative pronoun (see Abbott, par. 244).

13. staine] blemish (the reputation of).

17. confine] forbid, constrain.

18. censures] opinion, judgement, criticism (with or
without adverse connotation).

21. Muse's] The muse of poetry is obviously being
referred to here, as she is in so many of the Prologues of
the period. Gifford's emendation makes good sense, but
usually one muse is addressed, e.g., in Milton's Paradise
Lost (I.6).

22. throwes] throes or struggles (preceding the "coming
forth" of something). travell) travail; mental exertion.
teeming] productive.

But we have no despaire, that all here may

Be friends, and come with candor to this Play.

St. Patrick whose large story cannot be   25

Bound in the limits of one Play, if ye

First welcome this, you'll grace our Poet's art,

And give him Courage for a second part.

25-28. The Prologue's dedication of the play to St.
Patrick has parallels in other dramatists. The prologue to
Lyly's Endimion, for example, is directed towards the favor
of Queen Elizabeth.

25-26. whose . . . Play] Cf. the prologue to Henry V,
where the Chorus comments about the difficulty of telling
Henry's story in one play.

28. second part] Shirley apparently planned a possible
sequel to this play, but it does not exist. See the Introduction, p. 44.

ACT I. [Scene i.]

Enter Archimagus, and two other Magitians,

at severall doores.

1. Magitian. We are undone.

2. Magitian.   We are lost.

Archimagus.   Not so, your feares

Become you not, great Priests of Jove and Saturne;

Shall we that awe the furies, at whose charme

I.i. Gifford locates this scene in "The Temple, with
statues of Jupiter and Saturn: in front an altar." There
is no indication in the text itself, however, that the action
is localized, nor does seventeenth-century theatrical practice require such localization. Further, as MacMullan states
(p. 99), Leogarius later suggests (I.i.244) that no temple
has been built yet.

1. lost] This word is reiterated throughout this play
in various senses in much the same way that Webster repeats
it in The White Devil. For a discussion of the effect of
this motif on the play as a whole, see the Introduction,
p. 58.

2. Priests of Jove and Saturne] MacMullan's statement
(p. 100) that Shirley is "careless" here because he does not
remember that the god of the Irish is Ceanerachius is, I
believe, unfounded. Shirley is interested in the struggle
between paganism and Christianity, not in historical accu-
racy. His Druids worship Roman as well as Irish gods. Such
a lumping together of all pagan gods in opposition to the
Christian one is quite common in the seventeenth century
(cf. Milton's "On the Morning of Christ's Nativity"). Rodamant's later statement, "These be new Dieties, made since
yesterday" (II.ii.1), although it is slightly ambiguous, refers
most likely to the statues, not the gods they represent.

3. furies] three terrible spirits of Greek mythology
who punished those guilty of unavenged crimes.

Hell itselfe quakes, be frighted with a shadow,

A tame, a naked Church-man and his tribe   5

Of austere starved faces? no, this Kingdome

Shall still be ours, and flourish; every Altar

Breathe incense to our gods, and shine with flames,

To strike this Christian blinde.

1. Magitian.   This is but ayre;

He is now landing; every tread he prints   10

Upon this earth will make it grone.

Archimagus.   Are not

The havens strengthned by the King's command

With souldiers, to watch that none arrive

With this suspition?

2. Magitian.   But we that can

_____

9. but ayre] without substance, meaningless.

12. havens] harbors.

14. suspition] "Meaning, perhaps, suspected of being
a Christian; but the expression is so awkward that its genu-
ineness is doubted" (Gifford). MacMullan finds no difficulty
here and quotes another example of Shirley's broad use of the
word in The Maid's Revenge, III.i:

        Velasco's shallow,
And will be planet-struck, to see Berinthia
Die in his arms: 'tis so; yet he himself
Shall carry the suspicion.--If art,
Or hell can furnish me with such a poison . . . .
                              (Gifford, I, 137)

Cf. also St. Patrick, I.i.71-72 and I.i.178.

    Command armies from hell for our designe,   15

    And blast him, now stand idle, and benumm'd,

    And shall grow here ridiculous statues; I'le

    Muster my friends.

1. Magitian.   And if I ha' not lost

    My power, the Spirits shall obey to drowne

    This stragler, and secure this threatned Island.   20

Archimagus.   Stay, which of you can boast more power than I?

    For every Spirit you command, my spells

    Can raise a legion; you know I can

    Untennant hell, dispeople the wide ayre,

    Where like innumerous atomes the blacke genii   25

*18.   friends] Q; fiends Chetwood, Gifford, MacMullan, Donovan.

---

    16.   blast him] cause him to die by breathing on him.

    18.   friends] Although all previous editors emend this
word to "fiends," there is no sound reason for doing so. The
context indicates that "fiends" makes good sense, but "friends"
here could refer to devils of the Magician's acquaintance.
The same word is used in Middleton's The Witch (I.ii.228)
with this meaning. Also the phrase "muster friends" is common. Cf. 3 Henry VI (IV.viii.11 and IV.viii.18) and Richard III
(IV.iv.489).

    25.   innumerous] innumerable. atomes] very tiny particles
of matter. This could also be "atomies," i.e., very small
creatures invisible to the naked eye.

     Hover, and nistle one another; all

     That haunt the woods and waters, all i' th' darke

*26.   nistle] Q; nestle Chetwood; jostle Gifford; mistle Donovan.

     23-30. you know . . . my will] MacMullan quotes Nichol-
son's edition of Reginald Scot's The Discoverie of Witchcraft
(London, 1886) to illustrate this passage:

          Furthermore, he saith, that there are six
     principall kind of divels . . . The first sort
     consist of fier, wandering in the region neere to
     the moone . . . . The second sort consisting of
     aire, have their habitation more lowe and neere
     unto us . . . . The third sort of divels Psellus
     saith are earthlie; the fourth waterie, of the sea;
     the fift under the earth; the sixt are Lucifugi,
     that is, such as delight in darkness & are scant
     indued with sense, and so dull, as they can scarse
     be moved with charmes or conjurations (pp. 414-415).

Friar Bacon boasts similarly of his powers in Greene's Friar
Bacon and Friar Bungay:

          Bacon can by bookes
     Make storming Boreas thunder from his cave,
     And dimme faire Luna to a darke Eclipse.
     The great arch-ruler, potentate of hell,
     Trembles, when Bacon bids him, or his fiends
     Bow to the force of his Pentageron (I.ii.217-222)

Conjuration and magic were very popular on the Elizabethan and
Jacobean stages. Greene's play, Marlowe's Doctor Faustus, and
Rowley, Dekker and Ford's The Witch of Edmunton, as well as
Macbeth, are perhaps the most famous examples. For a further
discussion of the use of such material, see the Introduction,
p. 55.

     26. nistle] Andrew Wright, in An English Dialect Dic-
tionary (London, 1873), lists this word as a variant spelling
of "nestle," which he defines as follows: "To be restless or
uneasy; to fidget, be on the move; to bustle about." While
Shirley's verb is transitive, Wright's definition could be
very close to the meaning he had in mind. Donovan suggests
that the word is "mistle" (an obsolete form of "missel")
"meaning to thrust out with the muzzle or nose; to feel,
smell, or root about with the muzzle; to growl or murmur."
The only other possibility listed in Wright is a Scots word,
"nissle," which means "to beat with the fists." There is no
justification for Gifford's emendation, "jostle."

And solitary chambers of the earth,

Breake through their Adamantine chaines, and fly

Like Lightning to my will; and shall your factious   30

And petty correspondence with the fiends,

Attempt this worke without my voice and counsell?

Who brought you first acquainted with the divell?

Did not my Art?

1. Magitian.   We are disciples to

The Great Archimagus.   35

2. Magitian. We acknowledge all our Art deriv'd from you.

1. Magitian. But in this justice to our gods, we hope

Our gods' chiefe Priest will give us leave--

Archimagus. Yes, and confirme it, and applaud your zeales,

My fellowes both in sacred Arts and Priesthood.   40

Go on, I praise your resolution:

*39. zeales] Q; zeal Gifford.

---

29. Adamantine] made of adamant, a very hard material.

30-34. Forsythe (p. 224) points out that "Archimagus'
reproof to the Magicians suggests Prospero's rebuke to Ariel"
in The Tempest (I.ii.250-293).

30. factious] divided into factions.

39. Gifford's emendation "zeal" makes grammatic sense,
but the Q reading obviously refers to the zeal of each magician.

My Spirit gave intelligence before

Of his approach, and by all circumstance,

Our prophesie doth point this Christian Priest

The blacke subversion of our Isle; but we,   45

Like masters of all destiny, will breake

His fate, and bruise him in his Infancy

Of danger to this Kingdome; fly and be

Arm'd to your wishes; Spirits shall attend you,

And the whole power of hell.   *Exeunt Magitians*

                          This newes affrights me,   50

How e're I seem to swell with confidence;

This is the man, and this the revolution,

Fixt for the change of sacrifice, foretold,

And threatned in this fatall prophesie.

*53.   sacrifice,] Gifford; sacrifice∧ Q.

---

42.   My Spirit] a reference to the belief that witches
and magicians were served by attendant spirits in much the
same way that normal mortals were looked over by guardian
angels. The spirits (often "familiars," i.e., disguised
as cats, owls, etc.) were supposed to aid their masters and
communicate knowledge to them. Cf. Harpax in Dekker and
Massinger's The Virgin Martyr.

44.   point] acuse . . . of being.

45.   blacke] malignant.

46.   breake] change.

52-54. This is . . . prophesie] I adopt Gifford's
addition of a comma here because it makes the meaning clearer.
Shirley most likely is referring to the Roman Catholic Mass,
as well as the pagan Druid ritual. The passage means "This
is the person and this is the overturning decreed to effect a
change of ritual from Druidism to Christianity, predicted and
threatened in this dire prophecy."

He reads.

A man shall come into this Land,   55

With shaven Crowne, and in his hand

A crooked Staffe; he shall command,

And in the East his table stand;

From his warme lips a streame shall flow,

To make rockes melt, and Churches grow,   60

Where while he sings, our gods shall bow,

And all our kings his law allow.

This, this is the vexation.

Enter Endarius.

Endarius.   Sir, the King--

Archimagus. What of the King?

55-62. A . . . allow] The use of prophecies or oracles
was a common technique in the period for creating dramatic
irony. Forsythe (p. 224) lists a number of instances in the
plays of the Renaissance. The most obvious are Antony and
Cleopatra (II.iii.10-31), The Winter's Tale (III.ii.125-173),
Cymbeline (V.v.435-484), and Lyly's Mother Bombie, where the
witch's prophecies are also in iambic tetrameter (II.iii.89-94,
III.i.40-45, and V.ii.16-21). Cf. BB, pp. 16-17.

56. shaven Crowne] i.e., with a cleric's tonsure.

57. crooked] having a crook at one end, resembling a
shepherd's crook. This suggests the crosier usually carried
by a saint or bishop.

58. And . . . stand] Cf. the Appendix: "and his table
shall stand in the East of his house" (p. 17). Although
seventeenth-century Catholicism had abandoned the practice,
the altar had once been called a "table." It was often the
practice to orient the altar of a church toward the East,
because of the tradition of identifying the resurrected Christ
with the rising sun. Also see BB, pp. 16-17. St. Patrick's
first Church was in the eastern part of Ireland.

<u>Endarius</u>.   Is troubled, sicke, distracted.

<u>Archimagus</u>. How?

<u>Endarius</u>.   With a dreame; he has no peace within him;   65

   You must with all haste visit him; we shall

   Suspect his death else.

                    <u>Enter</u> Ferochus.

<u>Ferochus</u>.   Mighty Priest, as you

   Respect the safety of the King, you must

   Make haste; the Court is up in armes, and he

   Calls for his sword.

<u>Archimagus</u>.   You fright me gentlemen: 70

   Rebellion in the Court; who are the Traytors?

<u>Ferochus</u>. His owne wilde thoughts, and apprehension

   Of what, he sayes, was in his sleepe presented;

   He calls upon his Guard, and railes upon 'em,

   66-67. we shall . . . else] otherwise we shall expect
him to die.

   72. apprehension] In Renaissance psychology the apprehension was the faculty of understanding, but here, as in the
following quotation, by the imagination rather than the intel-
lect. Cf. Chapman, <u>Bussy D'Ambois</u> (III.i.21-23):

        like empty clouds
In which our apprehensions forge
The forms of dragons, lions, elephants,
When they hold no proportion.

   74. railles] utters abusive language.

When they appeare with no more armes, and sweares   75

That every man shall weare a Tun of Iron.

Endarius. The Prince.

Enter Conallus.

Conallus. The King impatient of your absence, Sir,

Hath left the Court, and by some few attended

Is coming hither, laden with feare and weapons;   80

He talks of strange things in his dreame, and frights

Our eares with an invasion, that his Crowne

Sits trembling on his head; unlesse your wisdome

Cleare his dark feares, we are undone.

Archimagus.   He's here.

Enter King Leogarius, Corybreus, Dichu.

How fares the King?

Leogarius.   Deare Archimagus,   85

We want thy skill to interpret a black dreame

I had last night; my fancie is still sick on't,

---

76. Tun] cask; barrel.

79. some few] an inconsiderable number.

82. with an invasion] with such an invasion.

86-87. We want . . . I had] MacMullan suggests that the
change from the royal "we" to the personal "I" indicates "a
show of confidence" (p. 102).

86. black] malignant.

87. fancie] in Renaissance psychology, the faculty of
apprehending the objects of perception.

And with the very apprehension

I feele much of my soule dissolve, and through

My frighted pores, creep from me in a sweat: 90

I shall have nothing in me but a bath,

Unlesse thou do repaire my languishing essence

With thy great art and counsell.

<u>Archimagus</u>.   Give me, Sir,

The particular of your dreame.

<u>Leogarius</u>.   They must not heare it.

Yet stay; the Ecclipse, if it be any thing,   95

Is universall, and doth darken all.

Me thought, <u>Archimagus</u>, as I was praying

I' th' Temple neere the sea, my Queene, my Sons,

Daughters, and Traine of my Nobilitie

Prostrate before the Altar, on the sudden   100

The roofe did open, and from Heaven a flame

Descending on the images of our gods

Began to burne the sacred browes, from which

Many deformed worms, and hideous serpents

Come crawling forth, and leap'd unto our throats,   105

Where, with their horrid circles and embrace,

---

91. bath] i.e., a bath of perspiration.

94. The particular] detailed information.

105. Come] Shirley is here using the "historical present," the present tense substituted for the past in order to
increase the effect of immediacy (cf. Abbott, par. 246).

106. circles] coils. The parallel of Leogarius' dream
to later events in the play is obvious.

We were almost strangled: in this fright, me thought,

We fled out of the Temple, and as soone

We saw a pale man coming from the sea,

Attended by a Tribe of reverend men,   110

At whose approach the Serpents all unchain'd

Themselves, and leaving our imprison'd necks,

Crept into the earth; straight all that were with me,

As I had been the prodigie, forsooke me,

My wife, my children, Lords, my servants all,   115

And fled to this pale man, who told me I

Must submit too, humble my selfe to him,

This wither'd peece of man: at which, my-thought,

I felt a trembling shoot through every part,

And with the horror, thus to be depos'd,   120

I waken'd. Now, <u>Archimagus</u>, thy Art

To cure thy soule-sick King.

<u>Archimagus</u>.   'Tis done already.

<u>Leogarius</u>. How, my deare Priest?

---

108. as soone] just then.

114. prodigie] marvel.

118. my-thought] methought.

119. Shoot] Shirley has a particular fondness for this
verb. e.g., <u>Love's Cruelty</u>, I.i: "I / Shoot no infection"
(Gifford, II, 195-196). See also <u>The Opportunity</u>, III.iii
(Gifford, III, 413) and <u>The Cardinal</u> (Forker, I.ii.221 and
IV.ii.50-53).

Archimagus.   This pale thing shall not

          trouble you;

     He that so long was threatned to destroy

     Us and our Gods, is come.

Leogarius.   Ha, where?

Archimagus.   Now landing: 125

     But were the coasts unguarded, he wants power

     To fight with those aetheriall troops, that wait

     Upon the Gods we serve. He is now dying;

     This minute they have blasted him: and they,

     Above the speed of wings, are flying hither   130

     With the glad newes; be calme agen, and let not

     These airy dreames distract your peace.

Leogarius.   They are vanish'd

     Already at thy voyce; thou (next our Gods

     The hope of this great Iland) hast disperst

     All clouds, and made it a faire skie againe,   135

     My learned Archimagus.

                    Enter Spirits.

     _____

     127. aetheriall] spirit-like.

     129. blasted] Cf. I.i.16 and note above; also Richard
     III: "Behold, mine arm / Is like a blasted sapling, withered
     up" (III.iv.70-71).

     130. above] faster than.

     132. airy] unsubstantial; without basis in fact.

1. Spirit. He is come.

2. Spirit.   He's come.

3. Spirit.   And we must flye.

Leogarius. What voyces make the aire
    So sad?

Corybreus. They strike a horror.

Conallus.   They are Spirits.

Archimagus. I command once more to oppose him.   140

1. Spirit. In vaine, great Priest.

2. Spirit.   We must away.

3. Spirit.   Away.

Omnes. We cannot, dare not stay.   Exeunt.

    Enter, Angell Victor, bearing a banner with a crosse,
        [followed by] St. Patrick and other Priests
                in procession singing.

140. command] Q; command you Gifford.

----

    139. strike a horror] i.e., the tune they sing horrifies
the listeners. "To strike" often meant to sound music, e.g.,
"Strike one strain more" (Tourneur, The Revenger's Tragedy,
V.i.170).

    142. We cannot, dare not stay] "Evil spirits are power-
less in the face of goodness" (MacMullan, p. 103). Harpax
cannot face Angelo in Dekker and Massinger's The Virgin Martyr.
See also Rowley's The Birth of Merlin, III.ii, and Act III of
Kirke's The Seven Champions of Christendom.

<u>Leogarius</u>. What harmony is this? I have no power

    To do them harme; observe their ceremonie.

      Ode. [Sung by the procession of Priests.]

<u>Post</u> <u>maris</u> <u>saevi</u> <u>fremitus</u> <u>Iernae</u>   145

(<u>Navitas</u> <u>coelo</u> <u>tremulos</u> <u>beante</u>)

<u>Vidimus</u> <u>gratum</u> <u>jubar</u> <u>enatantes</u>

      <u>littus</u> <u>inaurans</u>.

<u>Montium</u> <u>guin</u> <u>vos</u> <u>juga</u>, <u>vosque</u> <u>sylvae</u>

<u>Nunc</u> <u>salutamus</u>, <u>chorus</u> <u>advenarum</u>,   150

<u>Jubilum</u> <u>retro</u> <u>modulantur</u>, <u>Ecce</u>

      <u>Carbasa</u> <u>ventis</u>.

<u>Dulce</u> <u>supremo</u> <u>melos</u> <u>occinamus</u>

<u>Carminum</u> <u>flagrans</u> <u>Domino</u> <u>litamen</u>

<u>Cujus</u> <u>erranti</u> <u>dabitur</u> <u>popello</u>   155

      <u>Numine</u> <u>sacrum</u>.

---

143. harmony] music; tuneful sound.

145-156. <u>Post</u> . . . <u>sacrum</u>] "This Sapphic is Shirley's
own Latin verse, but no classical inspiration has been found
for it" (Armstrong, p. 83). A rough translation follows:

    1. After the roar of the raging Irish sea
(with heaven blessing the trembling sailors), we
who are coming out of the water see a pleasant
radiance gilding the shore.

    2. Now we, a chorus of foreigners, greet
you, O mountain peaks and you, O woods; look,
the sails measure in rhythm the song of praise
back to the winds.

    3. Let us sing a sweet song, a blazing
offering of hymns to almighty God by whose divine
power sanctuary will be given to a wandering people.

Leogarius. I'll speake to him. Stay, you that have presum'd

    Without our leave, to print your desperate foot

    Upon our Countrey; say, what bold designe

    Hath arm'd you with this insolent noyse, to dare   160

    And fright the holy peace of this faire Ile;

    Nay, in contempt of all our gods, advance

    Your songs in honour of an unknowne power?

    The King commands you speake.

Patrick.   Unto that title

    Thus we all bow;   [St. Patrick and Priests bow.]

              it speakes you are alli'd   165

    To Heaven; great Sir, we come not to distract

    Your peace; looke on your number; we bring no

    Signes of sterne war, no invasive force to draw

    Feare, or suspition, or your frownes upon us:

    A handfull of poore naked men we are,   170

165. all] Q; lowly Chetwood.

*167. your] Q; our Chetwood, Gifford, Donovan.

---

164. that title] i.e., of king.

165-166. it . . . heaven] Renaissance Englishmen saw
earthly order as reflecting divine order; the king ruled over
the body politic as God rules over the macrocosm. Correspon-
dences among these planes are very important in the world-view
of the period.

167. your] Despite the fact that all previous editors
have adopted an emendation here, the quarto reading makes
perfectly good sense. St. Patrick might be referring to the
large size of the king's train as well as the small size of
his own band of priests.

170. naked] without weapons or armor.

Throwne on your Coast, whose armes are only prayer,

That you would not be more unmercifull

Than the rough seas, since they have let us live

To finde your charitie.

Leogarius. Whence are you?

Patrick.   We are of Britaine, Sir.   175

Leogarius. Your name, that answer for the rest so boldly?

Patrick. My name is Patrick, who with these poore men

Beseech you would permit--

Leogarius.   No dwelling here,

And therefore quit this Kingdome speedily,

Or you shall curse you saw the land.   180

Dichu. Are they not Spies?

Archimagus. A whirlewind snatch 'em hence, and on the back

Of his black wings transport these fugitives,

And drop their cursed heads into the sea,

Or land 'em in some cold remotest wildernesse   185

Of all the world; they must not here inhabit.

_____

175. Britaine] Patrick was from Brittany (see BB,
p. 1).

182-186. A whirlewind . . . world] Donovan points out
that sudden storms, or whirlwinds, were popularly connected
with magic. Cf. Greene's Friar Bacon and Friar Bungay (I.i.
302-303) and Bellamente's speech in Love's Cruelty, III.iv:
"Some merciful whirlwind snatch this burden up, / And carry
it into the wilderness" (Gifford, II, 236).

Dichu. Hence, or we'll force you with these goads.

Corybreus.   Unlesse

    You have a mind to try how well your hoods

    Can swim, go trudge back to your rotten bark,

    And steere another course.

Ferochus.   You will finde Ilands   190

    Peopled with Squirrils, Rats, and Crowes, and Coneyes,

    Where you may better plant, my reverend Moles.

Endarius. Faces about.

Patrick.   You are inhospitable,

    And have more flintie bosomes than the rocks

    That bind your shores, and circle your faire Iland;   195

193. Faces] Q; Face Chetwood.

---

    187. goads] rods or sticks for driving cattle. Dichu
here might be referring to spears or swords.

    188-189. your . . . swim] Cf. a similar expression in
the ballad "Sir Patrick Spens," where the drowned lords are
described: "But lary or a' the play was played, / Their hats
they swam abune."

    189. bark] boat.

    191. Coneyes] rabbits.

    193. Faces about] about face.

    194. flintie bosomes] Cf. All's Well that Ends Well:
"Gratitude through flintie Tartar's bosome would peep forth"
(IV.iv.7).

But I must not returne--

Leogarius. How?

Archimagus. How?

Patrick. Till I have

    Perform'd my dutie: Know great King, I have   200

    Commission for my stay; I come not hither

    Without command, Legat from him, before

    Whose angry breath the rocks doe breake and thaw,

    To whose nod the mountaines humble their proud heads;

    The earth, the water, aire and heaven is his,   205

    And all the stars that shine with evening flames,

    Shew but their trembling when they wait on him:

    This supreme King's command I have obey'd,

    Who sent me hither to bring you to him,

    And this still wandring nation, to those springs   210

    Where soules are everlastingly refresh'd;

197. How?] Q; Not! Chetwood.

---

202. Legat] usually an ecclesiastic deputed to represent
the Pope, and armed with his authority. Although Shirley's
source gives an account of Patrick's receiving permission for
his journey in Rome, the sense of the passage suggests that
the saint is representing God directly, rather than the Pope.

203. rockes . . . thaw] Cf. the prophecy, I.i.59.
MacMullan suggests a parallel between this and Psalm XCVII:
"The hills melted like wax in the presence of the Lord"
(p. 102). This is also similar to the way Dichu's paralysis
is referred to in I.i.254.

Unto those gardens, whose immortall flowers

Staine your imagin'd shades, and blest abodes.

Leogarius.   What place is this?

Patrick.   Heaven; now a great way off.

But not accessible to those permit   215

Their pretious soules be strangled thus with mists,

And false opinion of their gods.

Archimagus.   No more.

Patrick.   I must say more in my great Master's cause,

And tell you in my dreames, he hath made me heare

From the dark wombs of mothers, prison'd infants   220

212-213.   those . . . abodes] "This is a description of
Elysium rather than of Heaven. It is interesting as a conclusion to the preceding Biblical lines" (MacMullan, p. 103).
Such literal-mindedness obscures what is a perfectly good
metaphorical presentation of a heaven of any kind.

213.   Staine] eclipse. shades] referring to the shadowy
and tenuous claims for an afterlife assigned to pagan reli-
gions by Christianity; also a word used to denote ghosts or
hell.

215.   those] those who. Omitted relative (cf. Abbott,
par. 244).

216.   be] to be (cf. Abbott, par. 349). mists] states
of obscurity or uncertainty; "atmospheres" of doubt.

217.   opinion of] belief in.

220.   dark wombs] "This is a reference to the Pelagian
heresy inserted in the text of Patrick's dream by the Monks"
(MacMullan, p. 104).

Confessing how their parents are mis-led,

And calling me thus far to be their freedome.

Have pitie on your selves; be men, and let not

A blind devotion of your painted gods--

Dichu. He does blaspheme. Accept me, Jove, thy Priest,   225

And this my sacrifice. [Offers to strike St. Patrick.]

                    Ha, mine armes grow stiffe,

I feele an ice creeping through all my bloud,

There's winter in my heart, I change o' th' sudden,

Am growne a statue, every limb is marble;

Yee gods take pitie on me; in your cause   230

I wither thus; Jove, if thou hast a lightning,

Bestow some here, and warme me.

Corybreus. Strange!

226. S. D. Offers . . . Patrick] Gifford.

219-222. in . . . freedome] Cf. BB, pp. 11-12.

224. painted] unreal; artificial.

225-259. Cf. the BB, p. 17. The ability to strike
people motionless characterizes several dramatic sorcerers in
the period. Prospero charms Ferdinand from moving when Ferdinand draws on him in The Tempest (I.ii.466.1), and Oberon
prevents Bohan from chopping off his limbs in Greene's The
Scottish History of James IV ("Induction," 25-35). See also
The Tempest (V.i.57.1-6), Beaumont and Fletcher's The Prophet-
ess (I.iii.224-226), Marlowe's Doctor Faustus (IV.vii.110-121),
and Greene's Friar Bacon and Friar Bungay (II.iii.767.1).

231. Jove . . . lightning] "It was believed that Jupiter controlled lightning and that those who were struck by it
were honored by the gods and made holy" (Donovan, p. 14).

Endarius.   Father! Brother, if he should dye now?

Ferochus.   [Aside.]   I am his eldest son; he shall find me

    reasonable;

    He may doe worse, considering how long   235

    I have been of age.

Dichu.   No power let fall compassion. I have

    Offended. Whom? I know not; this good man

    Forgive, and if the Deitie thou serv'st

    Can put a life into this frozen pile,   240

    Pray for me.

Leogarius.   Villaine, wouldst thou owe thy life

    To the mercie of the power he serves?

Archimagus.   Wish rather

    To rot for ever thus.

Leogarius.   And if thou diest,

    I'll build a Temple here, and in this posture

    Kings shall kneele to thee, and on solemne dayes   245

    Present their crownes; Queenes shall compose thee garlands,

    Virgins shall sing thy name, and 'bout thy neck

247. 'bout] Q; around Chetwood.

----

240. pile] The OED lists the following obsolete definition: "A pillar; a pier, esp. of a bridge"--hence, figuratively applied to "the neck, leg, &c." Perhaps Dichu is
referring to his entire trunk which has turned to stone.

246. compose] put together.

And armes disperse the riches of their Art;

Next to our Gods we honour thee: keep from

The Impostor.

Corybreus.   I have no meaning to come neere him.   250

Patrick. Give me thy hand: now move, and may thy heart

Find softnesse too; this mercie is the least

Of my great Master's treasures.

Dichu.   I feele my heat

Return'd, and all my rockie parts grow supple;

Let the first use I make of their restore, be   255

To bend my knees to you.   [Kneels before St. Patrick.]

Patrick.   Bow them to him

That gave me power to helpe thee.

Ferochus.   He is well agen.

Dichu. I finde a beame let into my darke soule,

Oh take me to your faith; here I give backe

My selfe to serve your god.

251-253. Give . . . treasures] Donovan assigns to Corybreus.

255. restore] Q; restoration Gifford.

---

250. meaning] intention.

255. restore] restoration. The OED cites this line as
an example of the obsolete use of the verb as a noun.

Leogarius.   Traitrous to heaven!   260

    Come from him.

Dichu.   Bid my haste forsake a blessing.

Endarius. Father.

Dichu. Call this good man your father, Boyes.

Archimagus.   He's mad,

    And I am frantick at this base Apostasie.

    My Lord, think how you may provoke our gods,   265

    And the King anger.

Patrick.   Feare his wrath that made,

    And can let fall the world.

Ferochus. [Aside.] He may yet do me as great a curtesie

*261. my haste] Q; me Gifford.

264. this base] Q; the false Donovan.

266. King] Q; King's Gifford.

---

    261. Bid . . . blessing] This line is obscure, but
Gifford's emendation is unjustifiable. Perhaps "Bid" should
be "Did," making the line read, "Did my haste forsake a blessing?" Despite the fact that "Did" makes better sense, however,
there is no bibliographical justification for emending the
line. As it stands, the line means "That my hurry should make
me forget to give my sons my blessing [is unfortunate indeed]!"

    261. forsake] forget.

    266. the King anger] Shirley is using the old genetive
case here (cf. Abbott, par. 217). However, Gifford's emendation is unnecessary.

    267. let . . . world] cause the world to be destroyed.

     As dying comes too, if his error hold,

     And the King's anger.

Leogarius.   Dotard,   270

     Returne; and prostrate to the gods we worship,

     Or though his witchcraft now protect thy selfe;

     Thy sonnes shall bleed.

Ferochus.   How's that?

Leogarius.   To satisfie

     The gods and us, with the next morning's Sunne,

     Unlesse thou rise, and sacrifice to our Altars,   275

     Downe from that Rocke which over lookes the Sea,

     They shall be throwne; my vow is fixt.

Ferochus.   Deare father.

*272.   through] Gifford, Donovan; though Q.

---

     269.   comes too] comes to.

     270.   Dotard] imbecile.

     272.   though . . . thy selfe] despite the fact that his
magic now shields you.

     272.   his] i.e., Patrick's.

     273.   bleed] die by bleeding to death. Cf. Julius Ceasar:
"Ceasar must bleed for it" (II.i.171).

     273-277.   To . . . fixt] In Shirley's source Ferochus
and Endarius were to be starved to death (see the BB, pp. 20-21).
Shirley's punishment here was probably influenced by classical
sources. Cf. Tiberius' rock in Jonson's Sejanus, His Fall
and the Tarpeian rock at the southwest corner of the Capitoline
hill in Rome, from which criminals were thrown to their deaths.

Leogarius. Take them away; their fate depends on him.

Dichu. Oh, I am lost.

Patrick. Thou art found.   280

Dichu. Forsake me not, poore boyes! my prayers and blessing.

Patrick. Set forward now in heaven's name,
     And finish our procession.

               Exeunt [St. Patrick, Dichu, Victor, and Priests].

Leogarius.   Death pursue 'em;
     Will nothing make them feele our wrath?

Corybreus.   The charme
     Will not last alwayes.

Archimagus.   Their fate is not yet ripe;   285
     Be not dejected, Sir; the gods cannot
     Be patient long. Meanetime let me advise,
     Not by your Lawes, or other open force,
     To persecute 'em; but disguise your anger.

Leogarius. Ha?   290

Archimagus. What matter is't, so we destroy these wretches

278. fate depends] Q; fates depend Gifford.
289. persecute] Q; prosecute Chetwood.
290. Ha] Q; How Chetwood.

_____

     291. so] just so.

> What wayes we take? invite him to your Court;
>
> Pretend I know not what desires to heare
>
> More of his faith, that you find turnes within
>
> Your heart, and tremble at the miracle   295
>
> Wrought upon <u>Dichu</u>; when he's in your possession
>
> A thousand stratagems may be thought upon
>
> To send his giddy soule most quaintly off to
>
> That fine phantasticall reward he dreames on
>
> I' th' t'other world.

<u>Leogarius</u>.   Thou hast pleas'd us, <u>Archimagus</u>.   300

<u>Corybreus</u>. Great <u>Ceanerachius</u> has inspir'd the Priest!
> This is the only way.

<u>Conallus</u>.   I doe not like it.

<u>Leogarius</u>. It shall be so; he shall be thus invited,
> And we will meet him with our Queene and Daughters,
> Who shall compose themselves to entertaine him.   305

<u>Archimagus</u>. Leave me to instruct my princely charge, your
> Daughters.

<u>Leogarius</u>. Be still their blest Director; to thy charge
> We gave them up long since; but do not tell 'em

---

300. I' th' t'other] There seem to be more words than
necessary in this contraction. However, cf. Webster's <u>The
Devil's Law-Case</u>: "Before I went to 'th tother Hogg-robber"
(IV.i.107).

305. compose] dispose.

What happen'd to the Apostate Dichu; women

Have soluble and easie hearts, that accident   310

May startle their religion; keep 'em firme

In the devotion to our gods, whose virgins

We hope to call them shortly, if their zeale

Maintaine that holy flame that yet hath fill'd

Their bosomes.

Archimagus.   They are the Darlings of the Temple.   315

Leogarius. Conallus, you shall be the messenger,

And beare our invitation.

Archimagus.   Trouble not

The Prince; impose that businesse on my care.

Leogarius. Be it so.

Conallus.   I am glad I am off the employment.

Leogarius. All wayes to serve our gods are free, and good;   320

When shed for them, they take delight in blood.   Exeunt.

---

309. women . . . religion] "This is hardly an original
generalization. 'Women are soft, mild, pitiful, and flexible'
(2 Henry VI, IV.i.141). 'Women are frail too!' (Measure for
Measure, III.iv.141). And, of course, Hamlet. But these lines
afford a typical illustration of the conventionality of much
of Shirley's work" (MacMullan, p. 105).

310. accident] event. startle] cause to waver.

319. am off the employment] no longer have the job. Conallus' desire not to speak with Patrick has little or no moti-
vation.

ACT II. [Scene i.]

Enter Ethne and Fedella, dancing.

Ethne. I am weary, and yet I would have more; my heart
      Was never more dispos'd to mirth, Fedella.

Fedella. Mine is as light as yours, Sister; I am
      All aire, me thinks.

Ethne.   And I all mounting fire.

Fedella. 'Tis well we are alone.

Ethne.   'Tis ill we are;   5
      This heat our servants should have given us.

Fedella. I wonder we cannot see 'em; they were not
      Since we first tooke them to our favor, guiltie
      Of such neglect.

Ethne.   You wrong our birth and bloud,

II.i. Gifford locates this scene in "The Palace Garden."
Jocelyn also places the scene near the palace (see BB, p. 34).

4. I . . . fire] This is a reference to the Renaissance
idea of the humors, which saw psychology influenced by the
four elements--earth, air, fire, and water. The element of
fire influenced the passions. Cf. Cleopatra in Antony and
Cleopatra: "I am fire and air" (V.ii.292).

6. heat] high temperature in the body arising from a
disordered condition, emotional excitement. Ethne is saying
that the two women should have been excited by the presence
of their lovers, rather than their absence.

6. servants] suitors.

112

    To thinke they dare neglect us, for if they   10

    Forget what we deserve in loving them,

    They owe more duṭie, as we are the King's

    Daughters, than to displease us so.

Fedella.   That binds

    But forme and heartlesse ceremony, Sister;

    By your favor, I had rather hold my servant   15

    By his owne love, that chaines his heart to mine,

    Than all the bands of state.

Ethne. I am of thy mind too, wo'd they were here;

    I shall be sad againe; fie, what a thing 'tis

    For two Ladies to be in love, and alone without   20

    A man so long.

            Enter Rodamant [with a book]

*13. binds∧] Gifford, Donovan; binds: Q

21.1 S. D. with a book] Gifford.

───────────

    13-14. That . . . ceremony] MacMullan points out (p. 106)
that the colon in Q after "binds" marks an emphatic pause. However, the passage is more intelligible with the colon removed.
The sense of the lines is "only formality and heartless ceremony
(as opposed to true feelings) are bound by duty."

    16. chaines . . . mine] a common phrase in Shirley. Cf.
The Lady of Pleasure, III.i: "Your eyes are brided, / And
your hearts chain'd to some desires" (Gifford, IV, 48) and
IV.iii: "Your eyes . . . should chain every heart a prisoner"
(Gifford, IV, 76). See also The Royal Master, I.i: "No brothers
were more chain'd in their affections" (Gifford, IV, 110).

    17. bands] bonds.

Fedella.   Here's one.

Ethne.   A foolish one,
    Our Governor's servant; how now Rodamant?

Rodamant. Keep off.

Fedella. What, is the fellow conjuring?

Rodamant. I wo'd, but I cannot read these devillish names.   25

Ethne. How long hast thou serv'd Archimagus?

Rodamant. Long enough to have had a Devill of mine owne, if
    hee had pleas'd; I have drudg'd under him almost these
    seven yeeres, in hope to learne the trade of Magick, and
    none of his spirits will obey me; would I were a witch,   30
    then I should have a Familiar, a sucking Devill, upon
    occaision to doe me service.

Fedella. A Devill?

---

22. servant] This word is used with a quibble on "servants" meaning "suitors." See line 6 above.

23. Keep off] Keep away.

28. drudg'd under] slaved for.

29. seven yeeres] "The usual term of an apprenticeship"
(MacMullan). Note lines 41-42, "when I come out of my time."

31. a Familiar, a sucking Devill] "A familiar is a minor
form of spirit who works petty magic for the witch, and, in
return, takes suck from him or her at a special teat. Pug, in
[Dekker, Rowley, and Ford's] The Witch of Edmunton was a familiar. They were perhaps the most common of devils; and they
figure at all the witch trials; but their power was extremely
limited" (MacMullan, p. 106).

Rodamant. Oh, I lov'd him of a child.

Ethne. What wouldst thou do with the Devill?   35

Rodamant. Only exercise my body, take the aire now and then

over steeples, and saile once a month to Scotland in a

sieve, to see my Freinds. I have a granam there, if I

had been rul'd, would not have seen me wanted a divell

at these yeers; pray Madam speak to my Master for me,   40

that my freinds may not laugh at me, when I come out

of my time; he has spirits enough: I desire none of his

---

34. him] i.e., the devil. of] as.

36. exercise] Perhaps this is a malapropism for "exor-
cise."

36. take the aire] "Witches were reputed to ride through
the air" (MacMullan, p. 106). Cf. Goody Dickinson in Heywood's
The Late Lancashire Witches: "The Earth we tread not, but the
winde, / For we must progresse through the aire" (Heywood, IV,
200).

37. Scotland] "Scotland seems to have been a favourite
haunt of the devil; a situation which may have developed from
King James' assiduous attempts to hunt out all professors of
the black art" (MacMullan, p. 106). Cf. The Imposture, V.iv:
"I left her in a sieve was bound for Scotland / This morn to
see some kindred . . ." (Gifford, V, 264).

38. sieve] As well as enabling them to ride through the
air on broomsticks, the power of witches could aid them in
traveling through the water in sieves. Cf. Macbeth, I.iii.8,
for the same image.

38. granam] grandmother.

39. rul'd] subjected to control, guidance, or discipline.

39. seen me wanted] forborne my lacking.

40. at these yeers] for so many years.

41-42. come out of my time] See note on line 29.

42. spirits] a pun on "high spirits" and "conjured spirits."

grandes, a little Don Diego Diabolo would serve my turne,

if he have but skill in Love or Physicke.

Fedella. Physick for what? art sick?   45

Rodamant. I am not sick, but I am troubled with a desperate

consumption.

Ethne. How?

Fedella. Why that's nothing.

Rodamant. To you that are great Ladies, and fed high;   50

But to a man that is kept lean and hungry

A little falling of the flesh is seen.

Ethne. I heard thee name love; prethee art thou in love?

50. fed] Q; feed Chetwood.

---

43. grandes] grandees. Spanish noblemen of the highest
rank, hence persons of high rank or position, or of eminence
in any line.

43. Don Diego Diabolo] "Don Diego" is a common name for
a Spaniard. The sense of this passage is that Rodamant is not
choosey. He would be satisfied with a devil of minor eminence.
Cf. Dick of Devonshire, II.iv.276-277: "Now Don Diego . . .
or Don Divell, I defye thee" (Bullen Collection, II, 39).

44. Physicke] medicine.

47-63. Consumption, lack of appetite, sore eyes, and
insomnia are all symptoms of love-melancholy. See Robert Burton's Anatomy of Melancholy, Third Partition, Sect. 1, Memb. 3.

47. consumption] a wasting disease.

52. falling of the flesh] loss of weight.

Rodamant. In love? look on my sore eyes.

Ethne. They are well enough, and thou canst see.   55

Rodamant. Yes, I can see a little with 'em; would they were out.

Ethne. How? out?

Rodamant. Out of their paine. I have but seaven teeth and a

    halfe, and foure on 'em are rotten; here's a stump a pickax

    cannot dig out of my gummes.   60

Fedella. Are these signes of love?

Rodamant. Oh infallible. Beside, I cannot sleep for dreaming

    a my Mistresse.

Ethne. So, and what's her name?

59. on] Q; of Chetwood.

63. a] Q; on Chetwood.

---

54. sore eyes] The conventional Elizabethan idea was
that the lover fell in love with the beloved when the beams
of her beauty entered his eyes. This caused lovesickness.
Cf. the proverb "a sight for sore eyes" (Tilley, E271).

59. on] of. The OED lists the replacement of "of" by
"on" as common in literary use to circa 1750. Cf. Macbeth:
"The perfect spy o' the time / The moment on 't" (III.i.130-131).

59-60. A lack of teeth was traditionally associated
with sexuality. Chaucer's Wife of Bath, for example, was
"gat-tothéd," indicating her amorous nature (Walter Clyde
Curry, Chaucer and the Medieval Sciences, London, 1926, rpt.
1960, p. 102).

63. a] of.

Rodamant. You shall pardon me, she is--   65

Ethne. A man or a woman?

Rodamant. Nay she is a woman, as sure--as sure as you are
     the Queen's daughters. I name no body; do not you say
     'tis the Queen; I am what I am, and she is what she is.

Ethne. Well said.   70

Rodamant. And if I live, I will dy for her; but I forget my
     self, I had a message to tell you; first my Master com-
     mends him to your Graces and will be here presently: sec-
     ondly I have news; Do you know what I meane?

Fedella. Not we.   75

Rodamant. Why then, my Lord Ferochus, and his brother Endarius--
     you know 'em?

Ethne. What of them?

Rodamant. And they know you.

Fedella. To the purpose.   80

Rodamant. I know not that, but they are--

67. woman, as sure--as sure as] woman as sure, as sure as Q;
woman, as sure as Gifford.

_____

     71. dy] This word carries the usual sexual overtones
common in the period.

     73. presently] immediately.

Ethne. What?

Rodamant. Not made for worme's meat.

Fedella. What meanes the fellow?

Rodamant. The King has commanded they shall be throwne from   85
    a rock into the sea, that's all; but here's my Master can
    tell you the whole story.

Ethne. What said the scritchowle?

                Enter Archimagus [with letters].

Fedella. We hope Archimagus brings better newes.
    And yet his face is cast into a forme of sorrow.   90
    What are these?

Archimagus. Read, and collect your noble forces up,
    You will be lost else; [Gives them the letters]
                    alas poore Ladies,
    How soon their blood is frighted?

---

    88. scritchowle] screechowl. A bearer of evil tidings,
since the bird was considered to be an evil omen. Cf. the
following lines from The Wedding, IV.iv: "Thy name . . . /
Shall sound hereafter like a screechowl's note, / And fright
the hearer" (Gifford, I, 433).

    94. blood is frighted] In Renaissance psychology, blood
is one of the "humors" or fluids usually associated with health
and youth. Shirley probably means here that they grew pale
(i.e., the blood ran out of their faces) as soon as they saw
the letters. Cf. The Cardinal: ". . . now if you / Will give
your judgements leave though at the first / Face of this object
your cool bloods were frighted" (Forker, II.i.94).

Ethne.   Every character

   Gives my poor heart a wound.   95

Fedella. Alas, how much of mischief is contain'd

   In this poore narrow paper.

Ethne.   Can this be?

Archimagus. Madam too true; the anger of the King

   Is heavy and inevitable; you may

   Beleeve what their sad pens have bled to you;   100

   They have no hope, not once before they die

   To see your blessed eyes, and take their leave,

   And weep into your bosome, their last farewell.

Fedella. They must not, sha'not die so.

Archimagus.   They must Madam.

Ethne. I will die with 'em too then: Sister shall   105

   They leave the world without our company?

Fedella. Could not you bend the King our cruell father?

   You should have said, we lov'd them; you have most

   Power to prevaile with him; you should have told him,

   The gods would be offended, and revenge their death   110

   With some strange curse upon this Iland.

---

  94. character] written character in the letters.

  97. narrow] small.

  107. bend] alter the resolve of.

Ethne. You knew our loves, and all our meetings Sir;

     They were not without you, nor will we live

     Without them, tell our father. Did our hearts

     Flatter themselves with mirth, to be struck dead   115

     With this, this murdering newes. I'll to the King.

Archimagus. Stay, and containe your selves; your loves are brave,

     Nor shall your flame die thus; as I was first

     Of counsell with your thoughts, I will preserve 'em:

     They sha'not die, if my braine leave me not.   120

Fedella. Oh, I could dwell upon his lips to thank him.

Archimagus. But they must then be banish'd.

Ethne.   That's death.

     Unlesse we go along to exile with 'em.

Archimagus. I have the way; they shall deceive the sentence

     Of the enraged King, and live; nor shall   125

     This be reward of your affections;

     You shall converse more often, and more freely

     Than ever, if you dare be wise and secret.

126. be reward] Q; be [the sole] reward Gifford.

---

     113. They] i.e., the loves and meetings of Ethne and
Fedella with Ferochus and Endarius.

     117. brave] courageous, glorious.

     124. deceive] escape.

     128. wise] prudent.

Fedella. You make us happy.

Archimagus.   Here's your elder brother;
    Away and trust to me.   [Exeunt Ethne and Fedella.] 130

                    Enter Corybreus.

Corybreus. Health to our Priest.

Archimagus.   And to your Highnesse.

                Enter Emeria and Conallus.

    Do you see that couple?

Corybreus. My brother and the faire Emeria, Milcho's daughter,
    Out of their way; but so, to reach their voice,
    This place o' th' Garden's apt.

Archimagus.   Observe 'em.   135

            [Corybreus and Archimagus retire.]

Emeria. But will you not, my Lord, repent to have plac'd
    Your love so much unworthily?

130.   S. D. Exeunt . . . Fedella] Gifford.
135.1 S. D. Corybreus . . . retire] Gifford.

_____

    129. happy] fortunate.
    134. reach their voice] overhear their conversation.
    135. apt] suitable.

<u>Conallus</u>.   Oh never.

    My best <u>Emeria</u>, thou hast a wealth

    In thy owne vertue, above all the world;

    Be constant, and I'm blest.

<u>Emeria</u>.   This hand and heaven   140

    Be witnesse where my heart goes.

<u>Corybreus</u>.   [<u>Aside</u>.] If my fate

    Cannot enjoy thy love, I shall grieve both

    Your destinies.

<u>Archimagus</u>.   [<u>Aside</u> <u>to</u> Corybreus.] Be confident you shall

    Enjoy her, if you'll follow my directions.

<u>Corybreus</u>. [<u>Aside</u> <u>to</u> Archimagus.] Thou art my genius, but

      she's very holy,   145

    And, I feare, too religious to her vowes;

    She is devoted much to <u>Ceanerachius</u>,

    Head of the gods.

    135.1-158. Forsythe (pp. 91-94) points out that Shirley uses eavesdropping probably more often than any other dramatist of the period. In the twenty-two dramatic pieces by Shirley which Forsythe discusses, there are forty-one instances of this device. Although these are usually minor incidents, the use of eavesdropping in Shirley's plays is often used, as here, to convey secret information unintentionally to the wrong people. This device is also used in IV.i.278 and V.i.21.

    141-142. If . . . love] i.e., "If it is my destiny that we never be lovers . . . ."

    142. grieve] do harm to.

    144. genius] attendant spirit. In Brome's The Queen and Concubine and The Queen's Exchange, guardian angels are called "Genius."

<u>Archimagus.</u>   [<u>Aside</u> <u>to</u> Corybreus.] Sir her piety

    Prepares your conquest, as I'le manage things;

    I wonot trust the ayre too much.   150

<u>Conallus.</u> This kisse and all's confirm'd.   [<u>Kisses</u> <u>her.</u>]

<u>Emeria.</u>   Pray my Lord use

    My poore heart kindly, for you take it with you.

<u>Conallus.</u> I leave mine in exchange.   <u>Exit.</u>

<u>Archimagus.</u>   [<u>Aside</u> <u>to</u> Corybreus.] He is
        gone; advance

    To your Mistris, and if you want art to move her.

    I shannot sir, to make you prosper; 'tis   155

    Firmely design'd, when we meet next, you shall

    Know more.   <u>Exit.</u>

<u>Corybreus.</u>   [<u>Coming</u> <u>forward.</u>] How now my fair <u>Emeria.</u>

<u>Emeria.</u> I do beseech your highnesse' pardon,

    I did think I was alone.

151. S. D. <u>Kisses</u> <u>her</u>] <u>Gifford.</u>

---

149. prepares your conquest] makes your conquest easier.

150. I wonot trust the ayre too much] be careful not to blab.

154. want] lack.

154-155. if . . . prosper] i.e., "If you lack art . . . , I shall not [lack art] to make you succeed." The repetition of "want art" is implied in the second clause.

Corybreus.   Alone you are

   In beauty sweet <u>Emeria</u>, and all   160

   The graces of your sex.

<u>Emeria</u>.   You are too great

   To flatter me, and yet this language comes

   So neer the wickednesse of court praise, I dare not

   With modesty imagine your heart means so.

<u>Corybreus</u>. Yet in this garden, when you seem'd most solitary, 165

   Madam, you had many fair, and sweet companions.

<u>Emeria</u>. Not I sir.

<u>Corybreus</u>.   Yes, and my rivalls too <u>Emeria</u>,

   And now they court thy beauty in my presence,

   Proud erring things of nature; dost not see

   As thou dost move, how every amorous plant   170

   157-242. Forsythe (pp. 69-70) lists a large number of
other instances of attempts at seduction "which are indignantly
resisted by the woman, often with one or more set speeches in
praise of chastity." Most comparable are the conversations
between the King and Albina in The Politician, I.i (Gifford, V,
96-97), and between Leontio and Euphemia in The Duke's Mistress, III.ii (Gifford, IV, 231-234). Cf. also Isabella and
Angelo in Measure for Measure (II.iv.31-170) and D'Amville and
Castabella in The Atheist's Tragedy (IV.iii.80-174).

   160. and all] and in all. Shirley has omitted the preposition here, perhaps because the parallelism (connecting this
phrase with "in beauty") makes it understood.

   163. court praise] MacMullan points out that "Shirley
distinguishes the difference between 'court praise' and simple
love making" (p. 107).

   168. court . . . presence] Corybreus is referring to
his rivals, the flowers, who are also trying to make suit to
Emeria while Corybreus is standing there.

Doth bow his leavy head, and becken thee?

The winde doth practise dalliance with thy hairs

And weave a thousand pretty netts within

To catch it self. That violet droop'd but now,

How tis exalted at thy smile, and spreads   175

A virgin bosome to thee. There's a rose

Would have slept still within his bud, but at

Thy presence, it doth open his thin curtains

And with warm apprehension looking forth

172. hairs] Q; hair Chetwood.

167-187. The courtly nature of this passage is very conventional. MacMullan (p. 107) cites passages of a similar
nature in Shirley's "Narcissus, or the Self-Lover."

The flowers here smile upon him as he treads,
And but when he looks up, hang downe their heads
. . . .
Thus all conspire, him severall waies to woo,
For whose love onely they delight to grow
                        (Armstrong, pp. 20-21).

See also The Triumph of Beauty (Gifford, VI, 337).

171. leavy] leafy.

172. dalliance] wanton toying. hairs] The plural form
was often used in the sixteenth and seventeenth centuries to
refer to hair in the collective sense. Cf. Spenser's Faerie
Queene, IV.viii.4: "He . . . would . . . knocke his head, and
rend his rugged heares."

172-174. Cf. Romelio's dirge in Webster's The Devil's
Law Case:

Vaine the ambition of Kings,
Who seeke by trophies and dead things,
To leave a living name behind,
And weave but nets to catch the wind . . . . (V.iv.143-146)

Also "He catches the wind in a net" (Tilley, W416).

Betrayes her love in blushes. And that Woodbine   180

As it would be divorc'd from the Sweet-bryer,

Courts thee to an embrace. It is not dew

That like so many pearls embroider all

The flowers, but teares of their complaint, with feare

To loose thee, from whose eye they take in all   185

That makes them beautifull, and with humble necks

Pay duty unto thee their onely spring.

180. her] Q; its Gifford.

183. embroider] Q; embroiders Gifford.

174-182. Flowers are used in this passage with their usual
Renaissance symbolic designations. Both the rose and the violet
were identified with the Virgin Mary, as well as with Venus in
Classical times. The violet's drooping was explained as having
been caused by the cross falling on it, and the color of the rose
came at the crucifixion. Shirley also draws upon the idea that
the beauty of nature is often in awe of human beauty. The woodbine represented fraternal love and the sweet briar poetry and
simplicity. The climbing and intertwining habits of these plants
suggested to Renaissance poetry an emblematic representation of
human love. Cf. Love in a Maze, II.iii:

> Hast thou not seen the woodbine,
> That honey-dropping tree, and the loved brier,
> Embrace with their chaste boughs, twisting themselves,
> And weaving a green net to catch the birds,
> Till it do seem one body, while the flowers
> Wantonly run to meet and kiss each other? (Gifford, II, 306)

183. embroider] Shirley used a plural verb here despite
the fact that "dew" (sing.) is the subject. He might have considered "pearls" to be the subject, or "dew" as a collective
noun of indeterminate number, since the figure implies many
drops of dew.

185. loose] lose.

187-192. Renaissance psychology defined three levels of
"souls" or consciousness, vegetable (plants), animal (beasts),
and rational (human beings). Cf. Burton, Anatomy of Melancholy,
Sect. I, Memb. 2, Subs. 1-8. By the "active" soul, Corybreus
is referring to the rational.

Emeria. Your Grace is courtly.

Corybreus.   When these dull vegetalls

    Shew their ambition to be thine Emeria,

    How much should we, that have an active soule   190

    To know and value thee, be taken with

    This beauty? yet if you dare trust me Madam,

    There's none, within the throng of thy admirers,

    More willing, more devote to be thy servant

    Then Corybreus.

Emeria.   I must agen beseech   195

    Your pardon, and declare my self most ignorant:

    Pray speak your meaning in a dialect

    I understand.

Corybreus.   Why, I do love you Madam.

Emeria. If this be it, I dare not sir beleeve

    You condescend so low to love Emeria,   200

    A worthlesse thing.

Corybreus.   Why not? I love you Madam.

---

   188. vegetalls] vegetables.

   194. devote] devoted. "Owing to the tendency to drop the
inflection en, the Elizabethan authors frequently used the cur-
tailed forms of past participles which are common in early
English . . ." (Abbott, par. 343).

   195. Then] than. The words were often used interchangeably
in seventeenth-century English. See Abbott, par. 70.

If there be difference of our birth, or state,

When we are compar'd, it should make me the first

In your fair thoughts: come, you must love agen,

And meet me with an equall active flame.   205

Emeria. I am more skil'd in dutie sir, then love.

Corybreus. You would be coy; your heart is not bestow'd?

Emeria. Indeed it is.

Corybreus.   On whom?

Emeria.   I must not name.

Corybreus. Were he my brother did twist heart with thine,

That act should make him strange to my blood,   210

And I would cut him from his bold embraces.

Emeria. [Aside.] Alas, I feare.

Corybreus.   I know you will be wise

210. strange] Q; stranger Chetwood, Gifford, Donovan.

---

205. meet . . . flame] Corybreus is encouraging Emeria
to return his attentions actively, rather than responding in
the usual "passive" feminine manner.

206. Then] than.

210. strange . . . blood] i.e., seem unlike a brother.

211. I . . . embraces] Cf. Colombo's threat to Rosaura
in The Cardinal: ". . . if after / You dare provoke the Priest,
and heaven so much, / To take another, in thy bed I'l cut him
from / Thy warm embrace, and throw his heart to Ravens" (Forker,
IV.ii.70-73).

And just to my desires <u>Emeria</u>,

When you shall see my love bid fairest for you,

And that presented from a Prince, who knowes   215

No equall here. Come, I already promise

My self possest of those faire eyes, in which

I gazing thus, at every search discover

New crystall heavens; those tempting cheekes are mine,

A garden with fresh flowers all the winter;   220

Those lips invite to print my soul upon 'em

Or loose it in thy breath, which I'le convey

Downe to my heart, and wish no other spirit,

As loth to change it for my owne agen.

How in thy bosome will I dwell <u>Emeria,</u>   225

And tell the azure winding of thy veins

That flow, yet climbe those soft, and ivory hills

Whose smooth descent leads to a blisse, that may

Be known, but puzzle art and tongue to speak it.

I prethee do not use this froward motion,   230

I must, and will be thine.

216-229. MacMullan (p. 107) suggests that this conventional
passage in the courtly tradition derives from Spenser in <u>The
Faerie Queene</u> (IV.viii.42).

219-220. those . . . winter] Cf. Thomas Campion's poem:
"There is a garden in her face, / Where roses and white lilies
grow; / A heavenly paradise is that place, / Wherein all pleasant fruits do flow . . ." (lines 1-4).

221. invite . . . soul] invite me to leave the mark of
my soul upon them by kissing them.

230. froward] obstinate.

Emeria.   Be your own sir,

    And do not thus afflict my innocence;

    Had you the power of all the world, and man,

    You could not force my will, which you have frighted

    More from you then my duty, although powerfull,   235

    Can call agen; you are not modest sir,

    Indeed I feare you are not; I must leave you,

    Better desires attend your Grace and me.   Exit.

Corybreus. This wo' not gain her; her heart's fixt upon

    My brother; all my hope is in Archimagus;   240

    She is a frozen thing, yet she may melt.

    If their disdain should make a man despaire,

    Nature mistook in making woman faire.   Exit.

[Act II, scene ii.]

An altar discovered, [Ferochus and Endarius representing] two

---

    234-236. You . . . agen] The meaning and syntax of this
passage is obscure. A rough paraphrase follows: Your bold suit
has frightened me, and caused me to neglect my duty. That duty,
however, is a powerful force upon me, and could be reinvoked.
But my will could not be forced to make me love you.

    242. Their] The reference is to "women's" (implied).

    II.ii.0.1. An altar discovered] Donovan suggests that this
direction indicates that an act curtain was used. The idea that
the Werburgh Street theater was similar to the Phoenix in London
(see the Introduction, p. 40) suggests that this could have been
the case since the Phoenix might have been equipped for the use
of scenery with a proscenium arch and curtains. Bentley discusses this possibility but points out that "the evidence is not
sufficient to demonstrate such a radical innovation" (IV, 51).
If the Irish theater was more traditional in design, the altar
could have been set up in the inner stage and that curtain used
to discover it.

Idolls upon it, Archimagus and [Magicians], lights and incense

prepar'd by Rodamant.

Rodamant. These be new Dieties, made since yesterday;

We shift our gods, as fast as some shift trenchers;

Pray sir what do you call their names? they are

But halfe gods, demi-gods as they say; there's

Nothing beneath the navell.

Archimagus.   This with the thunderbolt is

Jupiter.   5

Rodamant. Jupiter? 'Tis time he were cut off by the middle;

He has been a notable thunderer in his dayes.

Magitian.   This is Mars.

*7. S. H. Magitian] Gifford substantively; Prin. Q.

---

2. trenchers] wooden dinner plates.

5. nothing . . . navell] Apparently the lower halves of
the bodies of Ferochus and Endarius are cut off by the altar.
Rodamant facetiously refers to the lack of sexual organs on the
statues.

5-7. Jupiter was the god of thunder in Roman mythology.
Rodamant, however, is punning on the sexual suggestions of
"thunderer," i.e., a sexually active man.

7. S. H. Magitian] "Prin." is apparently a misprint for
"Priest," since "Prince" Conallus is not on stage. The assist-
ants of Archimagus are referred to variously in Q, so I have
emended all designations of them as "Priests" to "Magitians" to
distinguish them from the Priests accompanying St. Patrick. See
line 62 and note below.

Rodamant. Mars from the middle upward. Was it by my Lady Venus'

   direction that he is dismembred too? He that overcame all

   in a full careere, looks now like a Demilaunce.   10

Archimagus. Are they not lively form'd? but sirra away; tell

   the young Ladies the King is upon entrance. [Exit Rodamant.]

         Enter [at one door] Leogarius, Queen, Conallus.

      At the other door, Ethne, Fedella, [and Rodamant.]

   They all kneel, [and Leogarius places his crown upon the altar].

Archimagus. To Jove and Mars the King doth pay

      His duty, and thus humbly lays

      Upon his Altar, his bright crowne,   15

      Which is not his, if they but frowne.

      In token you are pleas'd, let some

      Coelestiall flame make pure this roome.

            A flame behinde the Altar.

   8-10. Rodamant is referring here to Mars's affair with
Venus while she was still married to Vulcan. Vulcan embarrassed
the two by catching them naked in a net and exposing them to the
ridicule of the other gods.

   10. Demilaunce] The OED definition is as follows: "A
light horseman armed with a demilance (a lance with a short
shaft). Often used humorously like 'cavalier'." Shirley's
usage in Love's Cruelty, III.ii ("Be not angry demilance . . ."
[Gifford, II, 230]) is given as an illustration. In conjunc-
tion with the word "dismembred" in line 9, it is quite obvious
that Rodamant is quibbling on the subject of castration.

   11. lively form'd] made to look lifelike.

   12. upon entrance] about to enter.

The Gods are pleas'd, great King, and we

Return thy golden wreath to thee,   20

[Replaces the crown on the King's head.]

More sacred by our holy fume;

None to the Altar yet presume.

Now shoot your voices up to Jove,

To Mars and all the Powers above.

Song at the Altar.

Come away, Oh come away   25

And trembling trembling pay

Your pious vowes to Mars and Jove.

While we do sing,

Gummes of precious odours bring,

And light them with your love.   30

As your holy fires do rise,

Make Jove to wonder

What new flame

Thither came

To wait upon his thunder.   35

*31-32. As . . . wonder] Gifford reads: As . . . rise /
[In cloudless glory to the skies,] / Make . . . .

---

20. wreath] crown.

21. fume] incense.

31-32. As . . . wonder] Gifford's additional line is
pure fancy, and MacMullan rightly rejects it. The text makes
good sense as it stands.

After the song the Queen offers, and her daughters, garlands,

      which are placed upon the heads of the Idols.

      The song being ended, the Idol that presented

              Jupiter moveth.

Leogarius. Archimagus, Conallus; see my children,

   The statue moves.

Archimagus.   Approach it not too neere.

Ethne. It is prodigious.

Archimagus.   With devotion,

    Expect what followes, and keep reverent distance;

    I am all wonder.

Jupiter.   King Leogarius,   40

*39. reverent] Q; reverend Chetwood, Gifford.

*40. I . . . wonder] Gifford assigns to Leogarius.

35.3-35.4. S. D. the Idol . . . moveth] Moving statues are
employed in other Elizabethan plays to great dramatic effect. In
Fletcher and Shakespeare's Two Noble Kinsmen, Palamon and Arcite
fall prostrate before the statue of Mars, which gives a clanging
of armor (V.i). The "statue" of Hermione in The Winter's Tale
(V.iii.103.1) moves, and she is revealed as still being alive.

38. prodigious] miraculous.

39. Expect] await. reverent] Chetwood's emendation must
merely be a spelling variant since a change in sense is unjustifiable.

40. I . . . wonder] There is no justification for Gifford's emendation, although he may have thought that the phrase
did not fit logically with the rest of Archimagus' speech.

Jove doth accept thy vowes, and pious offerings,

And will showre blessings on thee and this kingdome,

If thou preserve this holy flame burnes in thee.

But take heed, thou decline not thy obedience,

Which thou shalt best declare by thy just anger   45

Against that christian stragler Patricke, whose

Bloud must be sacrific'd to us, or you

Must fall in your remisse and cold religion.

When you are mercifull to our despisers,

You pull our wrath upon you, and this Iland.   50

My duty is perform'd, and I return

To my first stone, a cold and silent statue.

Archimagus. What cannot all commanding Jove? 'tis now

That artifically tonguelesse thing it was;

How are you bound to honour Jupiter,   55

That with this strange and publike testimony

Accepts your zeale? Pursue what you intended,

And meet this enemy to the gods, that now

Expects your entertainment.

Leogarius.   I obey.

Come my Queene, and daughters.   60

_____

43. flame burnes] flame which burns. The relative is
often omitted in seventeenth-century English (see Abbott, par.
244).

46. stragler] wanderer.

53. cannot . . . Jove] cannot . . . Jove [do].

59. Expects] awaits.

Queen.   I attend you Sir.

Rodamant.   [To Conallus.]   Is not the Queene a lovely creature
        Sir?

Conallus.   Why how now Rodamant, what passion's this?

Rodamant.   [Aside.]   Oh that I durst unbutton my minde to her.

Archimagus.   Your Princely daughters pray they may have leave
        To offer in their gratitude to the gods.   65
        One other prayer, and they will follow Sir.

Leogarius.   They are my pious daughters; come Conallus.

            Exeunt Leogarius, Queen, Conallus, &c. [and Magitians.

Archimagus.   They are gone; uncloud.

        [Ferochus and Endarius descend from the altar.]

Ferochus.   [To Fedella.]   Oh my deere Mistresse, is not the
        King mock'd rarely?

Ethne.   My most lov'd Endarius!

Archimagus.   Have I not don't, my Charge?   70

*62.   S. H. Conallus] Prin. Q; 1. Mag. Gifford.

---

        62. Why . . . this] Q attributes this speech to "Prin."
Gifford changes this to "1. Mag." since Shirley confuses Priests
and Magicians throughout the play. However, it is likely that
Shirley means the king's son, Conallus, who is referred to as
the "Prince" at I.i.77.

Fedella. Most quaintly. [To Ferochus.] Welcome to thy Fedella.

Rodamant. Hum, how's this? more scapes of Jupiter? they have

> found their neither parts; the gods are become fine mortal

> gentlemen; here's precious jugling, if I durst talke on't.

Archimagus. Not a sillable, as you desire not to be torne in   75

> pieces sir.

Rodamant. Gods quoth'a, I held a candle before the devill.

Archimagus. To the doore and watch.

Rodamant. So I must keep the doore too; here's like to be

> holy doings.   80

Ferochus. We owe Archimagus for more then life,

> For your loves, without which, life is a curse.   [Music.]

82. S. D. Music] Gifford.

---

72. scapes of Jupiter] Shirley calls Jupiter "the patron
of scapes" in The Bird in a Cage, III.i (Gifford, II, 405). The
word "scapes" means breaches of chastity in this sense.

73. neither] nether.

77. "It is good to hold (set) a candle before the devil"
(Tilley, C42). Rodamant has just lighted candles on the altar,
and Shirley may have had in mind one of the proverbs listed by
Tilley: "Holding a candle to the devil is assisting in a bad
cause, an evil matter."

79. keep the doore] to act as a pander. This is a fairly
common jest in the Renaissance. Cf. Middleton's Blurt, Master
Constable, II.ii.99-103: "Imperia. Keep the door. Fiesco.
That's my office: indeed I have been your door-keeper so long,
that all the hinges, the spring-locks, and the ring are worn to
pieces." Note also Othello, IV,ii.28-30.

Archimagus.   The musicke prompts you to a dance.

Endarius.   I' th' temple?

Archimagus.   'Tis most secure, none dare betray you here.

[They dance.]

Ethne.   We must away.

Ferochus.   My life is going from me.   85

Fedella.   Farewell.

Archimagus.   The King expects; now kisse and part.

Ethne.   When next we meet, pray give me back my heart.

Rodamant.   I am an Esquire by my office.   Exeunt.

84.1. S. D. They dance] Gifford.

---

85. life] i.e., Ethne.

86. expects] awaits.

88. Esquire] MacMullan (p. 109) says that this word means
"a pander." However, this does not make sense. Perhaps Rodamant means that he hopes to be promoted to higher office (that
of Squire, or gentleman) by acting as a pander.

ACT III. [Scene i.]

Enter Rodamant.

Rodamant. Oh my Royall love! why should not I love the Queene?

I have knowne as simple a fellow as I hath been in love

with her horse; nay they ha' been bedfellowes in the same

litter, and in that humour he would have been leap'd, if

the beast could have been provok'd to incontinencie; but   5

what if the King should know on't, and very lovingly cir-

cumcise me for it, or hang me up a gracious spectacle with

my tongue out a pearch for sparrowes? why, I should become

the gallowes, o' my conscience: oh I would stretch in so

gentle posture, that the spectators all should edifie, and   10

hang by my example.

9. gallowes,] Gifford substantively; gallowes⌃ Q.

III.i. Gifford locates this scene "Before the Palace."

1-11. Oh . . . example] Rodamant's passion for the Queen
is, of course, destined to be unfulfilled because of the strict
hierarchy of seventeenth-century society. It is comic, however,
and similar to Chapman's An Humorous Day's Mirth where Labesha,
a buffoon, hopes to marry Martia, a highborn lady. Also, in
Shirley's The Imposture, Bertoldi, an insolent coward, has a
passion for Fioretta, the daughter of the Duke of Mantua.

2-5. I . . . incontinencie] Rodamant's bawdy comparison
of a horse to a mistress here recalls the remarks of the Constable and Orleans on the Dauphin's praise of his horse in
Henry V (III.vi.45-84).

4. leap'd] sprung upon by the male in copulation.

5. incontinencie] incontinence.

6. on't] of it.

6-7. circumcise] castrate.

140

Enter <u>Bard</u>.

The King's merry Bard; if he have overheard, hee'le save the

hangman a labour, and rime me to death.

<u>Bard</u>. <u>Rodamant</u>, my halfe man, halfe gobling, all foole, how is't?

when didst thou see the devill?   15

<u>Rodamant</u>. Alas, I never had the happinesse.

<u>Bard</u>. Why then, thou art not acquainted with thy best friend.

<u>Sings</u>.

<u>Have you never seene in the aire</u>,

<u>One ride with a burning speare</u>,

<u>Upon an old witch with a pad</u>,   20

<u>For the devill a sore breech had</u>,

    <u>With lightning and thunder</u>

    <u>And many more wonder</u>.

    <u>His eyes indeed--law sir</u>,

    <u>As wide as a sawcer</u>.   25

<u>Oh this would have made my boy mad</u>.

---

13. rime me to death] a common phrase in the period. Cf.
Sidney's <u>Defense of Poesy</u>: "I will not wish unto you . . . to
be rimed <u>to death</u>, as is said to be done in Ireland" (Sidney,
II, 151).

14. gobling] goblin. The <u>OED</u> lists this as a spelling of
the period.

16. happinesse] good luck.

19. <u>with</u> . . . <u>speare</u>] This phrase has a sexual connotation here, as well as referring to the belief that spirits often
carried spears.

<u>Rodamant</u>. An honest merry trout.

<u>Bard</u>. Thou say'st right Gudgin; gape, and I'll throw in a bush-
    ell; why does thy nose hang over thy mouth, as it would
    peep in, to tell how many teeth thou hast?   30

<u>Rodamant</u>. Excellent Bard! Oh brave Bard, Ha Bard.

<u>Bard</u>. Excellent foole! Oh fine foole, Ha foole.

<u>Rodamant</u>. Prithee with what newes, and whither is thy head
    travelling?

<u>Bard</u>. My head and my feet goe one way, and both now at their   35
    journeye's end. The newes is, that one <u>Patricke</u> a stranger,
    is invited to court: this way he must come, and I like
    one of the King's wanton whelpes, have broke loose from the
    kennell, and come thus afore to bark, and bid him welcome;
    the King and Queene will meete him.   40

<u>Rodamant</u>. Has the King invited him?

---

    27. trout] a confidential friend or servant. The <u>OED</u> lists
the earliest usage as <u>circa</u> 1661: "I was a trusty trout / In
all that I went about" (<u>Roxburghe</u> <u>ballads</u> [London, 1869-99], IV,
518).

    28. Gudgin] "To gape like a gudgeon, is to be a fool
easily caught" (MacMullan, p. 109). A gudgeon is a fish; hence
one that will bite at any bait or swallow anything: a gullible
person. The Bard is picking up Rodamant's reference to "trout"
in line 27 and playing on it.

    28-29. I'll . . . bushell] Probably the Bard means that
if Rodamant will open his mouth wide enough, he can be made to
swallow quite a lot in his gullibility.

    38. wanton] playful.

Bard. What else man?

Sings.

Oh the Queene and the King, and the royall Off-spring,
    With the Lords, and Ladies so gay,
I tell you not a tricke, to meete the man Patricke,   45
    Are all now trouping this way.
This man, report sings, does many strange things:
    Our Priests, and our Bards must give place.
He cares not a straw, for our sword or club-law.
    Oh I long to behold his gay face.   50

Rodamant. Prethee a word; thou didst name the Queene. Does she
come too?

Bard. By any meanes.

Rodamant. Well 'tis a good soule.

Bard. Who?   55

Rodamant. The Queene.

Bard. The Queene is't? dost make but a soule o' her? treason!

----

44. gay] brilliantly dressed.

45. I . . . tricke] I'm not deceiving you.

49. sword . . . law] barbaric justice.

50. gay] cheerful.

53. By any meanes] absolutely.

I have heard some foolish Philosophers affirme, that women

have no soules: 'twere well for some they had no bodies;

but to make no body of the Queene is treason, if it be not   60

fellony.

Rodamant. Oh my royall love!

Bard. Love, art thou in love Rodamant? nay then thou may'st

talke treason or any thing. Folly and madnesse are lash

free, and may ride cheeke by joll with a judge. But dost   65

thou know what love is, thou one of Cupid's overgrowne

monkies? Come, crack me this nut of love, and take the

maggot for thy labour.

---

58. Philosophers] MacMullan (p. 109) is unable to identify
this allusion. He mentions that the idea occupied Medieval
churchmen and that a bishop of the Council of Macon suggested the
idea. I have been unable to find references in any of the standard histories of the Church. Moslems are popularly believed to
hold that women have no souls, but there is no evidence Shirley
was aware of this tradition.

60-61. to . . . fellony] "The Bard is punning. 'To make
no body of the Queen,' would be treason if she were denied to
have a body, would be felony if she were made nobody, i.e.,
killed" (MacMullan, p. 110). Treason and felony were both crimes
punishable by death, but treason was the more serious. In Dante's
Inferno traitors were relegated to the lowest circle of hell.

65. cheeke by jolly] cheek by jowl, i.e., side by side, in
the closest intimacy.

66-67. Cupid's . . . monkies] Monkeys are notoriously
imitative and were favorite court pets. The phrase means that
Rodamant is a foolish and absurd imitator of Cupid--as a monkey
might try to behave like his courtly master.

67. crack . . . love] i.e., tell me what love is all about.
The phrase "Crack me this nut" has a proverbial designation (see
Tilley, N359).

67-68. take . . . maggot] i.e., your reward shall be the
worm in the nut, rather than the nut meat.

Rodamant. Preethee do thou say what 'tis.

Bard. No, I will sing a piece of my minde, and love to thee.   70

Sings.

Love is a bog, a deep bog, a wide bog.

Love is a clog, a great clog, a close clog.

'Tis a wildernesse to loose our selves,

A halter 'tis to nooze our selves.

Then draw Dun our o' th' mire,   75

And throw the clog into the fire.

Keepe in the King's high way,

And sober you cannot stray.

If thou admire no female elfe,

The halter may go hang it selfe.   80

Drink wine and be merry, for love is a folly,

And dwells in the house of mellancholly.

---

72. clog] an impedence, a hindrance, from the practice of hanging blocks of wood on horses to slow them down. In line 76 it "evidently refers to a Yule log, sometimes called a 'clog' or 'block'" (Donovan).

74. halter . . . our selves] The point here is that lovers often victimize themselves and hang themselves in their own noose.

75. draw . . . mire] "'Dun is in the mire' is a Christmas game, played by pretending that a log of wood in the fire is Dun, the cart horse. The sport comes from attempts to pull Dun from the fire" (MacMullan, p. 110). The OED points out that "Dun is in the mire" is a proverbial phrase denoting that things are at a standstill or deadlock. So the Bard is suggesting that things be made to move again. Cf. Romeo and Juliet, I.iv.41 and Beaumont and Fletcher's The Woman Hater, IV.ii.160.

77. King's high way] Cf. "A man must not leave the king's highway for a pathway" (Tilley, M281). Donovan points out that country people in the seventeenth century disliked field paths and much preferred the high road. The king's highway was a high road protected by the king's soldiers.

Rodamant. 'Tis such a merry baboone, and shootes quills like

    a Porcupine; but who's this?

Enter St. Patrick, and his traine at one doore. At the other,

    the King, Queene, his sonnes and daughters, Milcho,

        Archimagus, and Magitians.

Bard. 'Tis he, I know him by instinct.   85

                Sings.

        Patricke welcome to this Ile,

        See how every thing doth smile:

        To thy staffe and thy miter,

          And Lawne that is whiter,

    And every shaven crowne, a welcome welcome to towne.   90

      Looke where the King, and Queene doe greete thee:

      His Princely sonnes are come to meete thee.

    And see where a paire is, of very fine Faries,

84.3. S. D. Magitians] Gifford substantively; Priests Q.

---

    83. baboone] playing on "monkies" above, line 67.

    83-84. shootes . . . Porcupine] Porcupines were popularly
considered capable of shooting their quills as a means of defense.

    85. 'Tis . . . instinct] an echo of Falstaff's "By the
lords, I know ye . . . on instinct" (I Henry IV, II.iv.389).
The Bard also greets Patrick in Jocelyn. See BB, p. 16.

    88. miter] Patrick was usually pictured in full episcopal
dress since he was later to become archbishop of Ireland.

    89. Lawne] a kind of fine linen used for a bishop's sleeves.

    90. shaven crowne] Cf. I.i.56.

    93. Faries] i.e., Ethne and Fedella.

Prepar'd too,

That thou may'st report, thy welcome to Court,   95

And the Bard too.

And so pray father give me your blessing.   [Kneels.]

[St. Patrick makes the sign of the cross over Bard.]

Patrick. I thank thee courteous Bard, thy heart is honest.

But to the King my dutie.   [Kneels.]

Leogarius.   Welcome Patrick,

For so thou cal'st thy self; we have throwne off   10(

Our anger, and with calme, and melting eyes

Looke on thee. Thou hast piety to forgive

Our former threats and language, and to satisfie,

For our deniall of some humble cottages,

Against the hospitable lawes of nature.   10!

We give thee now our Palace, use it freely.

My selfe, our Queene and children, will be all

Thy guests, and owe our dwellings to thy favour.

There are some things of venerable mark

Upon thy brow; thou art some holy man,   11(

107-108. My selfe . . . favour] a conventional courtly figu₁
Cf. The Coronation, V.ii: Sophia. Do you but hope? he came to
be your guest. Polidora. We are all his, whilst he is pleas'd
to honour / This poor roof with his royal presence, madam.
(Gifford, II, 528).

109-110. There . . . brow] The king is remarking on Patrick's physiognomy, which was popularly supposed to be an externa₁
sign of character traits. The reference to "things" is vague,
but it may refer to the belief that a protruding brow was an
indication of superior intelligence.

Design'd by providence to make us happy:

Agen, most welcome to us.

Queen.   His aspect

Doth promise goodnes: Welcome.

Conallus.   To us all.

Patrick. If this be heartie, heaven will not permit

Your charities unrewarded.

Corybreus.   [Aside to Archimagus.] I am

weary   115

Of these dull complements, Archimagus.

Archimagus. [Aside to Corybreus.] I am prepar'd; I know your

bloud's a longing,

To change embraces with Emeria.

Receive this, which worne upon your arme,

*113. S. P. Conallus] Co. Q.

---

111. happy] fortunate.

113. S. P. Conallus] Co. in Q might be easily confused
with Corybreus, but he is not on stage at this moment. Hence
I have emended the speech prefix.

113. To . . . all] i.e., goodness to us all.

114. heartie] sincere, from the heart.

117. bloud's a longing] This is another reference to the
blood as the humor of passion. Archimagus is referring to the
fact that Corybreus desires to possess Emeria.

119. For a discussion of sources for the bracelet and Corybreus' invisibility, see the Introduction, p. 53.

Is so by power of magicke fortified,   120

You shall goe where you please invisible,

Untill you take it off: Goe to your Mistres.

[Gives him a bracelet.]

Corybreus. [Aside to Archimagus.] Softly my deere Archimagus;
the rest

Speake in a whisper; I shall be jealous of

The Intelligencing aire.   [They speak apart.]

Leogarius.   You may be confident   125

Our favour spreads to all. But where is Dichu

Your Convert? wee'l receive him to our grace too.

Patrick. He durst not Sir, approach your royall presence.

And griefe, for the sad fate of his two sonnes,

Hath made him weary of society: 130

Not farre off in a wood, he meanes to weare out

His life in prayer and pennance.

Archimagus.   [Aside to Corybreus.] How
do you tast it?

Corybreus. [Aside to Archimagus.] 'Tis rare, and must succeede
to my ambition.

Archimagus. [Aside to Corybreus.] Loose no time then.

_____

124. intelligencing] spying.

132. How . . . it] How does it strike you?

133. succeede . . . ambition] make my ambition succeed.

Corybreus.   [Aside to

      Archimagus.] I fly; command me ever.   Exit.

Leogarius. I am not well o' th' suddaine.

Queen.   How? what is't   135

    That doth offend the King?

Leogarius. An evill conscience: Alas my children.

Conallus. Father.

Archimagus. Sir.

Ethne. Pray speake to us.

Leogarius.   How shall I   140

    Win credit with this good man, that I have

    Repented, for the bloud of Dichue's sonnes?

Patrick. If you dissemble not with heaven, I can

    Be easily gain'd Sir, to beleeve and pray for you.

Leogarius. Some wine; it is the greatest ceremony   145

    Of love with us, the seale of reconcilement.

---

143. with] to.

144. gain'd] won over.

145-146. Some . . . reconcilement] Here, as elsewhere in
the play, Shirley ironically plays off rituals in the Christian
Church against similar ones in the heathen Irish society. Wine
is, of course, used in the Eucharist, the greatest Christian
ceremony of love. See a discussion of such parallels in the
Introduction, p. 67.

Let some one bring us wine; I wo' not move,

Untill I drink to this blest man.

Archimagus.   Away.   [Exit Rodamant.]

Leogarius. This place shall be remembred to posterity,

Where Leogarius first shew'd himself friend   150

To holy Patrick. 'Tis religious thirst,

That will not let me expect, till more returne.

There is a streame of peace within my heart.

Archimagus. [Aside to Leogarius.] 'Tis rarely counter-

feited.

Conallus.   [Aside.] He is my father,

I should else tell him; 'Tis not like a King,   155

Thus to conspire a poore man's death. [To Queen.] What

thinks

Our royall mother? Is it just to take

By stratagemme, this innocent man's life?

Queen. What meanes my sonne?

*152. more] Q; morn Gifford.

154. S. D. Aside] Gifford.

155. him;] Q; him‸ Gifford.

---

149. to] by.

152. expect] await.

152. till more returne] i.e., "till I get more." This
sense makes Gifford's emendation unnecessary.

155. else] otherwise.

Conallus.   [Aside.] Shall I betray the plot

    Yet? and preserve him?

             [Re-enter Rodamant with wine.]

                See the wine.

Archimagus.   [To Leogarius.] The

       wine   160

    Attends you Sir.

Leogarius. 'Tis well; fill us a cheerefull cup: here Patrick,

    We drink thy welcome to the Irish coasts.

Ethne. [Aside to Fedella.] What does my father meane to doe

       with this

    Dull thing? hee'le never make a courtier.   165

Fedella. [Aside to Ethne.] His very lookes have turn'd my

       blood already.

160. S. D. Re-enter . . . wine] Gifford.

    160-276. The attempted poisoning of St. Patrick is similar
to the whipping of Dorothea in Dekker and Massinger's The Virgin
Martyr (IV.ii) where, through divine intervention, the heroine
escapes injury. Forsythe (p. 226) lists two other parallels:
the torture of St. Eugenius in Henry Shirley's The Martyred Soldier (Bullen Collection, I, 220-223) and the escape of St. Anthony
and St. Andrew from death in Kirke's The Seven Champions of
Christendom (Act II). St. Eugenius performs a miracle similar
to St. Patrick's curing of Rodamant: in The Martyred Soldier
(Bullen Collection, I, 221) he cures Henrick of a scorpion's bite.
Poison is used often in Renaissance drama (for example, in The
Cardinal and The Maid's Revenge, both of which contain parallels
to this scene).

    166. turn'd my blood] perhaps equivalent to modern "made
my blood run cold."

Archimagus. [Aside to Leogarius.] I'll spice his cup.

Leogarius.   [Aside to

        Archimagus.] Doo't strongly.

Queen. [Aside.] There's something within prompts me to pitty

    This stranger.

Conallus.   [To St. Patrick.] Do you love wine Sir?

Patrick. If I did not,   170

    I should presume against my nature once

    To please the King that hath thus honoured us.

Conallus. [Aside to St. Patrick.] Do not, I say do not.

Archimagus.   Please

        you Sir?   [Gives St. Patrick the cup.]

Leogarius. Come, to our Queene.

Rodamant. [Aside.] My royall love, would I had the grace to 175

    drink to her or kisse the cup.

167. S. D. Aside . . . Archimagus] Gifford.

173. S. D. Gives . . . cup] Gifford.

---

    176. kisse . . . cup] to offer her a pledge of love.   Cf.
Johnson's "Song. To Celia":

    Drink to me onely with thine eyes,
        And I will pledge with mine;
    Or leave a kisse but in the cup,
        And Ile not looke for wine. (Jonson, I, 364)

Patrick. My dutie.   [Drinks.]

Archimagus. [Aside to Leogarius.] Now observe Sir the change,
        he has it home.

Rodamant. I cannot live, my heart wo' not hold out.

Leogarius. [To Rodamant.] Forbeare, as you affect your life. 180

Queen. [Aside.] How's this? now I suspect Conallus.

Patrick. I have one boone to ask your Majestie,
        Since you look on us with this gracious smile,
        That you would give my poore companions leave,
        To build a little chappell in this place,   185
        (It shall be the first monument of your love),
        To use our owne religion; the ground offers
        Plenty of stone, the cost and paine be ours.

Leogarius. [Aside to Archimagus.] Not yet?

Patrick.   'Twill bind us ever
        to pray for you.

Leogarius. [Aside to Archimagus.] If it were violent, as thou

177. S. D. Drinks] Gifford.
181. S. D. Aside] Gifford.
181. suspect‸] Q; suspect, Chetwood.

---

    178. has it home] has settled upon him.
    180. affect] love.

                    say'st, it had   190
        By this time gnawne to his bowels.

Patrick.   Sir, you mind not
        The humble suit I make.

Archimagus.   [Aside to Leogarius.] Not yet?

Patrick.   Great
            Sir.

Leogarius. [Aside to Archimagus.] It does not alter him, he
            rather lookes
        With fresher bloud upon him.

Archimagus.   [Aside to Leogarius.] 'Tis
            my wonder;
        I did not trust another to prepare   195
        His cup.

Leogarius. [Aside to Archimagus.] Come, 'tis not poyson; we
            are abus'd.

Archimagus. [Aside to Leogarius.] Upon my life.

Patrick. The King is troubled.

Leogarius. Prepare another.

        193-194. lookes . . . him] In other words, the blood has
not disappeared from his face, as it would if the poison were
taking effect, but seems to be circulating even more freshly
than usual.

Archimagus. It shall be done.   200

Leogarius. [To Rodamant.] Come hither sirra; you brought
          this wine.

Rodamant. I did, Sir.

Leogarius. And you shall taste it.

Rodamant. Would I were but worthy.

Leogarius. I will have it so. Come, drink our health.   205

Rodamant. May I remember your good Queene's?

Archimagus. [Aside.] And he had the constitution of an Elephant
          'Twould pay him.

Queen. [To St. Patrick.] How cheere you, Sir?

Patrick.   Well, Madam; but
              I observe
          Distractions in the King.

Leogarius.   [To Rodamant.] Nay, drink it off. 210

Rodamant. And it were as deep as the root of Penmenmaure, my
          royall Love should have it.

_____

     201. sirra] an expression used by one in authority in
speaking to a servant.

     207. And] if.

     211. Penmenmaure] a mountain in Caernarvon, Wales.

Leogarius. [Aside to Archimagus.] Now we shall try the ingredi-
        ents; it stirr'd

    Not him; has he done't?

Rodamant. So   [Drinks.] 2

Archimagus. [Aside to Leogarius.] Yes, and the change begins
        to shew already.

Rodamant. Hoy ho--what's that?

Bard. Where?

Rodamant. Here, here abouts; was the wine burnt? oh there's
        wildefire in the wine.   2

Archimagus. [Aside to Leogarius.] It workes on him.

Rodamant. There's squibs and crackers in my stomacke; am not
        I poyson'd?

Bard. Poyson'd? we shall want a foole then.

Rodamant. Away, I'll never drink agen.   2

---

213. try] test. stirr'd] affected.

220. wildefire] in war, an inflammable material used to
start fires. Here it is used figuratively as in Shirley's The
Maid's Revenge: "There's wild-fire in my bowels; sure, I am
poison'd--" (Gifford, I, 182).

222. squibs and crackers in my stomacke] Squibs and
crackers are fireworks. In Renaissance drama characters conventionally verbalize their deaths clearly to the audience. Cf.
Bergetto in Ford's 'Tis Pity She's a Whore: "Is all this mine
own blood? . . . O!--I am going the wrong way sure, my belly
aches so. --O, Farewell, Poggio! --O!--O!--" (III.viii.30-34).

Bard. Not often, and thou beest poyson'd.

Rodamant. It increases; my royall love has poison'd me; her

　　　health has blowne my bowells up. Oh a cooler; would I

　　　were a while in the frozen sea; charity is not cold enough

　　　to releeive me: the devill is making fireworkes in my   230

　　　belly. Ha the Queene, let me but speake to the Queene;

　　　Oh Madam, little do you think, that I have poyson'd my

　　　self, Oh for your sweete sake. But howsoever; Oh think up-

　　　on me when I am dead. I bequeath my heart; Oh there 'tis

　　　already: my royall love farewell.   [Falls senseless.] 235

Archimagus. [Aside to Leogarius.] What thinke you now? it

　　　hath dispatch'd him raving.

Patrick. [To Queen.] Madam, you shew a pious heart; I finde

235. S. D. Falls senseless] Gifford.

———————————

　　　226. and] if.

　　　228. health] i.e., drinking her health (with a pun on health
as the basis of her beauty).

　　　228. blowne . . . up] "It was a popular belief that poison
burst the bowels" (Donovan). There may also be a grotesque suggestion of male pregnancy here.

　　　228. cooler] a medicine to calm an inflammation of the
digestive tract. Cf. The Maid's Revenge:

　　　　　No physic to restore me? Send for Sharkino;--a
　　　　　cooler! a cooler! there's a smith's forge in my belly,
　　　　　and the devil blows the bellows. (Gifford, I, 183).

　　　232-235. Oh Madam . . . farewell] Rodamant is here paro-
dying the conventional romantic death in which one dies for one's
mistress' sake. He admits this is not the reason he is dying,
but he hopes the Queen will think of him anyway in this light.

My death was meant; but 'tis heaven's goodnesse

I should not fall by poyson: do not loose

Your charity.   24

Bard. [_Examining_ Rodamant.] Hee's dead.

Patrick. Pray let me see the fellow.

Leogarius. It affrights me; this was some treason meant to us,

    And thee good man: How I am innocent.

Patrick. How soone death would devoure him.

Archimagus.   Past your cure.   24

Patrick. That power we serve can call back life; and see,

    He has a little motion.

Bard. He breathes too; nay then he may live to have th' other

    cup: Madam, this Patrick is a rare physition; if he stay

    with us, hee'l make us all immortall.   25

Leogarius. Alive agen? Oh let me honour thee.

Queen. We cannot Sir enough: Receive me Patrick,

    A weake disciple to thee: my soule bids me

245. How soone] Q; How ever soon Gifford.

---

245. would] wanted to.

248. See the various resurrections which Patrick performs
in the Appendix, passim.

Embrace thy faith: Make me a Christian.

Leogarius. How? didst thou heare Archimagus? let some   255

Convey our Queene hence, her weak conscience melts;

Shee'l be a Christian she sayes: I hate her,

And do confine her to the house of Milcho

Our zealous Provost.

Patrick.   'Tis the King's pleasure Madam,

I should attend you hence.

Queen.   Where the King please.   260

Patrick. In any prison Madam, I dare visit you;

Be comforted, they do but fight with heaven.

Conallus. I'll waite upon my mother.

Exeunt [Conallus, Queen, and Milcho].

*259. S. P. Patrick] Q substantively; Milcho Gifford, Donovan.

260. please] Q; pleases Gifford.

252-254. See BB, pp. 25-26. Forsythe points out that
the Queen's conversion is similar to Theophilus' in Dekker and
Massinger's The Virgin Martyr (V.i). In that play also, Calista
and Christeta are punished for the same offense (III.ii) as the
Queen's in St. Patrick.

259. S. P. Patrick] While Gifford's and Donovan's emendations make sense, I chose to retain the Q reading. Patrick could
be saying that the King's putting the Queen under the charge of
Milcho at Milcho's house merely necessitates Patrick's travelling
there with her.

Leogarius.   [Aside to Archimagus.] Looke

     to my daughters,

  Least this change worke on them.

Archimagus.   [Aside to Leogarius.] They

     are my charge.

Leogarius. Be not dejected Patrick; we do meane   26?

  All good to thee: set forward, have a care

  Of that poore fellow.

Patrick.   I'll attend you Sir,

  And trust to Providence we shall be safe.

Exeunt [all but Rodamant and Bard].

Bard. How is't now Rodamant? dost thou remember thou wert

  dead? Thou wert poyson'd.   27(

Rodamant. There is a kinde of grumbling in my guts still.

Bard.   Sings.

  Come, we will drink a cup boy, but of better brewing,

264. least] Q; lest Chetwood.

---

    264. Least] lest.

    267. that . . . fellow] i.e., Rodamant.

And we will drink it up joy, without any feare of slewing.

Wine is injust that is taken on trust, if it tarry with

    us it fatts,

A cup boy, drink up joy, and let 'em go poyson ratts.   275

                       Exeunt.

[Act III, scene ii.]

Enter Emeria [with a key].

Emeria. What is it that doth sit so heavy on me?

  Since Corybreus talk'd with me, I finde

  A dulnes in my braine; and my eyes look

  As through a mist, which hangs upon my lids,

*273. of slewing] of ------ Q, Donovan, MacMullan; of s--- Gifford.
III.ii.0.1. S. D. with a key] Gifford.

---

    273. slewing] getting drunk or intoxicated. Shirley could
have had in mind a pun on "being slain" (i.e., "slewing"--a variant form of "slaying"), the sense being that the better cup of
wine (unlike the one he has just drunk) will neither intoxicate
nor kill Rodamant. The only other word which fits the rhyme and
context is "spewing" (i.e., "throwing up") but it is obviously
not as fitting as "slewing." I see no reason why Shirley left
the word out of Q, unless the compositor didn't want to run over
on the next line for a mere syllable. In Q there is no room for
the entire word at the end of the line. Donovan and MacMullan
ignore the problem, and Gifford only prints the first letter.
Gifford's curious emendation may be explained by a mistaken assumption that, since it was missing in Q, the word was obscene. In
this case he might have mistakenly assumed the missing word was,
say, "screwing." His sensitive nineteenth-century sensibility
probably would have allowed him to print only the first letter.

    274. fatts] makes us fat. Cf. Hamlet: "We fat all crea-
tures else to fat us" (IV.iii.23).

    III.ii.3. dulnes] sleepiness.

And weighs 'em downe. He frighted me to heare him;   5

He has a rugged and revengefull nature;

Not the sweet temper that his brother,

My deere Conallus,--mine? alas did I

Say mine? indeed he is Master of my heart,

But something makes me feare I shall not be   10

So happy as I wish in his possession:

Yet we have vowes on both sides, holy ones,

And marriage promis'd. But I am too loude;

Yet not; my lodgings are remote and priva'st

Of all the Court: and I have dismist the servants,   15

None neere to reach my voice; then till this give

Access, I need not feare the silent chambers.

More cloudes doe gather 'bout my eyes; 'tis strange,

I am not us'd to be inclin'd to sleepe,

While the day shines; then take what nature offers   20

Emeria, and comply; it may discharge

Thy waking melancholly; so I feele

It gently slide upon my sences.   [She sleeps.]

*7. brother,] brother. Q; brother owns. Gifford, Chetwood.

23. S. D. She sleeps] Gifford.

---

  7. Not . . . brother] Gifford's addition of the word "owns"
at the end of the line makes sense, but, despite the fact that
the line is metrically deficient as it stands, it is more likely
that the sentence continues to the ellipsis in the next line.

  11. in . . . possession] in possession of him. This is
an archaic use of the old genetive case (Abbott, par. 218).

  16. this] i.e., the door.

Enter <u>Spirits</u> <u>before</u> Corybreus [<u>who is</u>] <u>habited</u>

<u>gloriously</u>, <u>and</u> <u>representing</u> Ceancrochi.

<u>Corybreus</u>. So, so; this ammelet I finde secures me

From all observers, and I now am in   25

Her chamber, by a feate my Spirit did me:

Ha? She sleepes too; what a fine Bawd the devill is,

What opportunities he can frame to bring

These things to passe; I were best loose no time;

Madam, Madam, faire <u>Emeria</u>.

<u>Emeria</u>.   Ha?   30

˙Who's that? was it a voice that cal'd me?

Or do I dreame? here's no body, this key

26. Spirit] <u>Q</u>; spirits <u>Gifford</u>.

24-144. This episode between Emeria and Corybreus has a
great many analogues in the drama of the day. Invisible characters were very popular, e.g., the ghost in <u>Hamlet</u> (closet
scene) and Ariel in <u>The Tempest</u> (although we sometimes see both
characters). It is likely, however, that Shirley was influenced
by I. C.'s <u>The Pleasant Comedy of Two Merry Milkmaids</u> in his
use of this device of invisibility (see the <u>Introduction</u>, p. 53.)
Valerius dresses like Mercury in Beaumont and Fletcher's <u>The
Triumph of Honor</u> (scene 2), a Lady enters disguised as Cupid in
Beaumont and Fletcher's <u>The Nice Valor</u> (II.i), and Amphitruo
disguises himself as Jupiter in Heywood's <u>The Silver Age</u> (II.ii);
but none of these disguises is for the purpose of rape. Rape
scenes, however, occur frequently. In Shakespeare's <u>Titus
Andronicus</u> (II.iii.186), Heywood's <u>The Golden Age</u> (II.i), Middleton's <u>The Mayor of Queenborough</u> (III.ii.98), Beaumont and
Fletcher's <u>The Queen of Corinth</u> (I.iv.8-10) and the anonymous
<u>Dick of Devonshire</u> (<u>Bullen Collection</u>, I, 35) hapless women are
borne off the stage by their ravishers.

24. ammelet] amulet.

27. what . . . is] This phrase sounds proverbial but is
not listed in Tilley.

Made all without fast; yet I'll see.   Exit.

Corybreus.   I had

Forgot; shee'le never see me if I do not

Take off my charme; perhaps I may agen   3

Be visible if I ha' not lost my selfe.

Enter Emeria.

Emeria. The doores are fast.

[Music is heard]

Ha! Blesse me you Powers.

This musick is not frequent in my chambers;

'Tis here, I know not where; I can see nothing.

Corybreus. Emeria.   4(

Emeria. Who is't that calls Emeria? goodnes ayde me!

Corybreus. [Takes off the bracelet.] Put off thy fright,

Emeria; yet I blame not

Thy feeble sence to tremble at my presence;

Not us'd to mortall eyes, and unprepar'd.

42. S. D. Takes . . . bracelet] Gifford.

---

33. Made . . . fast] made the door secure from all persons
outside.

36. lost my selfe] 1) forgot myself; 2) lost sight of myself because I am invisible.

41. Who . . . Emeria] Cf. "Who calls Hieronymo" (Kyd, The
Spanish Tragedy, II.v.4).

But gather strength, and call thy blood agen   45

Whose seate a palenesse doth usurp: I am

Thy freind.

Emeria.   But no acquaintance sure; what are you?

Corybreus. Not what I seeme; I have assum'd this forme,

To tell thee what a happinesse is now

Coming from heaven upon thee.

Emeria.   Upon me?   50

Corybreus. And when the sweete Emeria is collected,

Shee will loose her life agen in joy and wonder.

Emeria. My strength returnes; this is a gentle language,

And Spirit, if thou beest one, speake thy will.

Corybreus. Then know Emeria, I am no mortall   55

But Ceancrochi, chiefe of all the gods

That now appeare.

Emeria.   I know not what to answer

56. Ceancrochi] Q; Ceanerachius Gifford.

---

47. freind . . . acquaintance] A friend is one joined to
another in mutual benevolence and intimacy, not a mere acquaintance. "Friend" in the seventeenth century also meant a lover
or paramour.

49-50. what . . . thee] Shirley intends an ironic parallel
here to Christian grace, the power of which is dramatized in the
scenes in which St. Patrick appears. For a further discussion
of such relationships, see the Introduction, p. 67.

But with my humble knee.   [Kneels.]

Corybreus.   Thy pure devotion

Richer then cloudes of incense, Myrrhe, and Cassia,

And all the Gummes whose piles make sweete our Altar,   6(

Hath been delightfull to the gods, and me,

And I have left the Palace of the blest,

Where many glorious virgins waite, and want thee,

A fellow singer in their heavenly quire,

To visit in this forme the faire Emeria,   6!

And thank thee for thy pious sacrifices:

Rise then and be confirm'd; we meane to honour

Thy person and thy vertues.

Emeria.   Can this roofe

Be so much blest? and can so great a deity

Consider my imperfect dutie thus?   7(

Corybreus. To assure thy thoughts, ask fairest virgin, what

58. S. D. Kneels] Gifford.

60. Altar] Q; altars Chetwood.

---

59. Myrrhe] a gum-resin used as an ingredient in incense.
The Christian associations are ironically played upon here; gold,
frankincense, and myrrh were brought to the infant Christ
(Matthew 2:11).

59. Cassia] an inferior kind of cinnamon, used as a fragrant
spice for a cosmetic or in incense. Cf. "It hath no smell, like
Cassia or Cyvit" (Webster, The Duchess of Malfi, II.iv.86).

63. want thee] miss your presence.

67. we] Corybreus, as king of the gods, uses the royal
"we."

Thou most desirest, and it shall firmer than

The Destinies, be made thine owne: hast thou

A wish to this world's glorie, to be greater?

Would'st thou enlarge thy knowledge, or thy pleasure?   75

Do'st thou affect to have thy life extended,

Double the course of Nature; or thy beautie

Above the malice of disease, or time

To wither? Would'st thou see thy booke of fate,

And read the various lines that fall into   80

Thy life, as to their center? speake, and be

Possest; if thou refuse what here is nam'd,

Thy wish will come too late, Emeria.

---

72. firmer] more certainly.

73. Destinies] in Greek and Roman mythology the goddesses
held to determine the course of human life.

74. A wish . . . glorie] a desire for glory (or greatness)
in this world. The OED lists the idiom "a wish to" as obsolete
for "a desire for."

76. affect] desire.

77. Double . . . nature] for 140 years. The traditional
lifetime (or "course of nature") is 'threescore and ten" years.

80-81. lines . . . center] This is a difficult passage.
Perhaps the reference to "lines" here is to "life lines" in
Palmistry; for example, "The Saturnine line going from the ras-
cette through the hand to Saturn's mount . . . argues melancholy"
(Burton, Anatomy of Melancholy, Part I, Sect. 2, Subs. 4).
Astrological "lines" are held to connect the individual to the
governing planets (and therefore to his fate). There is a pun
on lines of a book. The reference to "center" is an analogy to
the Ptolemaic conception of the universe which holds the earth
to be immovably placed at the center with all the heavenly bodies
moving around it. Shirley may also be punning on the sexual
center (i.e., the vagina).

81-82. be Possest] be raped.

<u>Emeria</u>. None of all these; let me be still accepted

    An humble servant to the gods.

<u>Corybreus</u>.   Then I   85

    Will find some other way to thy reward:

    First, we release that dutie of thy knee;

    Reach thy faire hand.

<u>Emeria</u>.   I dare not.

<u>Corybreus</u>.   Doe not tremble,

    It shall but meet another like thine owne;   [<u>Raises her</u>.]

    For I had care not to affright my virgin: 90

    What do'st thou see in me, that to thy sense

    Appeares not man? Divinitie is too bright

    For thy weake eye, and therefore I have clad

    In this no threatning shape, all that is divine,

    That I with safetie of thy sence, <u>Emeria</u>,   95

    Might visit thee: come, I will see thee often,

    If thou be wise to understand how much

    It is my will to honour thee; and I

    Will thus descend, and leave my beames behind,

89. S. D. <u>Raises her</u>] <u>Gifford</u>.

---

    86. to thy reward] i.e., "to reward thee."

    87. release . . . knee] no longer require you to kneel.

    88. Reach . . . hand] i.e., "give me your hand" (so I can raise you up).

Whose brightnesse were enough to burne thee,   100

To converse with thee in a loving way

Of smiling thus, and thus embracing thee--

Of mixing palmes; nay I will kisse thee too.

Emeria. Doe our gods practise this?

Corybreus.   Not but with those

They meane especiall grace to; such as they   105

Know must hereafter shine above with them,

Though meerly mortals, are ador'd. And seldome

Visit the world, hid thus in flesh and bloud,

Which wee at pleasure can assume, and have

*104-112. They . . . men] Gifford's relineation; Q prints as
prose.

*107. mortals, are] Q; mortals, they are Donovan.

*107. *ador'd. And] ador'd; and Q.

---

100. were] would otherwise be.

103. mixing palmes] holding hands. Cf. "And palm to palm
is holy palmer's kiss" (Romeo and Juliet, I.v.102).

104-112. Not . . . men] Gifford (IV, 405) indicates that
he thinks words are missing in line 107 between "ador'd" and
"and": "This speech is given in the old copy as prose, and most
ridiculously pointed: these however are accidents in Shirley
too common to be noticed; but it appears that the careless
printer has also suffered some of the copy to escape his eye.
It is in vain to guess at what we have lost; but Corybreus, after
adverting to deified mortals, seems to revert to the privileges
of the gods themselves." There certainly is a shift in subject-
matter at line 107. I have printed the speech as two sentences.
After the full stop in line 107 the sense is, "And [we gods]
seldom visit the world [except when we] hide ourselves thus in
flesh and blood, which we can do at our pleasure. We also have
desires like you, and passions; and we can love, and can achieve
fulfillment of that love, or else we would be lesser creatures
than men."

Desires like you, and have our passions too,   11(

Can love, I, and enjoy where wee will place

The happinesse, else we had lesse than men.

Emeria. I thought the powers above had beene all honest.

Corybreus. 'Tis in them chastitie; nor is it sin

In those we love to meet with active flames,   115

And be glad mothers to immortall issues:

How oft hath Jove, who justly is ador'd,

Left heaven, to practise love with such a faire one?

The Sun, for one embrace of Daphne, would

Have pawn'd his beames: not one, but hath sometimes   12(

Descended, to make fruitfull weake Mortalitie.

Oh, if thou could'st but reach, Emeria,

112. had] Q; had been Gifford.

*115. with] Chetwood, Gifford, MacMullan, Donovan; wit Q.

---

113. honest] chaste.

115. with] The sense of the line (as well as the fact that
all previous editors adopted the emendation) makes it likely that
the compositor dropped the final letter in Q. Furthermore, I can
find no evidence that the preposition "with" was ever spelled
"wit" in the seventeenth century.

115. active] See note on II.i.205 above.

117. Jove] referring to Jupiter's visits to mortal virgins
such as Io and Europa.

119. Daphne] Daphne was the daughter of Peneus, a river
god. Running away from Apollo, she exhausted herself, and in
response to her call to the gods to rescue her was transformed
into a laurel before her pursuer could embrace her.

122. reach] understand.

With thy imagination, what delight,

What flowing extasies of joy we bring

Your sex, made nice and cold by winter lawes   125

Of man, that freeze the bloud, thou wood'st be fond

To my embraces, and petition me

To blesse thee with a rape; yet I woe thy

Consent.

Emeria.   Away: Thou art no god sure, but

Some vicious Impostor: Can a Deitie   130

Breath so much impious language, and reward

Vertue with shame?

Corybreus.   Take heed, and doe not vaine

127. To] Q; Of Gifford.

*132. vaine] Q; ruin Gifford; vail Donovan.

---

125. nice] foolishly reluctant; coy.

125-126. winter . . . man] i.e., laws which attempt to control the natural passions--lust, for example.

126-127. fond To] receptive of.

128. woe] appeal for.

131. Breath] breathe.

132. vaine] Previous editors have been quite unwilling to accept this word as Shirley's intention. It makes perfectly good sense in its older meaning of "frustrate," e.g., Owen Fetham's Resolves Divine, Morall, politicall (London, 1623) "Every good man . . . must be wise and circumspect, to vaine the sleeke navations of those that would undoe him" (II.xii.34). Donovan's word "vail" (an archaic word meaning to lower oneself in submission to) makes equally good sense, but is not justified bibliographically. There is no reason at all to accept Gifford's emendation "ruin."

Thy selfe by rash and froward opposition;

Know, I can make thee nothing, at a breath.

Emeria. Better be so, than made so foule a being.   13⁵

Corybreus. Nay then, what should have beene with thy consent

A blessing, shall now only serve my pleasure,

And I will take the forfeit of thy coldnesse.

Emeria. Oh help, some man; I dare not call upon

The gods, for they are wicked growne; oh help.   14(

Corybreus. I shall need none, thou thing of disobedience,

Thou art now within my power of love, or furie:

Yeeld, or I'll force thee into postures shall

Make pleasure weep, and hurle thee into wantonnesse.

He carries her in. The Devils rejoycing

in a dance conclude the Act.

ACT IV. [Scene i.]

Enter Milcho and Servant.

Milcho. Who's with the Queene, my prisoner?

Servant. The Prince Conallus came to visit her.

Milcho. So: bid my daughter Emeria come hither; Exit Servant.
     She's come verie melancholy from the Court,
     Under pretence to wait upon the Queene here.   5

               Enter Emeria.

     Still sad; come, I must have your face looke otherwise;
     Dresse it in smiles: I hope you put not on
     This sorrow for the Queene; she is a traytor
     To the King, and to the gods.

Emeria.   A traytor, Sir!
     Oh doe not say so; 'tis, I heare, for nothing,   10
     But looking on the stranger Patrick with
     Some pitie.

Milcho.   It will not run
     Out of my thought; but this is the same Patrick
     That was my slave once; he was a Brittan too:

_____

     IV.i. Gifford locates this scene in "A Room in Milcho's
House."

     13-18. this . . . was] See BB, pp. 7-9.

174

                I know not how, he found some treasure then

                To buy his libertie: were he agen

                My slave, no gold should buy him from my swine,

                Whose once companion he was: Emeria,

                D'yee heare? Conallus, the young Prince is come

                To see his mother; use him gently, girle: 2(

                Come, I have heard he does affect thee, ha?

                He may be King.

Emeria.   His brother Corybreus

                Is neerer to that title, and he sayes

                He loves me.

Milcho.   Does he so? then love him best.

Emeria.   Imagine I had promisd, Sir, my heart   2!

                To his younger brother.

Milcho.   Break a thousand promises,

                And hazard breaking of thy heart too, wench,

                To be but one degree neerer a Queene;

                It does exalt my heart; spread all thy charmes

                Of wit and language, when he courts thee girle: 3(

                Smile, kisse, or any thing, that may endeere

                _____

                18. once] former.

                21. affect] love.

                26-32. Break . . . fortune] Milcho's advice to Emeria
recalls Shirley's The Brothers, II.i (Gifford, I, 218) where
Don Carlos advises Jacinta to forsake Francisco for Fernando.

Him and so great a fortune: I must leave thee,

But wo' not be long absent.

[Re-enter Servant.]

Servant. Sir, the Bard does presse to see the Queene.

Milcho. He must not see her,   35

His insolence I'll punish; yet admit him hither;

[Exit Servant.]

His pleasant nature may raise mirth

In my sad daughter.

Enter Bard.

Welcome, merry Bard.

Bard. I care not whither I be or no: the Queene

I come to see.

Milcho.   Shee's private with the Prince: 40

Come hither; do'st thou see that piece of sullennesse,

That phlegmatick foolish thing?

Bard.   [Aside.] And like the father.

33.1 S. D. Re-enter Servant] Chetwood, Gifford, Donovan.

36.1 S. D. Exit Servant] Gifford, Donovan.

---

39. whither . . . be] whether I be [welcome].

42. phlegmatick] This is another reference to the humors.
A phlegmatic person is one in whom phlegm predominates, making
him cold, dull, sluggish, and apathetic.

Milcho. Make her merry, and I'll give thee

    Gold joy to purchase a new harp; here's some

    In earnest; thou hast wanton pretty songs   4

    To stirre the merry thoughts of maids: I'me gone

    To give thee opportunity; my presence

    May spoile the working of thy mirth; that done

    Sha't speak with the Queene too.   Exit.

Bard.   Fare you well Sir,

    And take a knave along we'e. Here's a rose   5

    Sprung out of a thistle now: You are sad, Madam.

Emeria. I have no cause of mirth, Bard.

Bard.   What d'yee think

    Of me?

Emeria.   Think of thee, Bard; I think

    Th'art honest, and canst shew a pleasant face

*44. Gold∧ joy∧] Q; Gold, joy, Gifford.

---

44. Gold joy] MacMullan and Gifford disagree as to the
meaning of this phrase. The fact that Gifford sets off "joy"
with commas indicates that he thinks Milcho is using it as a
pet name for the Bard. MacMullan glosses it as follows: "I.e.,
rejoice. The imperative." I think the phrase is an epithet
(i.e., golden joy) for coins, although I have not been able to
find any evidence of similar usage elsewhere.

45. earnest] money paid as an installment, especially
for the purpose of securing a bargain or contract.

50-51. Here's . . . thistle] Emeria is the rose and her
father Milcho is the thistle. This figure may be related to
the proverb, "Of a thorn springs not a rose" (Tilley, T233).

Sometimes, without an over joy within;   55
But 'tis thy office.

Bard. I know why you are so melancholy.

Emeria. Prethee why do'st think, Bard?

Bard. You want a man.

Emeria. Why, thou art one?   60

Bard. That's more than you know.

Sings.

'Tis long of men that maids are sad;
    Come then, and sweetly kisse them,
Their lips invite, you will be mad
    To come too late and misse them.   65
In their cheeks, are full-blowne roses
    To make garlands, to make posies:
He that desires to be a father,
Let him make haste before they fall, and gather:
You stay too long, and do them wrong: 70

---

55. over] excessive.

59. want] lack.

62-72. 'Tis . . . disease] This song obviously belongs
to the carpe diem tradition very popular in seventeenth-century
lyrics; cf., for instance, Herrick's "Gather ye Rosebuds While
ye May," Marvell's "To His Coy Mistress," and Carew's "Gaze not
on thy Beauties Pride." The images of flowers (particularly
roses) about to "fall" (or die) are, of course, conventional.

62. long of] owing to, because of. Cf. Florio: "I wot
not what it is long of, but I have no stomack" (First Fruites,
London, 1578).

    If <u>men</u> <u>would</u> <u>virgins</u> <u>strive</u> <u>to</u> <u>please</u>,

    <u>No</u> <u>maid</u> <u>this</u> <u>yeere</u> <u>should</u> <u>dye</u> <u>o'</u> <u>th'</u> <u>greene</u> <u>disease</u>.

What, are you merrie yet?

<u>Emeria</u>.   I am so far

    From being rais'd to mirth, that I encline

    To anger.

<u>Bard</u>.   Come, I'll fit you with a song,

    A lamentable ballad, of one lost

    Her maiden-head, and would needs have it cri'd,

    With all the marks, in hope to ha't agen.

<u>Emeria</u>. You were not sent to abuse me?

<u>Bard</u>. A daintie aire too; I'll but tune my instrument.

<u>Emeria</u>. No more, or I'll complaine: [Aside.] sure hee

    knowes nothing

    Of my dishonour. How mine owne thoughts fright me?

---

    72. <u>greene disease</u>] "Chlorosis--an anaemic sickness of young women (with consequent greenish complexion). The Elizabethan dramatists emblematized it as a sign of a girl's lovesickness, or a vague desire for a man" (Partridge, p. 123).

    75. fit] supply.

    77. have it cri'd] give public notice of it as a lost article.

    78. marks] characteristic features.

    80. daintie] pleasant. I'll . . . instrument] Partridge (p. 134) points out that "instrument" may refer to the male sexual organ, which seems to be the secondary implication here. Cf. <u>The Taming of the Shrew</u>: "Madam, before you teach the instrument, / To learn the order of my fingering, / I must begin with rudiments of art" (III.i.64-66).

Bard. Now you shall heare the dittie.

Emeria.   Hence, foolish Bard.

Bard.   Sings.

    A poore wench was sighing, and weeping amaine,

    And faine would she have her virginitie againe,   85

    Lost she knew not how; in her sleep (as she said)

    She went to bed pure, but she rise not a maid:

      She made fast the doore,

      She was certaine before,

        She laid her selfe downe in the bed: 90

    But when she awaked, the truth is stark-naked,

      Oh she mist her maiden-head.

*87. rise] Q; risse Gifford.

    84-92. A . . . maiden-head] This song recalls a similar
one in Beaumont and Fletcher's The Queen of Corinth where Merione
hears a song in an entertainment which reminds her of her rape:

    Court-ladies, laugh and wonder. Here is one
    That weeps because her maidenhead is gone;
    Whilst you do never fret, nor chafe, nor cry,
    But when too long it keeps you company.
    Too well you know, maids are like towns on fire,
    Wasting themselves, if no man quench desire.
    Weep then no more, fool: A new maidenhead
    Thou suffer'st loss of, in each chaste tear shed.
                            (III.ii.14-22)

Cf. also Ophelia's bawdy song in Hamlet, IV.v.48-66. The plot
of the Bard's ballad is very much like the episode with the maid
in Shirley's The Maid's Revenge, III.ii (Gifford, I, 145-146).

    84. amaine] violently; in full force.

    85. faine] gladly.

    87. rise] Gifford's emendation is an obsolete form of
"risen." The OED lists "rise" as a variant form of "risse."

<u>Enter</u> Conallus.

Ha, the young Prince; I'll tarrie no longer w'ee.

Now to the Queene.   <u>Exit</u>.

<u>Conallus</u>. <u>Emeria</u>, prethee doe not hide thy face   9

From me; 'tis more than common sorrow makes

Thee look thus: If the Queene's mis-fortunes have

Darken'd thy face, I suffer too in that.

If for thy selfe thou weep'st, my almost ebbing

Griefe thou wilt enforce back, and beget   10

New seas, in which, made high by one strong sigh

Of thine, I meet a watry sepulcher.

My mother's fate commands my griefe, but thine

100. and beget] <u>Q</u>; and [thus] beget <u>Gifford</u>.

95-167. This episode has many parallels in the drama of
the period. Cf. Middleton's <u>The Mayor of Queenborough</u> (III.iii.
266-300) where Vortiger (who <u>is Castiza's real ravisher</u>) discusses with her her reasons for being sad.

100. enforce back] use force to hold back.

101-102. New . . . sepulcher] The thought and imagery of
these lines recall Donne's "A Valediction: of Weeping":

On a round ball
A workeman that hath copies by, can lay
An Europe, Afrique, and an Asia,
And quickly make that, which was nothing, <u>All</u>,
So doth each teare,
Which thee doth weare,
A globe, yea world by that impression grow,
Till thy teares mixt with mine doe overflow
This world, by waters sent from thee, my heaven dis-
solved so.
(lines 10-18)

A greater suffering, since our hearts are one,

And there wants nothing, but a ceremony   105

To justifie it to the world.

Emeria.   Call back

Your promises, my Lord; they were ill plac'd

On me, for I have nothing to deserve 'em.

Conallus. If thou be'st constant to thy selfe, and art

Emeria still--

Emeria.   That word hath wounded me.   110

Conallus. Why, art not thou thy selfe?

Emeria.   I have the shape still,

But not the inward part.

Conallus.   Am I so miserable,

To have my faith suspected? for I dare not

Think thou canst sin by any change: What act

Have I done my Emeria? or who hath   115

112. inward] Q; purer Chetwood.

---

105. wants] lacks.

106. justifie it] make it legal.

107-108. ill . . . me] i.e., I did not deserve to have
your promises made to me.

112. inward part] Emeria is saying that her true inner
self has changed because of the loss of her virginity.

113. faith] fidelity; faith in you.

Poyson'd thy pure soule with suggestion

Of my revolt? Apostasie I'll call it,

For next our gods, thou art my happinesse.

Emeria. Now, my deere Lord, and let mee adde thus much

In my owne part, I never lov'd you better;   12

Never with more religious thoughts and honour

Look'd on you; my heart never made a vow

So blessed in my hopes, as that I gave you,

And I suspect not yours.

Conallus.   What then can make thee,

My Emeria, lesse; or me? Thou do'st affright--   12

Emeria. Yes, I am lesse, and have that taken from me

Hath almost left me nothing, or if any,

So much unworthy you, that you would curse me,

Should I betray you to receive Emeria.

----

118. next] next to.

124. I . . . yours] I do not suspect that your vow was
false.

125. lesse] i.e., less in virtue.

126. that] that which (for omitted relative see Abbott,
par. 244).

127. nothing] There is a pun here on the use of the word
as a female sexual organ (cf. Hamlet, III.ii.124-126).

128. unworthy you] unworthy of you. The preposition was
sometimes omitted after some verbs and adjectives that imply
value or worth (Abbott, par. 198a).

129. Should . . . Emeria] i.e., since I am no longer the
Emeria you loved (i.e., the one who was a virgin), should I
betray you by giving you to someone else?

Conallus. Doe not destroy me so; be plaine.

Emeria.   Then thus--   130
     But if I drop a teare or two, pray pardon me:
     Did not the story touch my selfe, I should
     Weep for it in another; you did promise
     To marrie me, my Lord.

Conallus.   I did, and will.

Emeria. Alas, I have lost--

Conallus   What?

Emeria.   The portion that   135
     I promis'd to bring with me.

Conallus.   Do I value
     Thy wealth?

Emeria.   Oh, but the treasure
     I lost, you wil expect, and scorne me ever,
     Because you have it not; yet heaven is witnesse
     'Tis not my fault, a thiefe did force it from me,   140
     Oh my deere Lord.

Conallus.   I know not what to feare;
     Speake plainer yet.

135. portion] Q; Dowry Chetwood.

_____

     135. portion] a quibble on "dowry" and "portion" in the
sense of portion or part of the body, hence "maidenhead."

Emeria.   You'l say I am too loud,

    When I but whisper, Sir. I am no virgin.

Conallus. Ha!

Emeria. I knew 'twould fright you; but by all those teares,   14

    The poore Lamb, made a prey to the fierce wolfe,

    Had not more innocence, or lesse consent

    To be devoured, than I to lose mine honour.

Conallus. Why, wert thou ravished?

Emeria.   You have named it, Sir.

Conallus. The villaine, name the villaine, sweet Emeria,   15

    That I may send his leprous soule to hell for't;

    And when he hath confest the monstrous sin,

    I'll think thee still a virgin, and thou art so:

    Confirme thy pietie by naming him.

Emeria. It will enlarge but your vexation, Sir,   15

    That he's above your anger and revenge;

    For he did call himselfe a god that did it.

Conallus. The Devill he was; Oh do not wrack, Emeria,

    The heart that honours thee; mock me not, I prethee,

    With calling him a god; it was a furie,   16

    The master fiend of darknesse, and as hot

    As hell could make him, that would ravish thee.

---

    155. enlarge but] only increase.

    158. wrack] i.e., stretch on the rack; wreck.

Emeria. If you do think I ever lov'd you, Sir

    Or have a soule after my bodie's rape,

    He nam'd himselfe a god, great Ceancrochius,   165

    To whom I owe my shame and transformation.

Conallus. Oh, I am lost in miserie and amazement.   Exit.

Emeria. So; I did see before it would afflict him:

    But having given these reasons to Conallus,

    For our divorce, I have provided how   170

    To finish all disgraces by my death.   [Draws a dagger.]

    Come, cure of my dishonour, and with bloud

    Wash off my staine.

Enter Archimagus.

Ha, Archimagus!

Archimagus.   Madam.

Emeria. What newes with our great Priest.

Archimagus. I come to tell you, heavenly Ceancrochius,   175

165. Ceancrochius] Q; Ceanerachius Gifford.

---

164. have a soule] i.e., have promise of salvation.

165. Ceancrochius] Elsewhere the god's name is spelled differently (e.g., "Ceancrochi," III.ii.23.2). There seems to be no significance to the variant spellings.

168. before] earlier.

170. divorce] separation.

Of whom I had this day a happie vision,

Is pleas'd agen to visit you, and commanded

I should prepare you.

Emeria.   [Aside.] I begin to finde

Some Magicall imposture. Does he know it?

Archimagus. I leave to say, how much you are his favorite;   18

Be wise, and humble for so great a blessing.

Emeria. [Aside.] This does increase my feares, I've been

        betraid;

    I'll live a little longer, then; [To Archimagus.] great

        Priest

    My words are poore to make acknowledgement

    For so divine a favour: But I shall   18

    Humbly expect, and hold my selfe agen

    Blest in his presence.

            Enter Corybreus as before habited.

Archimagus.   Hee's here, Emeria;

    Never was virgin so much honoured.   Exit.

Corybreus. How is it with my sweet Emeria?

_____

    179. Does he know it] Is he implicated.

    180. leave] omit; i.e., "I won't bother to recount how
much . . . ."

    186. expect] await. hold] consider.

Emeria. That question would become an ignorant Mortall,   190

    Whose sense would be inform'd; not Ceancrochius

    Whose eye at once can see the soule of all things.

Corybreus. I do not ask, to make

    Thee think I doubt, but to maintain that forme,

    Which men familiar to such faire ones use   195

    When they converse: For I would have my language

    Soft as a lover's.

Emeria.   You are still gracious.

Corybreus. This temper is becoming, and thou dost

    Now appear worthy of our loves and presence.

    I knew when thy wise soule examin'd what   200

    It was to be the darling to a god,

    Thou would'st compose thy gestures, and resigne

    Thy selfe to our great will: Which we accept

    And pardon thy first frailty; 'tis in us

---

192. soule] inner nature; essence which is hidden from human cognition.

197. gracious] Emeria is punning here on the two senses of "gracious"; polite, and endowed with religious grace.

199. our loves] Corybreus is here using the regal "we" since he is imitating a god.

202. compose thy gestures] relax your protestations, calm yourself.

203-204. Which . . . frailty] The sense here is "We accept that resignation and pardon your former weakness (which made you refuse our overtures)."

Emeria, to translate thee hence to heaven,

Without thy bodie's separation,

I' th' twinckling of an eye; but thou sha't live

Here to convince erring mortality,

That gods do visit such religious votaries

In humane forme; and thus salute 'em.   [Tries to kiss her.]

Emeria. And thus be answered, with a resolute heart.   Stabs him.

Corybreus. Oh thou hast murder'd me; Strumpet, hold.

Emeria. Sure if you be a god, you are above

These wounds: ˈIf man, thou hast deserv'd to bleed

For thy impiety.

Corybreus.   My blood is punish'd;

205-206. to translate . . . separation] A sexual meaning
seems to be implied here--a variation, perhaps, of the common
Elizabethan pun on "die." Cf. Beaumont and Fletcher's The Woman
Hater: "I will enjoy thee, though it be betweene the parting of
thy soule and body" (V.iv.69-70).

209. votaries] devout worshippers.

211-222. Emeria's revenge against the pretended Deity
recalls the device of Shirley's The Duke's Mistress, V.i
(Gifford, IV, 256) where Ardelia threatens Valerio with a
pistol whereupon he is wounded behind the arras by Bentivolio
(Forsythe, p. 228). Also notice the stab here as the sexual
act in reverse. There is a kind of subconscious exactitude
in the punishment which recalls Fletcherian tragicomedy.

215. My . . . punish'd] Cf. Webster's The White Devil:
"O, my greatest sin lay in my blood, / Now my blood pays for
it" (Webster, V.vi.239-240).

A curse upon thy hand, I am no god;

I am the Prince, see <u>Corybreus</u>.

<u>Emeria</u>.   Ha?

The Prince? were you my ravisher my Lord?

I have done a justice to the gods in this

And my owne honour. Thou lost thing to goodnesse;   220

It was a glorious wound, and I am proude

To be the gods' revenger.

<u>Corybreus</u>.   Help, Oh I am lost.   <u>He</u> <u>dies</u>.

<u>Emeria</u>. Call on the furies, they did help thy sinne,

And will transport thy soule on their black wings

To hell, Prince; and the gods can do no lesse,   225

Than in reward to draw thy purple streame up,

Shed in their cause, and place it a portent

In heaven, to affright such foule lascivious Princes.

222. Oh I am] <u>Q</u>; Oh! am I <u>Chetwood</u>.

216-217. Forsythe (p. 228) relates the exposure of Corybreus as the rapist of Emeria to an incident in Beaumont and
Fletcher's <u>The</u> <u>Island</u> <u>Princess</u> (V.v.53-65); here the governor's
disguise of beard and hair is ripped off to expose him.

220. And] and to. Shirley has omitted the preposition in
the second of two parallel constructions.

223. furies] See I.i.3.

226-228. draw . . . Princes] Blood in heaven was considered a portent in classic and medieval times. Cf. Marlowe's
<u>Doctor</u> <u>Faustus</u>: "See, see, where Christ's blood streams in
the firmament?" (V.ii.148) and in <u>Julius</u> <u>Ceasar</u> (I.iii.127-128).

I will live now, this story shall not fall so,

And yet I must not stay here; now Conallus

I have done some revenge for thee in this,

Yet all this wo' not help me to my owne

Agen; my honour of a virgin never will

Returne; I live and move, but wanting thee,

At best I'me but a walking miserie.   Exit.

Enter Rodament reading.

Rodamant. My royall love, my Lady, and faire Misteries,

          Such love as mine, was never read in histories.

There's love, and love; good.

---

229. fall so] i.e., end with my death.

236-267. My royall . . . service] The comic device of
a foolish courtier's reading verses to his beloved is common
in Shirley. In Love Tricks, Bubuculus hears a foolish love
poem read by Gorgon in III.v (Gifford, I, 42-44), then reads
one of his own in IV.i (Gifford, I, 59). Sir Nicholas Treedle,
in Shirley's The Witty Fair One, III.ii (Gifford, I, 311-314)
has written some poems called "Love's Hue and Cry," which are
read by Tutor. The following lines are similar to lines 261-
262 of St. Patrick:

     Her head is opal, neck of sapphire,
     Breast carbuncles, shine like a fire;
     And the naked truth to tell ye,
     The very mother of pearl her belly.
     How can she choose but hear my groans,
     That is composed of precious stones? (Gifford, I, 313)

See also Sir Gervase Simple in Shirley's Love in a Maze, II.ii
(Gifford, II, 301-302), Depazzi in Shirley's The Humorous
Courtier, III.i (Gifford, IV, 550), Suckabus in Kirke's Seven
Champions of Christendom (V), and the various young men in
Love's Labor's Lost (III.i.85-99; IV.ii.57-64; 109-122; V.ii.
158-169).

236. Misteries] love's mysteries (with a pun on "mistress").

The <u>poyson</u> <u>to</u> <u>my</u> <u>heart</u> <u>was</u> <u>not</u> <u>so</u> <u>cruell</u>,

<u>As</u> <u>that</u> <u>I</u> <u>cannot</u> <u>hang</u> <u>thee</u>--   240

How's that, hang the Queene?

The <u>poyson</u> <u>to</u> <u>my</u> <u>heart</u> <u>was</u> <u>not</u> <u>so</u> <u>cruell</u>,

<u>As</u> <u>that</u> <u>I</u> <u>cannot</u> <u>hang</u> <u>thee</u>, <u>my</u> <u>rich</u> <u>jewell</u>,

<u>Within</u> <u>my</u> <u>heart</u>.--

Oh there's <u>hang</u> and <u>jewell</u>, and <u>heart</u>, and <u>heart</u>; good agen. 245

<u>I</u> <u>am</u> <u>thy</u> <u>constant</u> <u>Elfe</u>,

<u>And</u> <u>dare</u> <u>for</u> <u>thy</u> <u>sweet</u> <u>sake</u>, <u>go</u> <u>hang</u> <u>my</u> <u>selfe</u>.

<u>What</u> <u>though</u> <u>I</u> <u>am</u> <u>no</u> <u>Lord</u>, <u>yet</u> <u>I</u> <u>am</u> <u>loyall</u>,

There's a gingle upon the letter, to shew if she will give

me but an inch, I'll take an ell; <u>Lord</u> and <u>loyall</u>.   250

<u>And</u> <u>though</u> <u>no</u> <u>prince</u> <u>I</u> <u>am</u> <u>thy</u> <u>servant</u> <u>royall</u>.

There's no figure in that; yes impossibility, <u>servant</u> and

<u>royall</u>.

<u>Then</u> <u>grant</u> <u>him</u> <u>love</u> <u>for</u> <u>love</u>, <u>that</u> <u>doth</u> <u>present</u> <u>these</u>,

---

240. <u>hang</u>] punning on the sexual meaning of the word.
MacMullan points out that Shirley uses the joke also in <u>Love</u>
<u>Tricks</u>, III.v: "Your jewel may have the grace to be <u>hanged</u>
one day" (Gifford, I, 49).

249-250. gingle . . . <u>loyall</u>] "Gingle" is an obsolete
form of "jingle," meaning <u>alliteration</u>; "Lord" and "loyall"
both begin with the same letter. The proverb, "to give an
inch and take an ell" (Telley, I49) means that undue advantage
will be taken of a slight concession, with a play on "ell"
and the letter "l" in "Lord" and "loyall." There is also the
sexual suggestion of an erection.

251. <u>servant</u>] lover.

252. figure] figure of speech.

      With Noverint universi per presentes.

There's to shew I am a Linguist, with a rumme in the rime

consisting of two severall languages, beside love and love.

      Thy jeat and alablaster face--

Jeat because it drawes the straw of my heart, and alablaster,

*259. Jeat] Chetwood, Gifford and Donovan substantively; I eat Q.

---

    255. Noverint . . . presentes] MacMullan (p. 113) identi-
fies this as "the customary beginning of legal documents." Its
literal meaning is "all men will learn through these presenta-
tions." The phrase is also used in Thomas Heywood's The Late
Lancashire Witches, V.i (Heywood, IV, 175) by the pedant Whet-
stone to indicate a familiarity with learning:

      I have been ever bound unto you, for which
      I will at this time be your Noverint, and give
      him notice that you universi will be with him
      per praesentes, and that I take to be presently.

    256. rumme] Gifford thinks that "rumme" is a misprint,
and suggests "conundrum." The OED quotes this passage, pointing out that the meaning of the word is obscure. MacMullan
(p. 114) states that the word might be a misprint for "runne,"
meaning rhythmical verse. It is also possible that this is a
nonsense word made up for its similarity to "rime," in order
to suggest alliteration (cf. Chaucer, "The Parson's Prologue,"
line 43: "I can not geeste 'rum, ram, ruf,' by lettre").
Robinson, in his note to this line in his edition of Chaucer,
points out that these are nonsense words used for the conso-
nantal repetition to suggest alliteration, and that they (and
words like them) are fairly common in both French and English.
In Shirley's lines (256-257) Rodamant is saying that he not
only has made an alliteration in English (on "love" and "love")
but also in Latin (on "per" and "presentes") and that because
he has also rhymed "present these" and "presentes," he is
therefore a linguist.

    258. jeat] jet, black marble. alablaster] alabaster, a
pure white material.

    259. Jeat . . . heart] Chetwood's emendation may be
accepted because it is probable that the compositor substituted
"I" for "J," a common practice of the period. The phrase,
according to MacMullan (p. 114), refers to the magnetic proper-
ties of jet. Cf. Jonson's Every Man in his Humour: "Draw
courtship to you, / As a jet doth strawes" (III.ii.45-46).

because there is some white in her face.   260

    Thy <u>jeat</u> and <u>Alablaster</u> <u>face</u> <u>now</u> <u>calls</u>,

    <u>My</u> <u>love</u> and <u>hunger</u> <u>up</u> <u>to</u> <u>eat</u> <u>stone</u> <u>walls</u>.

But so I may bite of her nose, if her face be alablaster;

but she is in prison, there it holds, and I may do her ser-

vice to break prison for her any way. Well, here's enough   265

at a time; if she like this, I have an ambling muse that

shall be at her service: But what stumbling block is cast

in my way? This is no place to sleepe in, I take it in

a story under a trundlebed: I have seene these clothes

afore now; the tailor tooke measure for one of our gods   270

that made 'em; de'e heare freind? ha! 'tis the Prince

<u>Corybreus</u>, dead, kild, Ha? my Lord? [shaking him.] hee's

    speechlesse.

What were I best to doe? in stead of searching the wound

I'll first search his pockets: What's here? a bracelet,

---

262. <u>My</u> . . . <u>walls</u>] Rodamant is referring to two proverbs: "Love will go through stone walls" (Tilley, L532) and
"Hunger breaks down (pierces) stone walls" (Telley, H811).

266. ambling muse] i.e., he derives his inspiration from
a slow-walking Muse. This phrase is a common one in the period.
Cf. George Williamson's book, The <u>Senecan</u> <u>Amble</u> (London, 1951),
pp. 44-45.

268-269. I . . . trundlebed] A trundlebed is "a low bed
that runs on truckles (castors), and was appropriated to the
servants, or inferior members of the family. It was only drawn
out at night; by day it was always thrust under the standing
bed" (Gifford). The sense of the passage is obscure. A story
under a trundlebed might have something to do with the gossip
of servants or what might be found out by hiding beneath such
a bed.

273. searching] probing.

a pretty toy; I'll give it the Queene; [picks up bracelet.]
but if I be found here alone I may be found necessary to
his death. Ha, what shall I do?   Hides himselfe.

Enter Milcho and servant.

Milcho. My daughter gone abroad without a servant?

Servant. I offer'd my attendance.

Milcho. Ha! what's here, one murder'd? 'tis the Prince,
    Slaine in my house; confusion! Look about,
    Search for the traitour; I am undone for ever.

Servant. The Prince! I'll take my oath I see him not enter.
    Why thus disguis'd?

Milcho.   I tremble to look on him;
    Seek everie where.

Servant.   I gave accesse to none
    But Rodamant, and he is gone.

Milcho. What shall we doe? remove the murder'd body,
    And on thy life be silent, we are lost else.
    Attend without, and give accesse to none,
    Till I have thought some way through this affliction.
                            [Exit Servant with body.]

_____

276. found necessary to] implicated in.
283. I see him not] that I didn't see him.

Did my stars owe me this? oh, I could curse 'em,

And from my vexed heart exhale a vapour

Of execrations, that should blast the day,

And darken all the world. The Prince murder'd

In my house, and the Traytor not discovered.   295

Enter Servant.

Servant. One, Sir, with a letter.

Milcho.   Let him carrie it back;

Where's the young Prince, Conallus?

Servant.   Gone long since, Sir.

Milcho. I'll lay the murder upon him; it will

Be though ambition, or upon the Queene.

Servant. Sir, one waits with a Letter from the King.   300

Milcho. The King? that name shoots horrour through me now;

Who is the messenger?

Servant. A stranger both in habit and in person:

---

292. from . . . vapour] This is a difficult passage
containing, perhaps, a reference to the concept of the humors
again. It is difficult to imagine how a heart could "exhale,"
but it was the seat of the passions, and therefore, "a vapor
of execretions" would probably originate there.

293. blast] See I.i.16.

301. name . . . now] See note on I.i.119.

303. habit] dress.

                         Enter Patrick.

     This is he, Sir.

<u>Milcho</u>.   Ha.

<u>Patrick</u>.   The King salutes you,
     My Lord; this paper speaks his royall pleasure.   30
                         [<u>Gives</u> Milcho <u>a</u> <u>letter</u>.]
     You have forgot me, Sir; but I have beene more
     Familiar to your knowledge: Is there nothing
     Within my face, that doth resemble once
     A slave you had?

<u>Milcho</u>.   Ha, is your name <u>Patrick</u>?

<u>Patrick</u>. It is, my Lord: I made my humble suit   31
     To th' King, that by his favour I might visit you;
     And though I have not now that servile tye,
     It will not shame me to professe I owe
     You dutie still, and shall to my best power
     Obey your just commands.

<u>Milcho</u>.   [<u>Aside</u>.] He writ to me,   31
     That I should try my art, and by some stratagem

315. writ to] Q; writ[es] to <u>Gifford</u>.

_____

     305. speaks] betokens, evidences.
     316. try] test.

Discharge his life; I'll do't, but all this wo' not

Quit the suspition of the Prince's death:

What if I lay the murder to his charge?

I can sweare any thing. But if he come off,   320

My head must answer; no trick in my braine?

[To Patrick.] Y'are welcome; the King writes you

    have desires

To see the Queene;   [To Servant.] you shall entreat

    her presence.   [Exit Servant.]

Patrick.   The King has honour'd me.

Milcho.   You have deserv'd it.

And I doe count it happinesse to receive   325

Whom he hath grac'd; but the remembrance

Of what you were, addes to the entertainment:

My old acquaintance, Patrick.

Patrick.   You are noble.

323.   shall entreat] Q; shall.-- Entreat Gifford.

---

317.   Discharge] put an end to.

318.   Quit] do away with. suspition] See note on I.i.14.

319-321. What . . . answer] "Perjury against the life
of a man for felony or murder when the accused was acquitted,
was a punishable offense; but it was not 'examinable or punishable,' if the accused were convicted" (MacMullan, p. 114).

320. come off] be acquitted. Cf. Shirley's The Cardinal:
"Now to come off were brave" (Forker, III.ii.126).

326. Whom] i.e., the one whom. The antecedent of a
relative was often implied in Renaissance usage.

Enter [Servant with] Queene and Bard.

Milcho. The Queene? welcome agen; [To Servant.] come hither,

    sirra.   [They talk apart.]

Patrick. Madam; I joy to see you, and present   330

    My humble dutie: Heaven hath heard my prayers,

    I hope, and if you still preserve that goodnesse,

    That did so late, and sweetly shine upon you,

    I may not be unwelcome, since there is

    Something behind, which I am trusted with,   335

    To make you happier.

Queene.   Holy Patrick, welcome.

Milcho. [To Servant.] Obey in everie circumstance: Exit Servant.

    [Aside.] My despaire

  Shall have revenge wait on it. [To Queen.] This is,

    Madam,

  A good man, he was once my slave; let not

  That title take thy present freedome of   340

  My house; my fortunes and my fate, I wish,

  May have one period with thee; I shall

  Attend you agen; I hope we all may live

---

335. behind] still to come.

340. take . . . of] prevent you from now having free access
to.

342. May . . . thee] will now be bound up with yours for
a short stretch of time.

And dye together yet. My dutie, Madam.   Exit.

Bard. [Aside to Patrick.] I doe not like their whispering,
       there's some mischiefe;   345
    hee did so over-act his courtesie, I'll looke about us.

Patrick. [Aside to Bard.] Doe, honest Bard.
                       Exit [Bard].

                                     Oh Madam, if you knew
    The difference betwixt my faith, and your
    Religion, the grounds and progresse of
    What we professe, the sweetnesse, certaintie,   350
    And full rewards of vertue, you would hazard,
    Nay, lose the glorie of ten thousand worlds
    Like this to be a Christian, and be blest
    To lay your life downe (but a moment, on
    Which our eternitie depends) and through   355
    Torture and seas of bloud contend, to reach
    That blessed vision at last, in which
    Is all that can be happie, and perfection.

Queene. I have a soule most willing to be taught.

                    Enter Bard.

347. S. D. Exit] Q prints right of line 346.

_____

349. grounds and progresse] foundation and increase.

Bard. Oh Madam, fire, help, we are all lost;   36(

    The house is round about on fire, the doores

    Are barr'd and lock'd, there is no going forth;

    We shall be burnt, and that will spoyle my singing:

    My voyce hath been recover'd from a cold;

    But fire will spoyle it utterly.   36!

Enter Victor.

Victor. Have no dread, holy Patrick, all their malice

    Shall never hurt thy person; Heaven doth look

    With scorne upon their treacherie; thou art

    Reserv'd to make this Nation glorious,

    By their conversion to the Christian faith,   37(

    Which shall by bloud of many Martyrs grow,

    Till it be call'd the Iland of the Saints;

    Look up, and see what thou observ'st--

*373. see] Q; say Chetwood, Gifford.

*373. observ'st--] observ'st. Q.

360-391. Forsythe points out (p. 228) that Milcho's
attempt at immolating St. Patrick, the Queen, and the Bard is
reminiscent of the attempt to torture Dorothea in Dekker and
Massinger's The Virgin Martyr (IV.i and ii).

364. My . . . cold] Cf. Flamineo in Webster's The White
Devil: "I have caught / An everlasting could. I have lost my
voice / Most irrecoverably . . ." (V.vi.270-272).

372. Iland of the Saints] See BB, p. 1. Shirley
got this epithet from his source. Ireland has often been
popularly known by this name, perhaps from the fact that many
famous Catholic saints (Patrick, Bridget, and Columba, for
example) are connected with that country.

Milcho throwing his treasures into the flames.

Milcho. Patrick, thou art caught; inevitable flames   375

  Must now devoure thee; th' art my slave againe,

  There is no hope to scape: How I doe glorie,

  That by my policie thou shalt consume,

  Though I be made a sacrifice with thee

  To our great gods; ha, ha, the Queene: Bard,   380

  You will be exlent rost meat for the Devill.

Patrick. Heare me.

Milcho.   I choose to leap into these fires,

  Rather than heare thee preach thy cursed faith.

  Y'are sure to follow me; the King will praise

  My last act yet; thus I give up my breath,   385

  And sacrifice you all for his son's death. *He burnes himselfe.*

Patrick. Oh Tyrant, cruell to thy selfe; but we

*374. Milcho . . . flames] Q; Gifford and Donovan print substan-
tively as S. D. after line 372.

───────────

  373-374. Look . . . flames] Gifford's interpretation of
the feat at this point (i.e., treating line 374 as a stage
direction) is bibliographically unjustifiable. Q is perfectly
intelligible if Milcho's act of throwing the treasures is understood as the phenomenon which Victor is inviting Patrick to
observe.

  378. policie] stratagem.   consume] be burned to ashes.

  386. S. D. He . . . himselfe] Milcho's leaping into the
flames recalls, as Forsythe mentions (pp. 228-229), Hercules's
death in Heywood's The Brazen Age, II.i (Heywood, I, 253) and
Dido's immolation in Marlowe's Dido, Queen of Carthage (V.i.
313). Shirley also probably had in mind Milcho as a pagan anti-
type of Christian sacrifice.

Must follow our blest Guide and holy Guardian:

Lead on, good Angell; feare not, vertuous Queene;

A black night may beget a smiling morne;   39(

And worst to dye, 'tis easier than be borne.   Exeunt.

[Act IV, scene ii.]

Recorders. The Altar prepar'd, with Ferochus and Endarius,

    as before. Leogarius, Conallus, Archimagus, Magitians,

      Ethne, Fedella; a sacrifice of Christian bloud.

Archimagus. Great Jove and Mars appeased bee

With bloud, which we now offer thee,

Drain'd from a Christian's heart, our first

Oblation of that Sect accurst;

And may we to the Altar bring   5

Patrick, our second offering,

The father of this Tribe, whose blood

IV.ii.0.2. S. D. Magitians] Priest Q.

---

391. And . . . borne] The sense is: "bad as dying is,
it is easier than being born." Perhaps this is a variation of
the proverb, "It is as natural to die as to be born" (Tilley,
D327). Abbott (par. 10) indicates that the superlative is
often used in the Renaissance where only two things are being
compared.

IV.ii.0.2. as before] i.e., representing idols of Jupiter
and Mars (cf. II.ii.0.1-3).

0.3. a . . . blood] Apparently Shirley intended the
actors presenting Archimagus and the Magitians to offer a
sacrifice at the altar, as Archimagus indicates at lines 2-4.
Perhaps he meant here to refer to the ritual which accompanied
the bringing on of the vessel containing the blood.

7. father . . . Tribe] leader of this band. The word
"father" is traditionally applied to priests or bishops.

Thus shed, will doe this Iland good.

The gods allow what we present;

For see, the holy flame is sent   10

To mightie Jove and Mars; now bring

Your vocall sacrifice, and sing.

Song at the Altar.

Looke downe, great Jove and God of war,

   A new sacrifice is layd

   On your Altars, richer far,   15

Than what in arromatick heaps we paid:

   No curled smoake we send,

   With perfumes to befriend

   The drooping aire; the cloud

We offer is exhal'd from bloud,   20

   More shining than your tapers are,

   And everie drop is worth a star.

Were there no red heaven, from the torne heart

*23-26. Were . . . breakes] Gifford prints as part of the song
above.

---

9. allow] receive with approval.

20. exhal'd . . . bloud] i.e., the vapor rising from the
blood produces the "cloud" of sacrifice which then ascends to
the gods.

23-26. Gifford attaches these lines to the preceding song,
despite the fact that they are printed in Roman type in the
quarto. The song, however, is mainly composed of trimeter and
tetrameter lines while the lines in question are pentameter. It
is most likely, as MacMullan suggests (pp. 114-115), that these
words are spoken by Archimagus, since they represent his attitude towards Christians·and since he began the speech at line 1
which the song interrupted.

Of Christians, we that colour could impart,

And with their bloud, supply those crimson streakes   2

That dresse the skie, when the faire morning breakes.

Enter Rodamant, and whispers Leogarius,

who falleth upon the ground.

Conallus. Father.

Archimagus. The King.

Leogarius. Away. Let not my daughters stir from hence:

Is this reward, you gods, for my devotion?   3

Exit with Conallus.

Archimagus. No more: I could not by my Art foresee

This danger.

Ethne.   Our father seem'd much troubled.

Archimagus. [Aside.] I must appeare a stranger to all passages;

[To Ethne and Fedella.] Be not disturb'd, my princely

charge; use you

The free delights of life, while they are presented   3

In these your lovers: Sirra, make fast the doore,

And wait aloofe; I'll follow the sad King.

Exit [Archimagus with Magitians].

25-26. those . . . skie] See note on IV.i.226-228.

33. stranger . . . passages] ignorant of all occurrences.

Fedella.   [Embraces Ferochus.]   No miserie can happen, while
            I thus
        Embrace Ferochus.

Ethne.   [Embraces Endarius.]   And I safe in the
            armes
        Of my deare servant.

Endarius.   You make it heaven   40
        By gracing me.

Ferochus.   But why have we so long
            Delay'd our blest enjoyings, thus content
            With words, the shaddowes of our happinesse.

Rodamant.   [Aside.]   So, so; here's fine devotion in the Temple:
            But where's my bracelet, let me see?   [Puts on bracelet.]

Ferochus.   Where's
                Rodamant?   .   45

Rodamant.   [Aside.]   Am I invisible agen?   Is this the trick on't?

Ferochus.   The doore is safe; come, my deare princely Mistresse,
            And with the crowne of love reward your servant.

45. S. D. Puts . . . bracelet] Gifford.

40-41. you . . . me] Endarius is playing on the religious
connotations of "heaven" and "grace" as well as their courtly
and amorous ones.

47. safe] safely locked.

<u>Fedella</u>. What's that?

<u>Ferochus</u>.   Fruition of our joyes.

<u>Fedella</u>.   Is not this

  Delight enough, that we converse, and smile   5

  And kisse, <u>Ferochus</u>?

              <u>Rodamant</u> <u>kisses</u> Fedella.

  Who's that?

<u>Ferochus</u>.   Where, Madam?

<u>Fedella</u>.   I felt another lip.

<u>Ferochus</u>. Than mine? here's none; try it agen:

  [<u>Aside</u>.] Why should her constitution be so cold?

  I would not lose more opportunities;   5

  Love, shoot a flame like mine into her bosome.

              [Rodamant <u>kisses</u> Ethne.]

56.1 S. D. Rodamant . . . Ethne] <u>Gifford</u>, <u>Donovan</u>.

    52-58. The device of invisibility, while the character is
in full view of the audience, is a common one on the Renaissance
stage. In <u>A</u> <u>Midsummer</u> <u>Night's</u> <u>Dream</u> (III.ii) Oberon and Puck
are visible to the audience, but invisible to the other actors.
In <u>The</u> <u>Tempest</u> (III.ii.48-162) Ariel enters invisible and plays
tricks on Caliban, Stephano, and Trinculo which are similar to
those Rodamant plays here. Faustus is invisible in Marlowe's
<u>Doctor</u> <u>Faustus</u> and plays various tricks on the Pope, the Car-
dinals and some friars (III.ii).

    54. constitution] temperament, manner.

    56. shoot . . . flame] See note on I.i.119.

Ethne. Who's that, Endarius, that kist me now?

Endarius. None, since you blest my lip with a touch, Madam;

    My brother is at play with your faire sister.

Ethne. I felt a beard.   60

Endarius. A beard? that's strange.

Rodamant. [Aside.] You shall feele some else too.

                            He strikes Endarius.

Endarius. [To Ethne.] Why that unkind blow, Madam?

Ethne. What meanes my servant?

Rodamant. [Aside.] Now to my other gamester.   65

Ferochus. Oh, I could dwell for ever in this bosome,

    But is there nothing else for us to taste?

            Rodamant puls Ferochus by the nose.

    Hold.

Fedella. What's the matter?

Ferochus. Something has almost torne away my nose.   70

62. some else] Q; some [thing] else Gifford.

    60-61. I . . . strange] Cf. similar comedy in Chaucer's
"The Miller's Tale," lines 3736-3743.

    65. gamester] rake; lover.

    70. torne . . . nose] Probably Ferochus is referring to
the false nose often used by actors.

        Endarius?

Endarius.   What sayes my brother?

Ferochus.   Did you pull me by the nose?

Endarius.   I mov'd not hence.

                    [Rodamant kicks Endarius.]

                        Did you kick me, brother?

Fedella.   We have troubled fancies sure; here's no body   7
        But our selves; the doores, you say, are safe.

Ferochus.   Wo' not that prompt you to something else?

Fedella.   I dare not understand you.

        [Rodamant touches Ferochus' face with blood.]

        What bloud is that upon your face?

Rodamant.   [Aside.]   You want
        A beard, young Gentleman.

Ferochus.   Mine?   Bloud; I felt   8
        Something that like a flie glanc'd o' my cheeke:

74.1 S. D. Rodamant . . . Endarius] Gifford, Donovan.
78.1 S. D. Rodamant . . . blood] Gifford, Donovan.

---

        78. understand] a pun here in the sense "to be under a
man in intercourse."   Cf. "undertake" in the sense of "accost"
in Twelfth Night, I.iii.59 (Partridge, p. 212).

Brother, your nose bled you that fine beard.

Endarius. You need not blush a' one side, brother, ha, ha.

Ethne. Is not this strange, sister; how came our servants

So bloudy?   85

[Rodamant touches Ferochus again with blood.]

Ferochus. Agen. I prethee leave this fooling with my face,

I shall be angrie.

Endarius. I touch'd you not.

Rodamant.   [Aside.] Another wipe for you.

[Touches Endarius' face with blood.]

Ethne. Some spirit sure: I cannot containe laughter:

What a raw head my servant has?   90

Fedella. Mine has the same complexion.

Rodamant. [Aside.] Put me to keep the doore another time.

*82. Brother . . . beard] Q; Brother, [did] your nose bleed
you that fine beard Gifford.

85.1. S. D. Rodamant . . . blood] Gifford, Donovan.

---

82. fine beard] referring to the blood on Endarius' face,
which is apparently hanging from his chin in a manner resembling a beard.

83. a'] on.

90. raw] i.e., bloody.

92. keep the doore] a phrase associated with pandarism;
cf. II.ii.79.

I ha' kept 'em honest, and now I will be visible agen.

[Takes off the bracelet.]

Knock.

Ferochus. Rodamant.

Rodamant. Here: I was asleep, but this noyse wak'd me.   9
    Ha' you done with the Ladies?

Magitian.   Open the doores.   Withi

Enter Magitian.

We are undone, my Lords, the King is coming

In furie back againe, with full resolve

To break these images; his son is slaine,

And burnt to ashes since, in Milcho's house,   10

And he will be reveng'd upon the gods,

He sayes, that would not save his dearest son:

I feare he will turne Christian: Archimagus

*96.   S. H. Magitian] Q assigns to Rodamant.

96.1   S. D. Magitian] Gifford; Priest Q.

---

96. S. H. Magitian] Since Rodamant is already on stage,
the command "Open the doores" would not be likely to come from
him. The stage direction "Within" suggests that it is spoken
by the Magitian.

98-99. with . . . images] Shirley could be glancing here
at Puritan attitudes to Anglican and Catholic ritual. As a
Catholic, he might have been interested in identifying his villains with Puritans.

    Is under guard, and brought along to see

    This execution done; no art can save you.   105

Ethne. We are lost too for ever, in our honours.

Leogarius. Break downe the Temple doores.   Within.

Magitian. He's come already; we are all lost, Madam.

Ferochus. Teare off these antick habits quickly; brother,

    Doe you the same. More bloud upon our faces.   110

                    [They smear their faces with blood.]

    Oh, my Fedella, something may preserve us

    To meet agen: Endarius, so, so: open.

            Enter Leogarius, Archimagus, Guard.

        Ferochus, Endarius confidently meet the King.

Leogarius. Ha! keep off; more horrours to affright me?

    I must confesse I did command your deaths

    Unjustly, now my son is murder'd for it.   115

110.1. S. D. They . . . blood] Gifford, Donovan.

---

    109. these antick habits] this ludicrous dress.

    112. open] i.e., open the door.

    113. keep off] keep away.

    113-138. Ferochus and Endarius' masquerade as their own
spirits, as Forsythe tells us (p. 229), is similar to Hermione's
pretending to be a statue in The Winter's Tale (V.iii.21-121);
Maria pretending to be her own corpse in Beaumont and Fletcher's
The Nightwalker (II.iii); and Chilax' pretense at death in
Beaumont and Fletcher's The Mad Lover (V.iv).

Ferochus. Oh do not pull more wrath from heaven upon you.

    Love innocence, the gods have thus reveng'd

    In your sonne's tragedy: Draw not a greater

    Upon your self and this faire Iland, by

    Threatning the temples, and the gods themselves;   12◖

    Looke on them still with humble reverence,

    Or greater punishments remaine for you

    To suffer; and our ghosts shall never leave

    To fright thy conscience, and with thousand stings

    Afflict thy soule to madnesse and despaire: 12◖

    Be patient yet and prosper, and let fall

    Thy anger on the Christians, that else

    Will poyson thy faire kingdome.

Leogarius. Ha, Archimagus, canst thou forgive me,

    And send those spirits hence?

Archimagus.   I can, great Sir;   13◖

    You troubled Spirits, I command you leave

    The much distracted King; returne and speedily,

    To sleepe within the bosome of the sea,

    Which the king's wrath, and your sad fates assign'd yee;

117. Love⌃] Q; Love, Chetwood.

    117-118. Love . . . tragedy] i.e., respect and revere
innocence (such as Emeria had), the destruction of which the
gods have revenged by your son's death.

    123-124. leave To fright] cease frightening.

And as you move to your expecting monument,   135

The waves agen, no frowne appeare upon you,

But glide away in peace.

Ferochus.⎫
                                    We do obey
Endarius.⎭

Great Priest, and vanish.   Exeunt [Ferochus and Endarius.]

Ethne.   [Aside to Fedella.]   Are they

    gone Fedella?

They talk of woman's wit at a dead lift;

This was above our braines; I love him for't   140

And wish my self in's armes now to reward him;

I should finde him no ghost a' my conscience:

But where shall we meete next?

Fedella.   [Aside to Ethne.]   Let us

    away.   Exeunt [Ethne and Fedella].

Leogarius. Art sure they are gone Archimagus? my feares

    So leave me, and religion once agen   145

    Enter my stubborne heart, which dar'd to mutinie

_____

135. your . . . monument] the grave which awaits you.

139. They . . . lift] This is a reference to the proverb,
"A woman's wit is best at a dead lift" (Tilley, W669). A "dead
lift" is an emergency, a situation or effort taxing one's utmost
power.

142. a'] on.

144-146. my . . . heart] The sense of both clauses is
optative subjunctive; i.e., "[may] my fears leave me and religion enter my heart."

And quarrell with the gods; <u>Archimagus</u>,

Be neere agen; we will redeeme our rashnesse,

By grubbing up these Christians, that begin

To infect us, and our kingdome.

<u>Archimagus</u>.   This becomes you,   15

And if you please to heare me, I dare promise

The speedy ruine of them all.

<u>Leogarius</u>.   Th' art borne

To make us happy; how my deere <u>Archimagus</u>?

<u>Archimagus</u>. This Iland Sir is full of dangerous serpents,

Of toads, and other venomous destroyers: 15

I will from every province of this kingdome

Summon these killing creatures to devoure him;

My prayer and power of the gods, feare not,

Will doo't, by whom inspir'd I prophesie

<u>Patrick's</u> destruction.

<u>Leogarius</u>.   I embrace my Priest;   16(

Do this, and I'll forget my sonne, and die,

And smile to see this Christian's tragedie.   <u>Exeunt</u>.

---

149. grubbing up] uprooting.

ACT V. [Scene i.]

Enter two Souldiers.

1. _Souldier._ So, so, we are like to have a fine time on't; we

　　may get more by every Christian we have the grace to catch,

　　than by three moneth's pay against our naturall enemies.

2. _Souldier._ And their noddles be so precious, would all my

　　kindred were Christians; I would not leave a head to wag　　5

　　upon a shoulder of our generation, from my mother's sucking

　　pig at her nipple, to my great grandfather's Coshering in

　　the pease straw. How did that fellow looke whose throat

　　we cut last?

]. _Souldier._ Basely, and like a Christian; would the fellow they 10

V.i. Gifford locates this scene "in a wood."

1. on't] of it.

2. grace] luck, in this sense. Usually, of course, the
word has religious connotations, meaning the position of being
favored by God. The word is used in various senses throughout
the play as a kind of motif. See the Introduction, pp. 69-70.

4. And] if. noddles] heads.

6. generation] family. sucking pig] suckling pig (often
used, as here, for an infant).

7-8. Coshering . . . straw] feasting while sitting on
stalks and leaves of the pea plant used as fodder. The OED
quotes from Stanyhurst's "Description of Ireland" in Hollins-
head's _Chronicles_ VI (1577), 67: "Their noble men, and noble
men's tenants, now and then make a set feast, which they call
coshering, wherto flocke all their retainers, whom they name
followers . . . . In their coshering they sit on straw, they
are served on straw."

216

call <u>Patrick</u> had been in his place, we had been made forever.

2. <u>Souldier</u>. Now are we of the condition of some great men in

office, that desire execution of the Lawes, not so much to

correct offences and reforme the common wealth, as to thrive

by their punishment and grow rich and fat with a leane con-

science. But I have walk'd, and talk'd my selfe a hungry;

prethee open the secrets of thy knapsacke, before we build

any more projects; let's see what store of belly timber we

have. Good, very good Pagan food: sit downe and let our

---

11. we . . . forever] our success would have been assured.

12-16. Now . . . conscience] Despite MacMullan's asser-
tion that "Shirley seems to have gone out of his way to avoid
mention of contemporaneous material in this play" (pp. 115-116),
this passage obviously refers to some politician of the time.
Perhaps Shirley had in mind Archbishop Laud, who "became the
scapegoat for almost every popular grievance" (Forker, p. xxxvii).
Forker points out that some events in <u>The Cardinal</u> allude to
Laud and his activities.

14. common wealth] society as politically organized.

15. leane] underdeveloped.

16. a hungry] hungry. Soldiers are traditionally hungry,
both for food and for sexual contact. Cf. Petillius' words to
his hungry soldiers:

              All my company
Are now in love; ne'er think of meat, nor talk
Of what provant is: <u>Ay-mes</u>, and hearty <u>hey-hoes</u>
Are sallads fit for <u>soldiers</u>. Live by meat?
By larding up your bodies? 'tis lewd, and lazy . . .
              (Beaumont and Fletcher, <u>Bonduca</u>, I.ii.38-42).

17-18. build . . . projects] make any more plans.

18. belly timber] material from which to build up the body
i.e., food.

stomackes conferre a while.   20

Enter Rodamant [with the bracelet on his wrist].

Rodamant. [Aside.] My royal love is rosted; she died of a

burning feaver, and since poison wo' not work upon me,

I am resolv'd to looke out the most convenient tree in this

wood to hang my self: And because I will be sure to hang

without molestation or cutting downe, which is a dispar-   25

agement to an able and willing body, I will hang invisible,

that no body may see me, and interrupt my hempen meditations.

But who are these? a brace of mankillers a mounching; now

I think what a long journey I am going, as far as to another

world, it were not amisse to take provision along with me;   30

when I come to the tricke of hanging, I may weigh the better,

and sooner be out of my paine: bracelet sticke to me; [To

Souldiers.] by your leave gentlemen, what's your ordinary?

---

20. conferre] i.e., digest together.

21-26. Forsythe (pp. 229-230) lists many analogous situations to Rodamant's attempts to hang himself. Characters most
like Rodamant in this scene are Fronto in Chapman's Caesar and
Pompey (II.i.1-24); Depazzi in Shirley's The Humorous Courtier,
I.ii (Gifford, V, 20); and Despair in Shirley's Cupid and Death
(Gifford, VI, 351-362). Shirley might also have had in mind a
parody of Judas Iscariot's death.

28. brace] pair. a mounching] in the process of eating.

31. tricke] knack. the better] more.

32-92. Rodamant's pranks with the soldiers are reminiscent
of Ariel's pranks with Caliban, Stephano, and Trinculo in The
Tempest (III.ii.48-162).

33. ordinary] allowance of food.

1. Souldier. Who's that?

Rodamant. A friend, my brace of Hungarians; one that is no soul-

dier, but will justifie he has a stomacke in a just cause,

and can fight tooth and naile, with any flesh that opposes

me.

2. Souldier. I can see no body.

Rodamant. I will knock your pate, fellow in armes, and to help

you to see, open the eyes of your understanding with a

wooden instrument that I have.

1. Souldier. I see nothing but a voice; shall I strike it?

2. Souldier. No, 'tis some Spirit; take heed and offend it not;

I never knew any man strike the devill, but he put out his

necke bone or his shoulder blade; let him alone, it may

---

35. Hungarians] obsolete slang for "crude fellows; ruf-
fians," with a pun on "hunger."

36. justifie . . . just] Rodamant is playing on these
two words here.

40. pate] skull.

41-42. open . . . instrument] Apparently the servant has
a club which he will use to beat the heads of the soldiers,
thereby indicating his presence.

43. see] perceive.

44. take . . . not] As with the ghost in Hamlet (I.i),
the soldiers are respectful of spirits and do not wish to offend
them. When the ghost leaves in Hamlet at I.i.50, Marcellus says
"It is offended."

45. put out] dislocated.

be the ghost of some usurer that kick'd up his heeles in

a deare yeere, and died upon a surfet of Shamroks and

cheese parings.

Enter Emeria.

1. Souldier. Who's this, a woman alone?   50

2. Souldier. And handsome; what makes shee in this wood? wee'll

divide.

1. Souldier. What, the woman?

2. Souldier. No, I'll have her body, and thou shalt have her

clothes.   55

Emeria. I know not where I am, this wood has lost me,

But I shall never more be worth the finding:

I was not wise to leave my father's house,

For here I may be made a prey to rapine,

Or food to cruell beasts.   60

---

47. kick'd . . . heeles] died and gone to hell. Cf. "that
his heels may kick at Heaven / And that his soul may be as damned
and black / As hell, whereto it goes" (Hamlet, III.iii.93-95).

48. deare yeere] famine year.   surfet] excess.

51. makes] does.

52. divide] a pun on 1) go different directions and 2)
share her.

59. rapine] robbery (with unconscious pun on "rape").

2. <u>Souldier</u>. No, you shall finde that we are men; what think
you? which of us two have you most minde to laugh and lye
downe withall?

<u>Emeria</u>. Protect me some good power; more ravishers.

2. <u>Souldier</u>. We are souldiers, and not us'd to complement; be   6
not coy but answer.

1. <u>Souldier</u>. We are but two, you may soone make a choice.

<u>Rodamant</u>. [<u>Aside</u>.] You shall finde that we be three, are
you so hot?

1. <u>Souldier</u>. Come humble your self behinde that tree, or--   7

<u>Emeria</u>. Are you a man?

1. <u>Souldier</u>. Never doubt it, I have pass'd for a man in my dayes.

[Rodamant <u>strikes</u> 2. <u>Souldier</u>.]

2. <u>Souldier</u>. Oh my skull.

1. <u>Souldier</u>. What's the matter?

72.1. S. D. Rodamant . . . <u>Souldier</u>] <u>Gifford</u>, <u>Donovan</u>.

---

61. we are men] The soldier here is referring to his sexual
role.

62-63. laugh . . . down] engage in sexual play. This is a
common phrase; cf. <u>The</u> <u>Merry</u> <u>Wives</u> <u>of</u> <u>Windsor</u> (I.iv.162).

65. complement] flattery; court praise.

69. hot] a pun on 1) eager and 2) sexually aroused.

70. humble your self] lie down.

Emeria. [Aside.] Where shall I hide my self? Hides her self. 75

Rodamant. [Aside.] Your Comrade will expect your company in
    the next ditch.

2. Souldier. Are you good at that?

  The second souldier strikes the first, and Rodamant both.

1. Souldier. What dost thou meane?

2. Souldier. What do I meane? what dost thou meane to beate   80
    my braines out?

1. Souldier. I: hold, it is some Spirit, and we fight with
    the aire.

Rodamant. Cannot a Mare come into the ground, but you must be
    leaping, you stone horses?   85

2. Souldier. My skull is as tender as a Mullipuffe.

1. Souldier. He has made a cullice of my sconce; hold deere
    friend.

85. leaping,] Chetwood, Gifford, Donovan; leaping∧ Q.

---

    78. good at that] responsible for the blow I received.

    82. I] aye.

    85. leaping] See III.i.4.   stone horses] male horses
endowed with "stones" (i.e., which have not been gelded).

    86. Mullipuffe] molly-puff; a popular name for the fuzz-
ball or puff-ball fungus.

    87. cullice] jelly.   sconce] head (jocularly).

2. Souldier. Has the devil no more wit then to take part against
     the flesh?

1. Souldier. The Devill may have a minde to her himselfe; let   9
     him ha' her.

2. Souldier. If I come back, let me be glib'd.

                    Exeunt [1. and 2. Souldiers] reeling.

Rodamant. Now Lady-- what, is shee invisible too? Ha. Well,
     let her shift for her selfe, I have tam'd their concupiscence
     Now to my businesse of hanging agen.   9

                    Enter Spirit.

I doe like none of these trees; the Devill is at my elbow
now, I doe heare him whisper in mine eare, that any tree
would serve, if I would but give my mind to't. Let me consider, what shall I get by hanging of my selfe, how it will
be to no purpose, a halter will be but cast away, by your   10
leave--   I would not have you much out of the way, because

99. how] Q; now Chetwood; how!-- Gifford.

88-89. Has . . . flesh] This is a joke referring to the
baptismal service where the sponsors promise to fight against
the world, the flesh, and the devil on the child's behalf. The
joke here is that the devil would not want to fight against the
flesh since, for all practical purposes, they are on the same
side.

92. glib'd] a corruption of "libbed," which means "cas-
trated."

94. concupiscence] vehement sexual desire.

101. you] Rodamant is adressing the tree.

here are trees that other men may hold convenient.--

[<u>Spirit</u> <u>touches</u> <u>his</u> <u>wrist</u>.]

Oh, my wrist: 'Tis a spirit. Sweet Devill, you shall

have it, the bracelet is at your service.

[<u>Exit</u> <u>Spirit</u> <u>with</u> <u>bracelet</u>.]

Have I all my fingers? A pox on his fangs; now o' my con-   105

science I am visible agen; if the Souldiers should meet with

me now, whom I have pounded, which case were I in? I feele

a destillation, and would be heartily beaten to save my

life.

Enter Conallus <u>and</u> Emeria.

Here's one, for aught I know, may be as dangerous: A pox   110

of despaire that brought me hither to choose my gallowes;

would I were at home in an embroydered clout.-- I'll sneake

this way.   <u>Exit</u>.

<u>Emeria</u>. I am no ghost, but the same lost <u>Emeria</u>,

My Lord, you left me.

<u>Conallus</u>.   Did not the flames devoure thee?   115

---

105. on . . . fangs] It was believed that syphilis caused
the gums to rot and the teeth to fall out; cf. <u>The</u> <u>Tempest</u> (I.i.43).

108. destillation] a defluxioun of rheum; a catarrh.
Related to "distillation."

112. embroydered clout] A clout is a rag or a piece of
cloth. MacMullan may be right in suggesting that this is a
diaper (p. 116) since Rodamant may want to retreat to childhood
in his desire to escape his present situation.

Emeria. I felt no flame, but that which my revenge
        Did light me to, for my abused honour.

Conallus. Oh say that word agen: Art thou reveng'd
        Upon thy ravisher? It was a god,
        Thou told'st me.

Emeria.   But he found the way to death: 12
        And when I name him, you will either not
        Beleeve me, or compassion of his wounds
        Will make you print as many in my brest:
        He was--

Conallus.   Say, feare not, wrong'd Emeria;
        Can any heart find compassion for his death,   12
        That murder'd the sweet peace of thy chaste bosome?
        Oh never; I shall blesse that resolute hand,
        That was so just, so pious; and when thou hast
        Assur'd that he which playd the Satyre with thee,
        Is out o' th' world, and kill'd sufficiently,   13
        (For he that robb'd thee hath deserv'd to dye,
        To the extent of his wide sin) I'll kisse,
        And take thee in mine armes, Emeria,
        And lay thee up as precious to my love,

---

        123. as many] i.e., as many [wounds].

        125-126. his death . . . murder'd] the death of the one
who murdered.

        132. wide] large.

As when our vowes met, and our yeelding bosomes   135

Were witnesse to the contract of our hearts.

Emeria. It was your brother Corybreus, Sir:

That name unties your promise.

Conallus.   Ha! my brother?

Sweet, let me pause a little, I am lost else.

Emeria. [Aside.] I did not well to enlarge his sorrow thus: 140

Though I can hope no comfort in this world,

He might live happie, if I did not kill him,

With heaping griefe on griefe thus.

Conallus.   He is slaine then.

Emeria. If you will, Sir, revenge his death, you must

Point your wrath here, and I will thank you for't;   145

Though you should be a day in killing me,

I should live so much longer to forgive you.

This weake hand did not tremble when it kill'd him,

And it came timely to prevent, I feare,

The second part of horrour he had meant   150

To act upon me.

Conallus.   Wo'd he had tooke my life,

When he assail'd thy chastitie, so thou

---

145. here] i.e., on Emeria's breast.

146. you . . . me] Cf. Othello: "I would have him nine
years a killing" (IV.i.188).

Hadst been preserv'd: I cannot help all this.

Did it not grieve thee he deserv'd to dye, ha?

Emeria. I took no joy, Sir, in his Tragedie.   15

Conallus. That done, thou fledst.

Emeria.   I left my father's house,

And found no weight hung on my feet for giving

His lust the bloudy recompence.

Conallus.   Thou art happie:

The gods directed thee to fly, Emeria;

Thou hadst beene lost else with my brother's ashes,   16(

And my deare mother, whom the hungry flames

Devour'd, soone after thy departure.

Emeria.   How?

Conallus. I know not by what malice, or mis-fortune,

Thy father's house was burn'd, and in it he

Did meet his funerall fire too, ha? Emeria.   165

Enter S. Patrick, Queene, and Bard.

Bard. Your companie's faire, but I'll leave you in a wood; I

could like your religion well; but those rules of fasting,

157-158. found . . . recompence] discovered that the fact
that I revenged myself on him for his lust in raping me did not
keep me from fleeing quickly from my father's house.

158. happie] fortunate.

prayer, and so much penance, will hardly fit my constitution.

Patrick. 'Tis nothing to win heaven.

Bard. But you doe not consider, that I shall loose my pension,   170

my pension from the King; there's a businesse.

Queene. Do not I leave more?

Bard. I confesse it; and you will get lesse by the bargaine; but

you that have been used to hunger, and nothing to live upon,

may make the better shift. The lesse you eat, you say, will   175

make the soule fat; but I have a body wo' not be used so: I

must drinke, and goe warme, and make much of my voyce; I

cannot doe good upon water and sallads; keep your diet-drinke

to your selves, I am a kind of foolish Courtier, Patrick;

with us, wine and women are provocatives, long tables and   180

short graces are physicall, and in fashion. I'll take my

---

168. constitution] temperament, make-up (not specifically
physical).

173. you . . . bargaine] you will not profit as much for
leaving your position to become a Christian as I would.

175-186. MacMullan (p. 116) and Forsythe (p. 230) point
to a similar speech by Bembo in The Royal Master, III.iii:

Every man is not bound to be religious;
Men of my bulk and bearing should not fast so.
I am not given by nature to drink water,
Or lie without a shirt; I have corns, madam,
And I would make less conscience to undo
My shoemaker, than walk on wooden pantables.
                                        (Gifford, IV, 145)

Shirley has reversed the situation in Jocelyn here. See BB, p. 24.

181. physicall] salubrious.

leave, Madam, no Christian yet, as the world goes; perhaps
hereafter, when my voyce is a wearie of mee, I may grow
wearie of the world, and stoop to your ord'narie, say my
prayers, and think how to dye, when my living is taken from
me; in the meanetime--   Sings.

    I neither will lend, nor borrow,

    Old age will be here to morrow,

    'Tis pleasure we are made for,

    When death comes all is paid for:

        No matter what's the bill of fare,

        I'll take my cup, I'll take no care.

    Be wise, and say you had warning,

    To laugh is better than learning,

    To weare no cloathes, not neat is.

    But hunger is good where meat is:

        Give me wine, give me a wench,

        And let her parrot talke in French.

*189. 'Tis] Chetwood; This Gifford, Donovan; 'This Q.

---

184. ord'narie] See V.i.33.

187-204. The Bard's song is a traditional carpe diem lyric
exalting the pleasures of this world over religious fasting and
temperance. Cf. Antony and Cleopatra (IV.i.141-144).

189. 'Tis] I have adopted Chetwood's emendation since it
makes better sense, and it is more likely that a compositor
would have added an h than an unnecessary apostrophe.

198. And . . . French] This line refers to the proverb,
"Jack would be a gentleman if he could talk French" (Tilley, J4).
Donovan points out that Shirley adverts to the association of
French with the gentry. In other words, the Bard wants a
respectable lady.

It __is__ __a__ __match__ __worth__ __the__ __making__,

To __keepe__ __the__ __merrie__ __thought__ __waking__;   200

__A__ __song__ __is__ __better__ __than__ __fasting__,

__And__ __sorrow's__ __not__ __worth__ __the__ __tasting__,

   Then __keepe__ __your__ __braine__ __light__ __as__ __you__ __can__,

   An __ounce__ __of__ __care__ __will__ __kill__ __a__ __man__.

And so I take my leave.   Exit.   205

Conallus. Ha! doe I see the Queene, Emeria?

Patrick. Alas, poore Bard, the flatteries of this world

   Hath chain'd his sense: thus many selfe-loving natures,

   Prison'd in mists and errours, cannot see

   The way abroad that leads to happinesse,   210

   Or truth, whose beamie hand should guide us in it.

   What a poore value do men set of heaven?

   Heaven, the perfection of all that can

   Be said, or thought, riches, delight, or harmony,

   Health, beautie, and all these not subject to   215

   The waste of time; but in their height eternall,

   Lost for a pension, or poore spot of earth,

   Favour of greatnesse, or an houre's faint pleasure:

   As men, in scorne of a true flame that's neere,

---

   211. truth . . . it] i.e., truth should guide us along the
way (to happiness) by the torch which it carries in its hand.
Cf. the similar expression "the light of truth."

   212. of] Shirley means "to get the value of something."
Modern usage would replace "of" with "on."

   219-220. men . . . glo-worme] as in the proverb, "You will
make me believe that glowworms are lanterns" (Tilley, G143).

           Should run to light their taper at a glo-worme.   2?

Conallus. 'Tis she, and the good Bishop Patrick with her.

Patrick. Madam, the Prince Conallus.

Conallus. Oh let me kneele to you, and then to Heaven,
           That hath preserv'd you still to be my mother;
           For I beleeve you are alive; the fire   22
           Hath not defac'd this monument of sweetnesse.

Queene. My blessing and my prayers be still my child's;
         It was the goodnesse, son, of holy Patrick,
         That rescu'd me from those impris'ning flames
         You speake of; his good Angell was our Conduct.   23

Conallus. To him that can dispense such blessings, mother,
           I must owe dutie, and thus kneeling, pay it: [Kneels.]
           May Angels still be neere you.

Patrick.   Rise, Conallus:
         My benediction on thee; be but what
         Thy Mother is, a Christian, and a guard   23

*220. glo-worme] Chetwood, Gifford, Donovan substantively;
glo-worne Q.

---

     220. glo-worme] Compositional substitution of n for m
was very common in the period.

     230. Conduct] guide.

Of Angels shall attend thee too; the fire

We walk'd upon secure, and which is greater,

Scap'd the immortall flames, in which black soules,

After their ill-spent lives, are bound to suffer.

Conallus. Sir, you shall steere me, and my mother's blest   240

Example will become my imitation.

But there's a peece of silent miserie   [Points to Emeria.]

Is worth your comfort, mother, and his counsell;

She is, I dare not name how much dishonour'd,

And should have beene the partner of my bosome,   245

Had not a cruell man forbid my happinesse,

And on that faire and innocent table powr'd

Poyson, above the Dragon's bloud, or Viper's.

Emeria. My humblest dutie, Madam.

Patrick.   Dichu's Cell

Is not far off; please you attend the Queene,   250

_____

236-239. the . . . suffer] This is a difficult passage.
The sense seems to be "the fire [is] now under control (secure)
and, more important, we have escaped hell."

241. will . . . imitation] i.e., will provide an action
for me to imitate.

246. forbid] forbade (an archaic form of "forbidden").

247. powr'd] a variant spelling of "poured."

248. above] more deadly than.

248. Dragon's bloud] "A drug or gum. In burning it gives
out an acid flame, similar to that of benzoic acid. There are
many superstitions attached to its use" (Donovan).

We are bent thither.

Conallus.   Yes: and as we walk,

I'll tell you a sad storie of my brother

And this poore virgin.

Patrick.   Come, I'll lead the way.

Queene. With such a Guide we cannot feare to stray.   Exeunt.

[Act V, scene ii.]

Enter Ferochus and Endarius.

Ferochus. Where are we yet Endarius?

Endarius.   I cannot

Informe you more, then that we are in the wood still.

Ferochus. And we are lost; our feare to die i' th' sight

Of men, hath brought us hither with our blood

To quench the thirst of wolves: Or worse, to starve.   5

Endarius. We are in no feare to be apprehended

Where none inhabite.

Ferochus.   Now that lust is punish'd,

---

251. bent] on our way.

V.ii. Gifford places this scene in "another part of the woods." MacMullan (p. 117) is right, however, in pointing out that this scene, as well as V.iii, could easily be played in front of a cave (perhaps suggested by the inner stage).

2. then] than.

    Which fed our hope, if we had staid i' th' Temple

    To have polluted it, with foule embraces:

    How wearinesse, with travell, and some fasting   10

    Will tame the flesh.

<u>Endarius</u>.   Stay, here's a cave.

<u>Ferochus</u>.   Take heede,

    It may be a Lion, or a fierce wolve's den;

    How nature trembles at the thought of death,

    Though it be prest downe, with the weight of life.

<u>Endarius</u>. I dare not enter; a new feare invades me.   15

<u>Ferochus</u>. The worst is welcome; with our clamor, rouse

    What ever doth inhabite here; [<u>Shouts into cave</u>.] or man

    Or beast appeare, if any such dwell in

    This Cave? We can meet charity or death.

<u>Enter</u> Dichu.

<u>Dichu</u>. What voice with so much passion calls me forth,   20

    Ha? Be my protection good heaven:

    My sonnes, my murder'd sonnes with gastly lookes,

---

    10. travell] a play on the two senses of travell: 1)
travel and 2) travail. Similar quibbles occur in <u>Comedy</u> <u>of</u>
<u>Errors</u> (V.i.400) and <u>The</u> <u>Tempest</u> (III.iii.15).

    14. prest downe] suppressed.

    17-18. or . . . Or] either . . . or.

    19. can meet] are ready for.

And bruised limbes; why do you come to me thus

To fright my wither'd eyes? 'las I was innocent,

It was the King, not I commanded your   25

Untimely death; I have wept for ye boyes,

And constantly before the Sun awak'd,

When the cold dew drops full upon the ground,

As if the morne were discontented too.

My naked feet o're many a rugged stone   30

Hath walk'd, to drop my teares into the seas,

For your sad memories.

Ferochus. We are no spirits, but your living sons,

Preserv'd without the knowledge of the King,

By Archimagus, till a new mis-fortune   35

Compell'd us hither to meet death, we feare,

In want of food.

Dichu.   Are yee alive? come in,

It is no time to be inquisitive;

My blessing, I have something to refresh you,

Course fare, but such as will keep out sad famine: 40

*28. full] Q; fell Gifford, Donovan.

---

28. full] Though Gifford and Donovan's emendation makes
sense, the Q reading could mean "[were] full."

29. As . . . too] i.e., as if the morning wept. Cf. Herbert's "Vertue": "The dew shall weep thy full tonight" (line 3).

40. Course] coarse.

40. sad famine] Famine is personified here as having a
sad face.

Humble your selves and enter, my poore boyes,

You'll wonder at the change; but we to Heaven

Do climb with loads upon our shoulders borne,

Nor must we tread on roses, but on thorne.   Exeunt.

[Act V, scene iii.]

Enter S. Patrick, Queene, Conallus, Emeria.

Patrick. Now we approach the Hermit Dichu's Cell:

Are you not wearie, Madam?

Queene.   Not yet, Father,

In such religious company.

Patrick.   You were not

Us'd to this travell; how does my new son,

And sweet Emeria?

Conallus.   I am blest on all sides.   5

---

41. Humble] "i.e., stoop. Shirley appears to have the
cave of Bellarious in view. See Cymbeline [IV.ii]" (Gifford,
IV, 437). I doubt, however, if Shakespeare's scene influenced
Shirley directly. Several other plays have scenes which take
place before caves. Cf. Shakespeare's Timon of Athens, IV and
V; Beaumont and Fletcher's The Knight of Malta, IV.i; and Fletcher's Cupid's Revenge, V.iii.

42-43. we . . . borne] This phrase is obviously proverbial, although it is not listed in Tilley.

44. must . . . thorne] This phrase is proverbial, being
related to "No rose without a thorn" (Tilley, R182).

V.iii. Gifford places this scene "in front of Dichu's
cell."

Emeria. You have quieted the tempest in my soule,

    And in this holy peace I must be happie.

Patrick. You will be Spouse to an eternall Bridegroome,

    And lay the sweet foundation of a rule,

    That after ages, with devotion,   1

    Shall praise the follow. You are, Sir, reserv'd

    To blesse this Kingdome with your pious government,

    Your Crowne shall flourish, and your bloud possesse

    The Throne you shall leave glorious: This Nation

    Shall in a faire succession thrive, and grow   1

    Up the world's Academie, and disperse,

    As the rich spring of humane and divine

    Knowledge, cleare streames to water forraine Kingdomes,

---

    9. rule] i.e., rule of life in a religious order (of nuns).

    10. after] later.

    11-20. You . . . Iland] Cf. BB, p. 32. This prophecy
recalls the one in I.i.55-62. In Macbeth (IV.i.111-124),
Banquo's future is predicted by the witches in much the same
way that St. Patrick predicts Conallus' future here. It is
highly likely that Shirley meant to compliment Strafford
and the Irish oligarchy here by predicting a great future for
Ireland and her government. Cf. a similar prophecy compliment-
ing Queen Elizabeth in Henry VIII (V.v.18-56).

    13. bloud] progeny.

    15. succession] dynasty.

    15-20. grow . . . Iland] Before the raids of the Vikings,
Ireland was a seat of Medieval learning and scholarship held in
high esteem by the rest of Europe. Monks in monasteries at
Lindisfarne and Echternach attained a high degree of learning
as evidenced by the illuminated books they have left.

    17. humane] human (not humane).

Which shall be proud to owe what they possesse

In learning, to this great all-nursing Iland.   20

Conallus. May we be worthy of this prophesie.

Patrick. Discourse hath made the way lesse tedious,

We have reach'd the Cell already, which is much

Too narrow to containe us; but beneath

These trees, upon their coole and pleasing shades,   25

You may sit downe; I'll call upon my Convert:

Dichu, my Penitent, come forth, I pray,

And entertaine some guests I have brought hither,

That deserve welcome.

Enter Dichu.

Dichu.   I obey that voyce.

Patrick. The Queene, and Prince, and Milcho's vertuous daughter 30

Gain'd to our holy faith.

Dichu.   Let my knee speake

My dutie, though I want words for my joy;   [He kneels.]

Ten thousand welcomes; I have guests within too;

---

20. all-nursing Iland] i.e., an island which can supply
sustenance to all.

24. narrow] small.

25. upon . . . shades] i.e., "upon the places which their
shade has made cool and pleasing."

You'l wonder to salute my sons, not dead,

As we suppose, by heavenly providence,   3

I hope, reserv'd to be made blest by you;

They are here.

          Enter Ferochus and Endarius.

          Your duties to the Queene and Prince,

Then to this man, next to our great Preserver,

The Patron of us all.

Patrick.   A happie meeting:

I must rejoyce to see you safe, and here: 4

But tell us by what strange meanes, all this while,

You have been preserv'd? Sit downe.

                       Soft Musick.

Conallus.   What musick's this?

Queene. 'Tis heavenly.

34. to salute my sons] Q; to salute, my sons Chetwood; to
salute; my sons Gifford.

35. suppose] Q; supposed Gifford.

    42.1. S. D. Soft Musick] In Shakespeare's later plays,
"Soft Music" is often used to suggest a change in mood as it
is here. Cf. The Winter's Tale (V.iii.98); The Tempest
(IV.i.59); and King Lear (IV.vii.25), except that in Lear the
music is made louder to help cure Lear.

    42-43. musick's . . . heavenly] Shirley suggests that
the music is "heavenly" because of the symbolic harmony. There
is a suggestion of the music of the spheres here.

Patrick.   And a preface to some message,

Or will of Heaven; be silent, and attend it:

[They all sleep but St. Patrick.]

Such harmony as this did wait upon   45

My Angell Victor, when he first appear'd,

And did reveale a treasure under ground,

With which I bought my freedome, when I kept

Unhappie Milcho's swine; Heaven's will be done.

What, all asleep already? holy dreames   50

Possesse your fancie, I can wait no longer.   [Sleeps.]

Enter Victor, and other Angels. Song.

Victor.   Downe from the skies,

*51. wait] Q; wake Gifford.

---

49. Unhappie] unlucky.

50-51. holy . . . Possesse] This phrase is in the subjunctive, i.e., [may] holy dreams possess.

51. fancie] See I.i.87.

51. wait] Gifford's emendation makes good sense, but is
unjustifiable. Clearly "wait" here means "wait to go to sleep."

52-76. Downe . . . Ile] Forsythe (p. 230) points out
that St. Patrick's vision is reminiscent of the masque in Henry
VIII (IV.ii.82.1-82.17) where Katherine has a garland put over
her head by various personages in white robes and in Brome's The
Queen and Concubine, II, 45-47, where the genius enters and
makes the sleeping Euralia have a dream about her future fortunes. See also Beaumont and Fletcher's The Triumph of Death,
scene 4; Lodge's The Wounds of Civil War, Dodsley, VII, 193-194;
and The Tempest (IV.i.60-138), although in these last the wit-
nesses to the masques are not asleep.

Commanded by the Power that ties

   The world and nature in a chaine,

We come, we come, a glorious traine,   55

     To wait on thee,

And make thy person danger-free:

   Hearke whilst we sing,

And keep time with our golden wing,

To shew how earth and heaven agree,   60

What eccho rises to our harmonie.

Victor. Holy Patrick, sleep in peace,

   While I thy Guardian, with these

   My fellow Angels, wait on thee,

   For thy defence: A troop, I see,   65

   Of serpents, vipers, and what ere

   Doth carrie killing poyson, here

   Summon'd by Art, and power of hell;

   But thou shalt soone their furie quell,

   And by the strength of thy command,   70

   These creatures shall forsake the Land,

   And creep into the sea; no more

    53-54. Power . . . chaine] a reference to the great chain
of being, the concept of all creation ordered in a hierarchy
with God at the top.

    62-73. Holy . . . shore] It is customary in the plays of
the period to assign lighter characters lighter verse. That is
why Victor, an angel, speaks in tetrameter, rather than in pentameter. Cf. the fairies in A Midsummer Night's Dream and Juno,
Ceres, and Iris in The Tempest (IV.i), as well as the witches in
Macbeth.

          To live upon the Irish shore.

               Once more then.

                         Song.

          Patrick, sleep; oh sleep a while,   75

          And wake the Patron of this Ile. [Exeunt Victor and Angels.

          Enter Leogarius, Archimagus, and other Magitians.

Archimagus. Your person shall be safe; feare not, great Sir,

          I have directed all their stings and poyson:

          See where he sleeps? if he escape this danger,

          Let my life, with some horrid circumstance,   80

          End in this place, and carrie all your curses.

               Enter Serpents, &c. creeping.

          What think you of these creeping executioners?

          Doe they not move, as if they knew their errand?

Leogarius. My Queene! my son Conallus! Dichu! ha!

76. S. D. Exeunt . . . Angels] Gifford, Donovan.

76.1. S. D. Magitians] Gifford; Priests Q.

---

     76. Patron] Patrick is, of course, the patron Saint of
Ireland.

     78. directed . . . poyson] gained control over their fangs
and venom.

     81.1 S. D. Enter . . . creeping] This scene must have
challenged the ingenuity of the Dublin theater. For a discussion
of how this might have been accomplished, see the Introduction,
p. 76.

     82-122. See BB, pp. 88-89.

And the still wandring ghosts of his two sons!   8.

Archimagus. They are alive, Sir.

Leogarius.   Ha, who durst abuse us?

Magitian. Will you not have compassion of the Queene,
     And the Prince, Sir?

Leogarius.   How met they to converse?

Archimagus. They are all Christian.

Leogarius.   Let the serpent then
     Feed upon all, my powerfull Archimagus.   9(

Patrick. [Waking.] In vaine is all your malice, Art, and power
     Against their lives, whom the great hand of Heaven
     Daines to protect; like wolves you undertake
     A quarrell with the Moone, and waste your anger:
     Nay, all the shafts your wrath directeth hither,   95

89. Christian] Q; Christians Chetwood, Gifford, Donovan.

*89. serpent] Q; serpents Chetwood, Gifford, Donovan.

91. S. D. Waking] Gifford, Donovan.

------

   89. the serpent] Leogarius is here referring to serpents
in general, and so uses the singular.

   92. Against . . . whom] against the lives of those whom
(see Abbott, par. 259).

   93-94. like . . . anger] Cf. "The dog (wolf) barks in
vain at the moon" (Tilley, D449).

Are shot against a brazen arch, whose vault

Impenetrable, sends the arrowes back,

To print just wounds on your owne guiltie heads.

These serpents, (tame at first and innocent,

Untill man's great revolt from grace releas'd   100

Their dutie of creation) you have brought,

And arm'd against my life; all these can I

Approach, and without trembling, walk upon;

Play with their stings, which though to me not dangerous,

I could, to your destruction, tune upon   105

Your selves, and punish with too late repentance.

But you shall live, and what your malice meant,

My ruine, I will turne to all your safeties,

And you shall witnesse: Hence, you frightfull monsters,

Go hide, and burie your deformed heads   110

For ever in the sea; from this time be

This Iland free from beasts of venomous natures:

The Shepherd shall not be afraid hereafter,

To trust his eyes with sleep upon the hils;

---

96. brazen arch] I am unable to identify this allusion. Shirley is obviously referring to some sort of protective arch of brass which is vaulted over the earth.

100-101. releas'd . . . creation] i.e., absolved them of their allegiance to hierarchical order and proportion. Shirley here is using a metaphor of fudal allegiance.

103. walk upon] Cf. the proverb, "Tread on a worm and it will turn" (Tilley, W909).

106. punish . . . repentance] punish you by killing you and sending you to death before you have repented.

The traveller shall have no suspition,   11!

Or feare, to measure with his wearied limbs

The silent shades; but walk through everie brake,

Without more guard than his owne innocence.

The verie earth and wood shall have this blessing

(Above what other Christian Nations boast);   12(

Although transported where these Serpents live

And multiply, one touch shall soone destroy 'em.

                                   [Exeunt Serpents, & c.]

Leogarius. See how they all obey him, Archimagus.

Archimagus. Confusion: All my Art is trampled on.

    Can neither man, nor beast, nor Devill hurt him?   12

*115.   traveller] Gifford; travellers Q.

115.   shall have] Q; shall [from hence] have Gifford.

*120.   boast);] boast)∧ Q.

     115-116. traveller . . . his] Gifford's emendation has
been adopted since it makes "traveller" and "his" agree. The
word "Shepherd" in line 113, moreover, is analogous, and so
suggests that the word should be singular. It would have been
possible for the compositor to repeat the initial letter of
"shall," thereby making "traveller" plural. It is also possible, of course, that the sentence as Shirley wrote it was
ungrammatical.

     116. measure . . . limbs] wearily lie down in.

     117. brake] thicket.

     119-122. The . . . 'em] a difficult passage. The clause
"Although . . . multiply" modifies "earth and wood," so the
sense of the passage is "The very earth and wood of this land
shall have this blessing (a blessing which is greater than those
which other Christian lands can boast of) such that even if they
(the earth and woods) should be transported to other lands where
serpents thrive, the serpents will be destroyed if they even
touch the earth and wood."

Support me, fellow-Priests; I sink, I feele

The ground bend with my weight upon it, ha!

The earth is loose in the foundation,

And something heavie as the world doth hang

Upon my feet, and weigh me to the Center.   130

A fire, a dreadfull fire is underneath me,

And all those fiends that were my servants here,

Look like tormentors, and all seeme to strive,

Who first shall catch my falling flesh upon

Their burning pikes: There is a power above   135

Our gods, I see too late. I fall, I fall,

And in my last despaire, I curse you all.   Sinks.

Leogarius. Patrick, the King will kneele to thee.   [Kneels.]

Patrick.   Oh rise,

126-137. Various magicians in Shirley's source, the life
of Patrick by Jocelyn, meet fates similar to that of Archimagus.
See the BB, pp. 17, 24-25, 28, 29, 35. Cf. also Catalina
in Shirley's The Maid's Revenge (Gifford, I, 183-184), Marpisa
in Shirley's The Politician (Gifford, V. 175), the various
devils in Dekker's If This be not a Good Play, the Devil is in
It (V.iii.149) and Harpax in Dekker and Massinger's The Virgin
Martyr (V.ii.238).

130. Center] Shirley is perhaps suggesting that the weight
on Archimagus' feet is pulling him to the center of the earth.
But theologically and morally, the "center" is the center of
energy and intelligence generally, or the human soul.

137. S. D. Sinks] Archimagus doubtless sank from the
stage through one of the trap doors with which the Dublin
theater was probably equipped. Bentley says that the Phoenix
theater in London (probably the prototype for the Dublin theater) had a trap (VI, 51).

138. Oh rise] Notice that Shirley makes the symbolism
of rise-fall visual in the scene. After Archimagus has sunk
below the stage to Hell, the king lowers himself, but is raised
again by Patrick.

And pay to Heaven that dutie.

Leogarius.   Canst forgive?

Let me embrace you all, and freely give   14&

What I desire from this good man, a pardon.

Thou shalt no more suspect me, but possesse

All thy desires. [Aside.] The ground is shut agen:

Where now is Archimagus? How I shake,

And court this Christian out of feare, not love?   14!

[To Patrick.] Once more visit our Palace, holy Father.

[To Queene.] The storie of our sons, and what concernes

Your escape, Madam, we will know hereafter;

I' th' mean time be secure.

Endarius. ⎞
                              We are your creatures.
Ferochus. ⎠

Omnes. Our prayers and duty.

Patrick.   [Aside.] I suspect him still;   15

But feare not, our good Angels still are neer us:

Death at the last can but untie our frailty;

---

149. your creatures] i.e., yours to command.

151. still] ever.

152. Death . . . frailty] i.e., "we should not fear death
because it actually only takes away that which makes us frail
(our mortality)."

'Twere happy for our holy faith to bleed,

The Blood of Martyrs in the Churche's seed.   Exeunt Omnes.

THE EPILOGUE.

How e're the Dyce run Gentlemen, I am

The last man borne, still at the Irish game:

What say you to the Epilogue? may not I stay,

And boldly aske your Verdict of the Play?

I would report the Sun-shine on your brow,   5

And the soft language of the Dye t'allow

*154. seed] Q; feed Donovan.

The Epilogue. (Chetwood omits)

---

153. happy] fortunate.

153. holy . . . bleed] Shirley is here using a figure in which the abstraction is substituted for the person, a form of metonomy. He is saying that martyrdom (i.e., earthly suffering) is the way to heavenly bliss.

153-154. 'Twere . . . seed] These concluding lines provide an interesting contrast to the analogous lines at the end of Act I: "All wayes to serve our gods are free, and good; / When shed for them, they take delight in blood" (I.i.320-321).

154. The . . . seed] Donovan's emendation ("feed" is almost certainly wrong as the proverb, "The Blood of Martyrs is the Church's seed" shows (Tilley, B457).

1-2. How . . . game] The reference here is to backgammon, often called the "Irish game." It is a board game played with "stones," or pieces which are "borne off" at the end of the game. The game is played with dice. So the Epilogue is saying (using the metaphor of backgammon) that no matter what, he is the last man to leave the stage. The secondary meaning is "to leave the stage."

6-7. soft . . . Story] Picking up the reference to dice in line 1, Shirley is probably using the noise that dice make when shaken to refer metaphorically to applause. "Allow" means to praise. The Epilogue is obviously encouraging the audience to applaud the play and the performers.

Our labour and your Story, native knowne;

It is but justice to affect your owne;

Yet this is but a part of what our Muse

Intends, if the first birth you nobly use: 1

Then give us your free votes, and let us stile

Your Patrons of the Play, him of the Ile.

FINIS.

---

7. native knowne] i.e., known to the natives [of Ireland].

8. affect your owne] i.e., love that which is yours. Shirley is trying to underscore the appeal which he thinks this play
should have for its audience.

9-10. Yet . . . Intends] Cf. Shakespeare's unfulfilled
promise at the end of 2 Henry IV: "Our humble author will continue the story with Sir John in it" (Epilogue, lines 27-28).
Falstaff does not appear in Henry V.

10. birth] i.e., the first birth of the Muse, the first
play. Shirley is picking up "borne" in line 2 and playing on
it.

11. free] unprejudiced.   stile] invest with a right to
be called.

12. him] i.e., St. Patrick, Patron Saint of Ireland.

The names of the Actors.

    1.   Ireland.] Ireland., Q.

   15.   Archimagus'] Gifford; Archimagus Q.

Prologue.

    1.   take;] Gifford; take, Q.

    4.   please,] Gifford; please; Q.

   27.   Poet's] Gifford substantively; Poets Q.

Act I, scene i.

    7.   flourish;] Chetwood; flourish, Q.

    9.   ayre;] ayre, Q.

   10.   landing;] Gifford; landing, Q.

   11.   earth∧] Gifford; earth, Q.

   12.   King's] Chetwood substantively; Kings Q.

   14.   suspition?] Chetwood substantively; suspition. Q.

   17.   statues;] statues, Q.

   26.   another;] Chetwood; another, Q.

   27.   i' th'] Chetwood; i' th Q.

   30.   will;] Gifford; will, Q.

   36.   We . . . you.] Q lines: We . . . all / Our . . . you.

   38.   gods'] Chetwood; gods Q.

   45.   Isle;] Chetwood; Isle, Q.

          we,] Chetwood; we∧ Q.

   48.   Kingdome;] Kingdome, Q.

   50.   And . . . me,] Q lines: And . . . hell. / This . . . me,.

51. confidence;] confidence, Q.

53. sacrifice,] Gifford; sacrifice, Q.

54.1. S. D. He reades] Q prints in right margin opposite line 62.

57. Staffe;] Gifford substantively; Staffe, Q.

63. King--] Gifford substantively; King, Q.

66. him;] Chetwood; him, Q.

69. haste;] Chetwood; haste, Q.

71. Court;] Chetwood substantively; Court, Q.

73. presented;] presented, Q.

83. head;] Chetwood; head, Q.

84.1. S. D. Corybreus,] Corybrues, Q.

87. night;] Gifford; night, Q.

94. it.] Gifford; it, Q.

96. and] Chetwood; aad Q.

102. gods,] gods, Q.

113. earth;] Chetwood; earth, Q.

116. me] Gifford; me, Q.

123. you;] Chetwood; you, Q.

128. dying;] Chetwood; dying, Q.

131. newes;] newes, Q.

133. voyce;] Gifford substantively; voyce, Q.

144. harme;] Chetwood substantively; harme, Q.

148. inaurans.] Chetwood substantively; inaurans, Q.

150. advenarum,] Chetwood substantively; advenarum, Q.

152. ventis.] Gifford substantively; ventis, Q.

153. occinamus] Gifford; occinanas Q.

166. Heaven;] Chetwood substantively; Heaven, Q.

167. peace;] Chetwood; peace, Q.

   number;] Chetwood; number, Q.

178. permit--] Gifford; permit. Q.

186. world;] Chetwood; world, Q.

196. returne--] returne. Q.

201. stay;] stay, Q.

203. thaw,] thaw; Q.

204. heads;] Chetwood; heads, Q.

208. King's] Chetwood substantively; Kings Q.

218. Master's] Chetwood substantively; Masters Q.

223. selves;] selves, Q.

224. gods--] gods.--Q.

228. sudden,] Chetwood; sudden, Q.

230. me;] Chetwood; me, Q.

234-236. I . . . reasonable; / He . . . long / I . . . age]
Gifford's relineation; Q prints as prose.

234. son] Chetwood; son, Q.

   reasonable;] Chetwood; reasonable, Q.

238. not;] Gifford; not, Q.

242. serves?] Chetwood; serves, Q.

248. Art;] Chetwood; Art, Q.

252. too;] Chetwood; too, Q.

253. Master's] Chetwood substantively; Masters Q.

254. supple;] supple, Q.

259. faith;] Chetwood; faith, Q.

263-266. He's . . . anger.] Gifford's relineation; Q lines:
He's . . . base / Apostasie . . . may / Provoke . . . anger.

265. Lord,] Lord, Q.

270. King's] <u>Chetwood</u> <u>substantively</u>; Kings Q.

272. selfe;] <u>Chetwood</u> <u>substantively</u>; selfe, Q.

274. morning's] <u>Chetwood</u>; mornings Q.

278. away;] <u>Gifford</u>; away, Q.

282. heaven's] <u>Chetwood</u>; heavens Q.

283. 'em;] 'em, Q.

284. wrath?] <u>Gifford</u>; wrath. Q.

285. ripe;] <u>Chetwood</u>; ripe, Q.

286. Sir;] <u>Chetwood</u> <u>substantively</u>; Sir, Q.

292. Court;] <u>Gifford</u>; Court, Q.

293. Pretend‿] Pretend, Q.

       desires‿] desires, Q.

303. so;] <u>Gifford</u>; so, Q.

306. Daughters.] <u>Chetwood</u> <u>substantively</u>; Daughters: Q.

307. Director;] <u>Chetwood</u> <u>substantively</u>; Director, Q.

308. since;] <u>Gifford</u>; since, Q.

311. religion;] religion, Q.

318. Prince;] <u>Chetwood</u> <u>substantively</u>; Prince, Q.

320. good;] <u>Gifford</u>; good, Q.

<u>Act</u> <u>II</u>, <u>scene</u> <u>i</u>.

1. more;] <u>Gifford</u>; more, Q.

3. Sister;] <u>Gifford</u>; Sister, Q.

6. us.] <u>Chetwood</u>; us: Q.

7. 'em;] 'em, Q.

12. King's] <u>Chetwood</u> <u>substantively</u>; Kings Q.

14. Sister;] Sister, Q.

18. here;] here, Q.

21-22. A foolish . . . Rodamant?] Gifford's relineation;
Q lines: A . . . servant, / How . . . Rodamant.

22. Governor's] Chetwood substantively; Governors Q.

   servant;] servant, Q.

28. pleas'd;] pleas'd, Q.

40. yeers;] yeers, Q.

42. time;] Gifford; time, Q.

   enough:] Gifford; enough, Q.

50. high;] Chetwood; high, Q.

53. love;] Gifford; love, Q.

56. 'em;] em, Q.

59. 'em] em Q.

   rotten;] Chetwood; rotten, Q.

   stump∧] Gifford; stump, Q.

62-63. Oh . . . Mistresse] Gifford prints as prose; Q
lines: Oh . . . sleep / For . . . Mistresse.

64. what's] Chetwood; whats Q.

66. woman?] Gifford; woman. Q.

67. sure--] sure, Q.

68. Queen's] Chetwood substantively; Queens Q.

69. Queen;] Chetwood substantively; Queen, Q.

71. her;] Chetwood; her, Q.

74. news;] Chetwood; news, Q.

76. Endarius--] Gifford; Endarius, Q.

77. 'em] em Q.

81. are--] Chetwood; are∧ Q.

83. worme's] Chetwood substantively; wormes Q.

85. commanded∧] Gifford; commanded, Q.

86. that's] Chetwood; thats Q.

all;] all, Q.

88. scritchowle?] Chetwood substantively; scritchowle∧ Q.

93. else;] Chetwood; else, Q.

98. true;] Chetwood; true, Q.

99. inevitable;] Chetwood; inevitable, Q.

112. Sir;] Chetwood; Sir, Q.

117. selves;] Chetwood; selves, Q.

124. way;] Gifford; way, Q.

129. brother;] Chetwood; brother, Q.

137. unworthily?] Gifford; unworthily. Q.

146. vowes;] Chetwood substantively; vowes, Q.

147-148. She . . . piety] Gifford's relineation; Q lines:
She . . . gods. / Sir . . . piety.

149. things;] things, Q.

153. gone;] Chetwood; gone, Q.

155. prosper;] Chetwood; prosper, Q.

'tis] Chetwood; tis Q.

158. highnesse'] Chetwood substantively; highnesse Q.

161-162. You . . . comes] Gifford's relineation; Q lines:
You . . . me, / And . . . comes.

168. presence,] Chetwood; presence∧ Q.

169. nature;] nature, Q.

171. thee?] Gifford; thee; Q.

174. To . . . now,] Gifford's relineation; Q lines:
To . . . self. / That . . . now,.

195. Corybreus] Chetwood; Coribreus Q.

207. coy;] Chetwood; coy, Q.

bestow'd?] _Gifford_; bestow'd. Q.

219. heavens;] _Chetwood_; heavens, Q.

232. innocence;] _Chetwood_; innocence, Q.

237. not;] _Chetwood_; not, Q.

239. her;] _Chetwood_; her, Q.

240. brother;] _Chetwood_; brother, Q.

    Archimagus;] _Chetwood_; _Archimagus_, Q.

Act II, scene ii.

1. yesterday;] _Chetwood_; yesterday, Q.

3. names?] _Gifford_; names, Q.

4. say;] _Gifford_; say, Q.

6. middle;] _Gifford_; middle, Q.

8. _Venus_'] _Chetwood_ substantively; _Venus_ Q.

8-10. _Mars_ . . . Demilaunce.] _Gifford_ prints as prose; Q lines: _Mars_ . . . Lady / _Venus_ . . . too. / He . . . like / A Demilaunce.

9. too?] _Gifford_; too. Q.

11. form'd?] _Gifford_; formed, Q.

    away;] away, Q.

12.3 S. D. _kneel_,] _kneel_. Q.

14. lays] lay Q.

35.1-35.2. S. D. _After_ . . . _Idols_] _Gifford_; Q prints after line 24.

42. thee₍₎] _Gifford_; thee; Q.

54. was;] was, Q.

55. _Jupiter_,] _Jupiter_? Q.

57. zeale?] zeale. Q.

67. daughters;] daughters, Q.

68. gone;] Chetwood; gone, Q.

70. don't,] Gifford substantively; don't‸ Q.

71. Most . . . Fedella.] Q lines: Most . . . Welcome /
To . . . Fedella.

74. gentlemen;] Chetwood; gentlemen, Q.

79. too;] Chetwood; too, Q.

81. life,] Chetwood; life‸ Q.

83. th'] Chetwood; th Q.

   temple?] temple. Q.

86. expects;] Chetwood; expects, Q.

Act III, scene i.

   3. horse;] Chetwood; horse, Q.

   ha'] ha Q.

   6. on't] Gifford; ont Q.

   9. gallowes,] gallowes‸ Q.

   12. King's] Chetwood substantively; Kings Q.

   Bard;] Gifford substantively; Bard, Q.

   14. is't] Gifford; ist Q.

   15. devill?] Gifford; devill. Q.

   17.1. S. D. Sings] Q places to left of line 18.

   21. had,] Gifford; had. Q. (perhaps faintly inked).

   22. lightning‸] Gifford; lightning, Q.

   24. indeed--] Gifford; indeed- Q.

   28. Gudgin;] Chetwood substantively; Gudgin, Q.

   28-29. bushell;] Chetwood; bushell, Q.

   29. mouth,] Gifford; mouth; Q.

31. Bard!] Chetwood substantively; Bard, Q.

35. head_A] Gifford; head, Q.

36. journeye's] Gifford substantively; journeyes Q.

38. King's] Chetwood substantively; Kings Q.

39. welcome;] Gifford; welcome, Q.

42. man?] Gifford; man. Q.

42.1. S. D. Sings] Q places right of line 42.

45. Patricke,] Gifford substantively; Patricke: Q.

51. word;] Gifford; word, Q.

     Queene.] Queene, Q.

57. is't] Gifford; ist Q.

     treason!] Gifford substantively; treason, Q.

60. Queene_A] Gifford substantively; Queene, Q.

64. talke] Talke Q.

66. Cupid's] Gifford substantively; Cupids Q.

70.1 S. D. Sings] Q prints to left of line 70.

71. bog,] bog; Q.

75. th'] th Q.

     mire,] Gifford; mire: Q.

77. King's] Gifford substantively; Kings Q.

81. folly,] Gifford substantively; folly: Q.

84. Porcupine;] Chetwood; Porcupine, Q.

85.1. S. D. Sings] Q prints to left of line 86.

89. whiter,] Gifford; whiter. Q.

93. Faries,] Gifford substantively; Faries. Q.

101. anger,] Chetwood; anger: Q.

102. piety_A] Chetwood; piety, Q.

108. guests,] Chetwood; guests: Q.

110. brow;] Chetwood; brow, Q.

117. prepar'd;] Chetwood substantively; prepar'd, Q.

119-120. Receive . . . fortified.] Gifford's relineation; Q lines: Receive . . . your / Arme . . . fortified.

134. time] Chetwood; time time Q.

fly;] Chetwood; fly, Q.

S. D. Exit.] Exit Cori. Q.

135. is't] Gifford; ist Q.

142. Dichue's] Chetwood substantively; Dichues Q.

145. wine;] Chetwood; wine, Q.

147. wine;] Chetwood; wine, Q.

150. first∧] Chetwood; first, Q.

154. 'Tis] Chetwood; Tis Q.

156. man's] Chetwood; mans Q.

158. man's] Chetwood; mans Q.

life?] Gifford; life. Q.

160. him?] Gifford; him: Q.

See] Gifford; see Q.

162. well;] Chetwood; well, Q.

179. wo' not] wonot Q.

182. Majestie,] Chetwood substantively; Majestie; Q.

183. smile,] Chetwood; smile: Q.

185. place,] Gifford; place. Q.

186. (It . . . love),] Gifford substantively; It . . . love; Q.

187. religion;] religion, Q.

194. wonder;] Gifford; wonder, Q.

195-196. I . . . prepare / His cup.] Gifford's relineation; Q prints as one line.

197. poyson;] Gifford substantively; poyson, Q.

201. sirra;] Gifford substantively; sirra, Q.

206. Queene's?] Chetwood substantively; Queenes. Q.

209. Sir?] Gifford substantively; Sir. Q.

213. ingredients;] Chetwood; ingredients, Q.

214. him;] Chetwood; him, Q.

219. abouts;] Chetwood; abouts, Q.

227. increases;] Chetwood; increases, Q.

me;] Chetwood; me, Q.

228. cooler;] Chetwood; cooler, Q.

229. sea;] Chetwood; sea, Q.

234. heart;] Chetwood; heart, Q.

237. heart;] Chetwood; heart, Q.

238. heaven's] Chetwood; heavens Q.

243. me;] Chetwood; me, Q.

us,] Chetwood; us; Q.

246. life;] Chetwood; life, Q.

248. too;] Chetwood; too, Q.

249. physition;] Chetwood substantively; physition, Q.

250. make us] Chetwood; makeus Q.

252. We . . . Patrick] Gifford's relineation; Q lines:
We . . . enough: / Receive . . . Patrick.

255. Archimagus?] Gifford; Archimagus, Q.

259. 'Tis] Chetwood; Tis Q.

King's] Gifford substantively; Kings Q.

265. Patrick;] Chetwood; Patrick, Q.

269. is't] Gifford; ist Q.

271.1. S. D. Sings] Q prints left of line 272.

275. 'em] Chetwood; e'm Q.

Act III, scene ii.

2-4. Since . . . lids] Gifford's relineation; Q lines:
Since . . . and / My . . . lids.

2. Corybreus] Coribreus Q.

4. mist,] Chetwood; mist: Q.

5. 'em] e'm Q.

him;] him, Q.

8. Conallus,--] Gifford; Conallus, Q.

14. not;] Chetwood; not, Q.

16. voice;] Chetwood; voice, Q.

18. eyes;] Chetwood; eyes, Q.

21. comply;] Chetwood; comply, Q.

22. melancholly;] Chetwood substantively; melancholly, Q.

23.1. S. D. Corybreus] Gifford; Coribreus Q.

24. so;] so, Q.

27. too;] Chetwood; too, Q.

30-31. Ha? . . . me?] Gifford's relineation; Q prints as
one line.

34. Forgot;] Gifford; Forgot, Q.

35-37. Take . . . Powers] Gifford's relineation; Q lines:
Take . . . visible / If . . . fast / Ha . . . powers.

35. charme;] Chetwood; charme, Q.

36. ha'] ha Q.

39. where;] Chetwood; where, Q.

41. is't] Gifford; ist Q.

42. fright,] Chetwood; fright Q.

42. Emeria;] Gifford; Emeria, Q.

47. sure;] Chetwood; sure, Q.

48. seeme;] Chetwood substantively; seeme, Q.

53. returnes;] Chetwood substantively; returnes, Q.

54. one,] Gifford; one; Q.

63. waite,] Gifford substantively; waite: Q.

67. confirm'd:] Chetwood; confirm'd, Q.

72. firmer‸] Gifford; firmer, Q.

74. world's] Chetwood; worlds Q.

81. center?] Gifford substantively; center: Q.

83. Emeria.] Chetwood; Emeria? Q.

94. divine,] Gifford; divine: Q

103. palmes;] Chetwood substantively; palmes, Q.

104. Not‸] Gifford; Not, Q.

105. to;] Chetwood; to, Q.

114. chastitie;] Chetwood substantively; chastitie, Q.

129. Away . . . but] Gifford's relineation; Q lines: Away / Thou . . . but.

136-144. Nay . . . wantonnesse.] Gifford's relineation; Q prints as prose.

139. men;] Chetwood; man, Q.

140. gods,] Chetwood; gods; Q.

growne;] growne, Q.

Act IV, scene i.

3. hither;] hither, Q.

S. D. Exit Servant] Q prints to right of line 2.

6. otherwise;] Chetwood; otherwise, Q.

8. Queene;] Chetwood substantively; Queene, Q.

14. once;] Chetwood; once, Q.

22.   Corybreus] Coribreus Q.

24.   best.] Chetwood; best, Q.

27.   too,] Gifford; too∧ Q.

29.   heart;] Chetwood; heart, Q.

33.   wo' not] wonot Q.

36.   hither;] Chetwood; hither, Q.

38.   In . . . Bard] Gifford's relineation; Q lines:
In . . . daughter. / Welcome . . . Bard.

41.   hither;] hither, Q.

42.   thing?] Chetwood; thing. Q.

44.   harp;] Chetwood; harp, Q.

47.   opportunity,] Chetwood; opportunity, Q.

48.   mirth;] Chetwood; mirth, Q.

49-50.   Fare . . . rose] Gifford's relineation; Q lines:
Fare . . . knave / Along . . . rose.

52-56.   What . . . office] Gifford's relineation; Q prints
as prose.

55.   within;] Chetwood; within, Q.

61.1.   S. D. Sings] Q prints to right of line 61.

72.   th'] th Q.

80.   too;] Chetwood; too, Q.

81-82.   No . . . me? Gifford's relineation; Q prints as
prose.

93.   Prince;] Chetwood substantively; Prince, Q.

96.   me;] Chetwood; me, Q.

97.   Queene's] Chetwood substantively; Queenes Q.

103.   mother's] Chetwood; mothers Q.

107.   Lord;] Lord, Q.

113.   suspected?] suspected, Q.

130. so;] Chetwood; so, Q.

135. lost--] Gifford; lost. Q.

135-137. The . . . treasure] Gifford's relineation; Q lines:
The . . . me. / Do . . . wealth / Oh . . . treasure.

141. feare;] Gifford substantively; feare, Q.

151. for't;] Gifford; for't, Q.

160. god;] Chetwood; god, Q.

164. bodie's] Chetwood substantively; bodies Q.

167. amazement.] Chetwood; amazement∧ Q.

173.1 S. D. Enter Archimagus] Q prints right of line 167.

180. favorite;] Chetwood; favorite, Q.

182. betraid;] Gifford substantively; betraid, Q.

183. longer,] Gifford; longer∧ Q.

185. a] Chetwood; a a Q.

187. here,] Chetwood; here∧ Q.

193.195. I . . . use] Gifford's relineation; Q lines:
I . . . ask / To . . . maintain / That . . . use.

197. lover's] Chetwood; lovers Q.

205. Emeria,] Chetwood; Emeria∧ Q.

206. bodie's] Chetwood substantively; bodies Q.

207. th'] th Q.

   eye;] Chetwood substantively; eye, Q.

212. me;] me, Q.

214. man,] Chetwood; man∧ Q.

215. punish'd;] Chetwood; punish'd, Q.

217-218. Ha . . . Lord?] Gifford's relineation; Q prints
as one line.

222. gods'] Gifford; gods Q.

223. furies,] Chetwood; furies Q.

230. here;] Chetwood; here, Q.

232. wo' not] wonot Q.

234. Returne;] Returne, Q.

236-262. My . . . walls.] Gifford's italics.

238. love;] Gifford; love, Q.

239. cruell,] Gifford substantively; cruell. Q.

240-241. As . . . Queene] Gifford's relineation; Q prints
as one line.

241. How's] Gifford; how's Q.

244-245. Within . . . agen] Gifford's relineation; Q
prints as one line.

243. jewell,] Gifford substantively; jewell. Q.

244. heart.--] Gifford; heart. Q.

245. heart;] Gifford; heart, Q.

249-251. There's . . . royall] Gifford's relineation;
Q prints as prose.

250. loyall.] Gifford substantively; loyall, Q.

252. that;] Chetwood; that, Q.

256-260. There's . . . face] Gifford's relineation; Q
prints as prose.

256. There's] Gifford; there's Q.

257. love.] Gifford; love, Q.

258. face--] Gifford; face, Q.

260. face.] Gifford; face, Q.

266. time;] Chetwood; time, Q.

270. now;] Gifford; now, Q.

271. freind?] Gifford substantively; freind, Q.

272. Lord?] Lord_∧ Q.

275. toy;] Gifford; toy, Q.

Queene;] Chetwood substantively; Queene, Q.

281. house;] house, Q.

confusion!] Gifford; confusion; Q.

282. traitour;] Chetwood substantively; traitour‸ Q.

284-286. I . . . gone] Gifford's relineation; Q lines:
I . . . where. / I . . . gone.

284. him;] Chetwood; him, Q.

296-297. Let . . . Conallus] Gifford's relineation; Q
prints as one line.

296. back;] Chetwood; back, Q.

298. him;] Gifford; him, Q.

298-302. I'll . . . messenger] Gifford's relineation;
Q lines: I'll . . . him, / It . . . Queene. / Sir . . . waits /
With . . . King. / The . . . name / Shoots . . . messenger?

301. now;] Chetwood; now, Q.

305. Lord;] Gifford substantively; Lord, Q.

311. To th'] Toth' Q.

317. wo' not] Chetwood; wonot Q.

318. Prince's] Chetwood substantively; Princes Q.

323. Queene;] Chetwood substantively; Queene, Q.

329. agen;] Chetwood substantively; agen, Q.

336. Patrick] Chetwood; Patricik Q.

342. thee;] Chetwood; thee, Q.

343. agen;] Chetwood substantively; agen, Q.

345. mischiefe;] Chetwood substantively; mishciefe, Q.

352. worlds‸] Gifford; worlds, Q.

359.1. S. D. Enter Bard] Q prints to right of line 359.

360. lost;] Gifford; lost, Q.

362. forth;] Gifford; forth, Q.

367. person;] Chetwood; person, Q.

368. treacherie;] Gifford substantively; treacherie, Q.

375. caught;] Chetwood; caught, Q.

376. thee;] Chetwood; thee, Q.

384. me;] Chetwood; me, Q.

386. son's] Chetwood; sons Q.

387. selfe;] Chetwood substantively; selfe, Q.

389. Angell;] Chetwood substantively; Angell, Q.

390. morne;] Gifford substantively; morne, Q.

Act IV, scene ii.

0.2. S. D. Leogarius] King Q.

0.3. S. D. Fedella;] Fedella, Q.

 3. Christian's] Chetwood; Christians Q.

11. Mars;] Chetwood; Mars, Q.

19. aire;] Gifford substantively; aire, Q.

26.1. S. D. Leogarius] the King Q.

30. devotion?] Gifford; devotion: Q.

33. passages;] passages, Q.

34. charge;] Chetwood; charge, Q.

40-41. You . . . me] Gifford's relineation; Q prints as one line.

44. so;] so, Q.

46. on't?] Chetwood; on't. Q.

51. Ferochus?] Gifford; Ferochus. Q.

53. none;] Chetwood; none, Q.

55. opportunities;] Chetwood; opportunities, Q.

58. Madam;] Madam, Q.

75. sure;] Gifford; sure, Q.

77. Wo' not] Chetwood; wonot Q.

79-81. You . . . cheeke] Gifford's relineation; Q lines: You . . . Gentlemen. / Mine . . . flie / Glanc'd . . . cheeke:

88. wipe for you] Chetwood; wipe for for you Q.

89-90. Some . . . has] Gifford's relineation; Q lines: Some . . . sure: / I . . . has?

93. ha'] ha Q.

95. asleep] Chetwood; a sleep Q.

96. Ha'] Ha Q.

99. images;] Chetwood; images, Q.

105. done;] done, Q.

108. S. H. Magitian] Pr. Q.

already;] already, Q.

109. quickly;] Chetwood; quickly, Q.

112.1. S. D. Leogarius] King Q.

112.2. S. D. Ferochus] Ferochus Q.

113. off;] off, Q.

me?] Gifford; me, Q.

118. sonne's] Chetwood substantively; sonnes Q.

119. Upon] Chetwood; Up on Q.

120. themselves;] Chetwood; themselves, Q.

130. Sir;] Chetwood substantively; Sir, Q.

134. king's] Chetwood; kings Q.

135. monument,] Gifford; monument‸ Q.

lift;] Gifford; lift, Q.

141. him;] Chetwood; him, Q.

143. next?] Gifford; next. Q.

148. agen;] agen, Q.

153. happy;] Chetwood; happy, Q.

157. him;] Gifford; him, Q.

160. Patrick's] Chetwood; Patricks Q.

Priest;] Chetwood substantively; Priest, Q.

162. Christian's] Chetwood; Christians Q.

Act V, scene i.

1. on't;] Chetwood; on't, Q.

3. moneth's] Chetwood substantively; moneths Q.

6. mother's] Chetwood substantively; mothers Q.

7. grandfather's] Chetwood; grandfathers Q.

10. Christian;] Chetwood; Christian, Q.

16. hungry;] Chetwood; hungry, Q.

18. let's] Chetwood; lets Q.

21. My royal] Chetwood; royal My Q.

rosted;] Chetwood substantively; rosted, Q.

22. and] Gifford; & Q.

wo' not] Chetwood; wonot Q.

30. me;] Chetwood; me, Q.

32. me;] Chetwood; me, Q.

35. Hungarians;] Chetwood; Hungarians, Q.

35-36. souldier,] Gifford substantively; souldier; Q.

41. understanding∧] Gifford; understanding, Q.

43. voice;] Chetwood; voice, Q.

44. Spirit;] Chetwood; Spirit∧ Q.

not;] Chetwood; not, Q.

46. blade;] Chetwood; blade, Q.

48.   yeere,] Gifford substantively; yeere; Q.

51.   handsome;] Chetwood; handsome, Q.

53.   What,] Chetwood; What∧ Q.

58.   father's] Chetwood; fathers Q.

63.   withall?] Gifford; withall. Q.

64.   power;] Chetwood; power, Q.

65.   complement;] Chetwood; complement∧ Q.

74.   What's] Chetwood; Whats Q.

75.   S. D. Hides] hides Q.

78.1. S. D. first,] Gifford; first, Q.

85.   horses?] Gifford; horses. Q.

87.   sconce;] Chetwood; sconce, Q.

90.   himselfe;] Gifford substantively; himselfe, Q.

91.   ha'] ha Q.

105. fangs;] fangs, Q.

106. agen;] Chetwood; agen, Q.

115. thee?] Chetwood; thee. Q.

124. Emeria;] Chetwood; Emeria, Q.

127. never;] Chetwood; never, Q.

129. Assur'd∧] Chetwood; Assur'd, Q.

137. Corybreus] Coribreus Q.

156. father's] Chetwood; fathers Q.

159. Emeria;] Chetwood; Emeria∧ Q.

160. brother's] Chetwood; brothers Q.

164. father's] Chetwood; fathers Q.

166. wood;] Chetwood; wood, Q.

171. King;] Chetwood substantively; King, Q.

176. wo' not] Chetwood; wonot Q.

177. voyce;] Chetwood substantively; voyce, Q.

178. sallads;] Chetwood; sallads, Q.

179. Patrick;] Chetwood; Patrick, Q.

186. me;] Chetwood; me, Q.

218. houre's] Chetwood substantively; houres Q.

225. alive;] Chetwood; alive, Q.

227. child's;] Chetwood; childs, Q.

230. of;] Chetwood; of, Q.

240. mother's] Chetwood; mothers Q.

248. Dragon's] Chetwood substantively; Dragons Q.
     Viper's] Chetwood substantively; Vipers Q.

250. off;] Chetwood; off, Q.

Act V, scene ii.

   3. lost;] Chetwood; lost, Q.
      th'] th Q.

   8. th'] th Q.

  11. Stay,] Chetwood; Stay₄ Q.

  12. wolve's] Chetwood substantively; wolves Q.

  13. death,] Gifford; death: Q.

  15. enter;] Chetwood; enter, Q.

  16. welcome;] Chetwood; welcome, Q.

  17. here;] Chetwood; here, Q.

  26. death;] Chetwood; death, Q.

Act V, scene iii.

  16. world's] Chetwood; worlds Q.

32. joy;] <u>Chetwood</u>; joy, Q.

33. too;] too, Q.

36. you;] <u>Chetwood</u>; you, Q.

38. Preserver,] <u>Chetwood</u> <u>substantively</u>; Preserver. Q.

44. Heaven;] <u>Chetwood</u> <u>substantively</u>; Heaven, Q.

49. Heaven's] <u>Chetwood</u> <u>substantively</u>; Heavens Q.

76.1. S. D. Leogarius] King Q.

79. sleeps?] <u>Chetwood</u>; sleeps, Q.

100. man's] <u>Chetwood</u>; mans Q.

154. Churche's] <u>Chetwood</u> <u>substantively</u>; Churches Q.

GLOSSARIAL INDEX TO THE COMMENTARY

N.B. If the gloss is exactly repeated, only the first occurrence is noted.

a, II.i.63.

a', IV.ii.83.

above, I.i.130, V.i.248.

accident, I.i.310.

active, III.ii.115.

Adamantine, I.i.29.

aetheriall, I.i.127.

affect, III.i.180

after, V.III.10.

airy, I.i.132.

alablaster, IV.i.258.

allow, IV.ii.9.

amaine, IV.i.84.

ambling muse, IV.i.266.

ammelet, III.ii.24.

And, III.i.207.

antick, IV.ii.109.

apprehension, I.i.72.

apt, II.i.135.

as soone, I.i.108.

atomes, I.i.25.

bands, II.i.17.

bark, I.i.189.

bath, I.i.91.

before, IV.i.168.

behind, IV.i.335.

belly timber, V.i.18.

bend, II.i.107.

bent, V.i.251.

blacke, I.i.45.

blast, IV.i.293.

blasted, I.i.129.

blast him, I.i.16.

bleed, I.i.273.

bloud, V.iii.13.

brace, V.i.28.

brake, V.iii.117.

brave, II.i.117.

breake, I.i.46.

Britaine, I.i.175.

but ayre, I.i.9.

By any meanes, III.i.53.

can meet, V.ii.19.

Cassia, III.ii.59.

censures, Prol. 18.

Center, V.iii.139.

273

cheeke by joll, III.i.65.

circles, I.i.106.

circumcise, III.i.6-7.

clog, III.i.72.

clout, V.i.112.

come off, IV.i.320.

common wealth, V.i.14.

complement, V.i.65.

compose, I.i.246, I.i.305.

concupiscence, V.i.94.

Conduct, V.i.230.

Coneyes, I.i.191.

confine, Prol. 17.

constitution, IV.ii.54.

consume, IV.i.378.

consumption, II.i.47.

cooler, III.i.228.

Coshering, V.i.7.

Course, V.ii.40.

court praise, II.i.163.

crackers, III.i.222.

creatures, V.iii.149.

crooked, I.i.57.

cullice, V.i.87.

daintie, IV.i.80.

dalliance, II.i.172.

Daphne, III.ii.119.

deceive, II.i.124.

deare yeere, V.i.48.

Demilaunce, II.ii.10.

destillation, V.i.108.

Destines, III.ii.73.

devote, II.i.194.

Discharge, IV.i.317.

divorce, IV.i.170.

Don Diego Diabolo, II.i.43.

Dotard, I.i.270.

Dragon's bloud, V.i.248.

dresse, Prol. 3.

drudg'd under, II.i.28.

dulnes, III.ii.3.

dy, II.i.71.

earnest, IV.i.45.

else, III.i.155.

Esquire, II.ii.88.

exercise, II.i.36.

Expect, II.ii.39.

Faces about, I.i.193.

factious, I.i.30.

faine, IV.i.85.

faith, IV.i.113.

fall, IV.i.229.

falling of the flesh, II.i.52.

Familiar, II.i.31.

fancie, I.i.87.

father, IV.ii.7.

fatts, III.i.274.

figure, IV.i.252.

firmer, III.ii.72.

fit, Prol. 7, IV.i.75.

fond To, III.ii.126-127.

forsake, I.i.261.

free, Epil. 11.

froward, II.i.230.

fume, II.ii.21.

furies, I.i.3.

gain'd, III.i.144.

gamester, IV.ii.65.

gay, III.i.50.

generation, V.i.6.

genius, II.i.145.

gingle, IV.i.249.

glib'd, V.i.92.

goads, I.i.187.

gobling, III.i.14.

Gold joy, IV.i.44.

grace, V.i.2.

granam, II.i.38.

grandes, II.i.43.

greene disease, IV.i.72.

grieve, II.i.142.

grounds, IV.i.349.

grubbing up, IV.ii.149.

Gudgin, III.i.28.

habit, IV.i.303.

hang, IV.i.240.

happiness, III.i.16.

happy, II.i.129.

harmony, I.i.143.

have it cri'd, IV.i.77.

havens, I.i.12.

health, III.i.228.

heartie, III.i.114.

heat, II.i.6.

hold, IV.i.186.

honest, III.ii.113.

hot, V.i.69.

humane, V.iii.17.

Humble, V.ii.41.

Hungarians, V.i.35.

humour, Prol. 6.

Iland of the Saints, IV.i.372.

incontinencie, III.i.5.

innumerous, I.i.25.

intelligencing, III.i.125.

inward part, IV.i.112.

jeat, IV.i.258.

Jove, III.ii.117.

justifie, IV.i.106.

Keep off, II.i.23.

the better, V.i.31.

Then, II.i.195.

throwes, Prol. 22.

to, III.i.149.

travell, Prol. 22, V.ii.10.

trenchers, II.ii.2.

Tribe, IV.ii.7.

tricke, V.i.31.

trout, III.i.27.

try, III.i.213.

trundlebed, IV.i.269.

Tun, I.i.76.

understand, IV.ii.78.

upon entrance, II.ii.12.

vaine, III.ii.132.

Various, Prol. 2.

vegetalls, II.i.188.

votaries, IV.i.209.

want, II.i.154.

wanton, III.i.38.

wide, V.i.132.

wildefire, III.i.220.

winter lawes, III.ii.125.

wise, II.i.128.

with, III.i.143.

woe, III.ii.128.

would, III.i.245.

wracke, IV.i.158.

wreath, II.ii.20.